LETTERS OF
JAMES WHITCOMB RILEY

JAMES WHITCOMB RILEY
From the portrait by John Singer Sargent in the John Herron Art Institute

LETTERS

of
James Whitcomb Riley

Edited by William Lyon Phelps

Illustrated

THE BOBBS-MERRILL COMPANY
Publishers · Indianapolis

Printed in the United States of America

PRESS OF
BRAUNWORTH & CO., INC.
BOOK MANUFACTURERS
BROOKLYN, N. Y.

ACKNOWLEDGMENT

I am grateful to various members of the family of James Whitcomb Riley for biographical and other information. The publishers have also given me valuable assistance. I have selected out of a great mass of letters those which seemed to me most interesting, and in some cases I have omitted parts of letters that seemed unimportant or irrelevant.

W. L. P.

CONTENTS

CONTENTS—*Concluded*

THE LETTERS

CHAPTER I

CHAPTER II

THE LETTERS—*Continued*

CHAPTER III

THE LETTERS—*Continued*

CHAPTER IV

THE LETTERS—*Continued*

CHAPTER V

THE LETTERS—*Continued*

THE LETTERS—*Continued*

CHAPTER VIII

THE LETTERS—*Continued*

THE LETTERS—*Concluded*

APPENDIX

ILLUSTRATIONS

LETTERS OF
JAMES WHITCOMB RILEY

LETTERS OF
JAMES WHITCOMB RILEY

FOREWORD

(October 7, 1849—July 22, 1916)

WHAT his final position in American literature will be no one can say; but it is certain that many of his poems in dialect, and many of his poems about children will remain for generations, because they have in them the principle of life. One test of a poet's vitality is seen by the number of people who can quote him; there are hundreds of thousands who know some of Riley's poems by heart.

The first academic critic to salute him in print was the late Henry Augustin Beers, a man erudite and fastidious, not at all given to easy enthusiasms. In his book, *Initial Studies in American Letters,* published in 1891, he acclaimed Riley as a national poet. And in a notice of him which appeared in the *New York Sun* after his death, a critic wrote, "He took by divine right the place as an American poet which has not been occupied since Longfellow's tenancy ended." Don Marquis called him an "untamed Hoosier," saying, "James Whitcomb Riley was a Hoosier who happily escaped; he was never captured, never enslaved; the things hidden from the rest of us, or revealed only in flashes, remembered but vaguely from the days of our own happy Hoosierdom, he continued to see steadily; he lived among them familiarly to the end, and until the end was their interpreter to us."

It was my good fortune to know Riley intimately for

1

nearly twenty years. He cared only for poetry, never talked about anything else. He took no interest in politics, and he never voted but once. When he later discovered that by reason of his unfamiliarity in making out the ballot, he had voted for the opponent of the friend who had induced him to go to the polls he vowed never to vote again. He was extraordinarily neat and precise; his clothes were immaculate, his handwriting was a work of art. He could not dictate with any comfort or ease, and so during the last years, when he was ill, we have unfortunately very few letters.

He always took infinite pains with his verse, considered carefully its technique and the weight of every word. He hated free verse with such uncompromising ardor that he was unable to see anything in Walt Whitman; the letter on Whitman published in this volume is mild indeed. I wish I could reproduce exactly what he said to me orally.

There was absolutely no taint of vulgarity in the man; his profanity was lyrical. He had a heart of gold, and a genius for friendship. Having missed me one day at the train, he wrote, "I could have wept, had not the Almighty given me the blessed gift of cussin'."

Most of these letters appear in print for the first time. In making a selection from a very large number, I have chosen those that seemed to me most important, both for the subjects discussed and for their revelation of the man. He had of course a wide circle of acquaintances. There are letters here to Rudyard Kipling, to Joel Chandler Harris, to Mark Twain, to Henry Irving, to John Burroughs, to Booth Tarkington, to George Ade, to Thomas Bailey Aldrich, to Eugene Debs, to S. Weir Mitchell, to Meredith Nicholson, to Robert Underwood Johnson, to many others. But assuredly the best of his epistles are those addressed to the friend he perhaps loved most of all, Bill Nye. The two humorists traveled together—Riley could never travel alone, as he could never find the right train or get off at the right place, having no notion of locality—and their conversation during their expeditions must have been miraculous.

Many of the letters deal with the technique of writing; especially the use of dialect. Many show his immense enthusiasm for the works of contemporaries and his grateful appreciation of praise. They reflect his chronic modesty; he often felt that publishers and lecture bureaus paid him more than he earned. There are the charming letters to a child. There are the wonderful letters of sympathy to a bereaved family, for he well knew the difference in such letters between sympathy and consolation.

As he wrote better poems about children than any other contemporary American, his letters to children had a flavor all their own. I have therefore included some of his merry epistles to Dorian Medairy, a niece of the poet Edith M. Thomas, whom he calls Dory-Ann. His affection for children and his understanding of them, shown not only in his verse but in the natural "equal" way he treated them, were beautifully expressed immediately after his death in a cartoon by Westerman, which appeared in the *Ohio State Journal,* at Columbus. At the foot of a staircase there is a crowded group of children looking up, and calling "Good night, Mr. Riley, good night, good night." One of the smallest children, overwhelmed by tears, is being led away.

The letters begin in 1876, when he was twenty-seven years old, and continue until 1916. Many of the earlier ones were written to intimate personal friends, as he had no acquaintance with the outside world of literature, though to take a place in that charmed circle was from the start his passionate ambition. Some of these close friends were Captain Lee Harris, Benjamin Parker, George C. Hitt, Mrs. R. E. Jones. He often spontaneously breaks out in verse, his natural medium of expression. Later on, the warm affectionate nature of the man is shown in the letters to Mr. and Mrs. Holstein, in which he gives many of his amusing experiences "swinging round the circle" as an itinerant lecturer. No man ever better burlesqued his own profession as a public speaker. He always seemed to feel there was an element of the ridiculous in this, and wondered that such prodigious crowds paid out real money to see and hear him. Nor did he ever get over the torture that afflicted him for hours preceding his appearance. He would eat nothing all day, would groan and wail and lament, could not bear to be left alone; and yet the instant he stepped out on the stage, there was no sign of the nervousness or of the agony that had tormented him. I remember once, a few hours before he was due to appear, trying to reason with him. "Why, Jim, there's nothing to be afraid of. You have done this hundreds of times, always done it well. Nobody is going to hurt you. You haven't even got to think up anything to say. All you are going to do is to repeat your own poems. Come on, let's have something to eat, and you'll feel better." He looked at me in amazement. *"Eat?* My God, hear him talk. Hear him say *eat.* I haven't eaten a mouthful all day." I am certain that if he had known he was to be hanged, he would not have suffered so acutely.

It was characteristic of his affectionate disposition to praise minor poets whom he knew personally, more than their work justified. Thus the reader of these letters must be prepared for superlatives in his writings to Edith M. Thomas, to Madison Cawein and to many others. It was not that he was devoid of the critical faculty. He was terribly severe in conversation on many writers who enjoyed both popular and critical acclaim, and always gave particular reasons for his disapproval. But when poets and novelists whom he knew personally, especially if they wrote in an optimistic or spiritual mood, sent letters to him, his heart expanded, and he was lavish with sincere praise.

He had little sympathy with gloomy writers and none at all with the cynical. His immense admiration of Poe's genius was tempered by his regret over Poe's pessimism; and for Ambrose Bierce he had an absolute antipathy.

He was irritated by any inaccuracy of spelling or quotation. I well remember the smooth flow of profanity when under a portrait of Poe he saw printed EDGAR ALLEN POE. He said that he himself always wrote his full name. If a man does not know you personally, what meaning is there in the name James Riley? But James Whitcomb Riley referred to one individual, who could not be confused with anybody else. When people wrote to him, asking for an autograph of James Whitcomb Reilly, he used to laugh and swear at the same time, as Stevenson did at letters addressed to him as Stephenson.

He recognized genius immediately, always excepting Walt Whitman. Rudyard Kipling he saluted with all his soul and strength, likewise Joel Chandler Harris, whose works will outlive those of nearly all his contemporaries; and Mark Twain he believed in at a time when academic histories of literature gave Mark hardly any recognition. He was so uncompromisingly loyal that he never forgot the early praise from Longfellow, coming at a time when he was very nearly in despair. It was natural therefore that he should look upon Longfellow as one of the greatest poets of the world, as he is still one of the most popular.

As we proceed through these letters in chronological order, we can trace the steady growth of his own fame. It is shown in many ways: in the increased confidence of the man in himself, never overweening, always a bit fearful; in the widening circle of his literary acquaintances; in the advance of his reputation abroad, for the English editions of his books had an enormous circulation.

He used his influence to help Booth Tarkington, before that famous novelist had attracted any attention; he did all he could to encourage Bliss Carman, Meredith Nicholson and many others. He was so overwhelmingly interested in creative literature that any one who showed talent found him immediately responsive. He loved with all his heart that kindly and beautiful character, Eugene Debs; and perhaps it is fortunate that he did not live to see him put in prison. Riley would certainly have done his best to have him released.

Apart from his friendships, Riley was more interested in the art of verse than in anything else. Many of these letters show his preoccupation even with what might be called trivialities, so long as they were concerned with the art of writing. It is deeply instructive to see his comments, his suggestions, and his profound seriousness in the discussion of details. In the use of dialect, he was a master, and his remarks on dialect will interest all who believe in the accurate reproduction of speech. The three supreme specialists in dialect at the turn of the century were Riley, Joel Chandler Harris and Mark Twain.

The famous fraud he perpetrated on Edgar Allan Poe

is mentioned repeatedly in these letters; and it again illustrates his interest in style and diction.

His letters of travel are of value only for their humor. He had none of that power of observation which makes Hawthorne's Notes so pungent, for he simply did not notice externalities. His bump of locality was concave; he was so utterly lost in Philadelphia, during the sittings for his portrait to John Sargent, which by the way is one of that painter's masterpieces, that some one had to go with him every day, so that he could find his way to the studio.

In Europe he was like a somnambulist, wandering about in a dream. He seemed to be thinking only of poetry and of the great men who had written it. He himself would rather talk anywhere with a famous writer than behold all the natural scenery in the world.

Having had little formal education, he perhaps overvalued academic honors, which, for the sake of the universities, I am glad he received. Such recognition was to him infinitely precious. He was always grateful to Yale, to Wabash College, to Indiana University and to the University of Pennsylvania, as his letters on this theme sufficiently show. On taking his degree at Yale in 1902, he received more applause than all the other candidates put together. He was also gratified by his election to the American Academy of Arts and Letters, and by the award of the Gold Medal from the National Institute.

In his public appearances, Riley's impersonations of certain familiar characters—notably the School Visitor— were so remarkable that it is certain he could have been one of the greatest stage comedians of his time. George Ade has referred to Irving's admiration for Riley's histrionic ability. At the dinner given by Henry Irving in honor of

Riley, the great Coquelin, who was present, remarked to Irving, "This Monsieur Riley has by nature what you and I have spent twenty years to acquire."

Everybody who read Riley loved him, and those who met him loved him even more. He never disappointed you; he was the man of his works. He was simple, affectionate, true-hearted; and his humor was the ground quality of his personality.

I never knew any one more sure of the future life, which gave to his letters of sympathy a refreshing tone of authority. When I first met him at Indianapolis in the 'nineties we were to be entertained together at the Country Club. The ladies who acted as our hostesses and guides told us as we entered the open carriage that the best way to the Club was through the cemetery and asked if we had any objection. Of course I had none, and Mr. Riley said he would be glad to see the cemetery. "Because, you know, one day I shall go there and shall not have to come back."

A short time before his death, as we were slowly moving around Indianapolis in his automobile, and he was making comments on the ladies' hats in his own particular manner, I asked him if he still believed in the future life. He said he was absolutely certain of it, that he had no doubt at all. "Why, you and I are going right on *living*."

After his death the State of Indiana honored her famous son in a peculiarly appropriate manner, by founding a Children's Hospital in his name. The Trustees of Indiana University, by an act of the legislature, were authorized to take over the Children's Hospital as a part of the Medical Department of the University. This project was the result of the organization of the James Whitcomb Riley Memorial Association. The hospital was dedicated

on Riley's birthday, October 7, 1924. Fifteen thousand
children have already received treatment. Doctor John
Finley, of New York, who made the address at the dedication, wrote:

"Indiana has made her monument one of ministry
rather than mourning. In Riley's poem on 'The
Happy Little Cripple' he gave a glimpse of a heaven
rather unconventional, occidental, not to say mid-
western in character, in which there were no children
afflicted with 'curv'ture of the spine.' The institution
which bears his name will do much to make the children of Indiana what he imagined them to be. Indiana has made, as human monuments go, the perfect
memorial to her poet."

The fact that in these letters he had no thought of publication is one good reason for their excellence and
for their charm. They have the peculiar flavor of his personality; they reveal his innermost nature in an incom-
parable manner. They are thus more valuable than any
prepared autobiography. Furthermore, one of the things
that give to these letters an unusual value is their "Hoo-
sierness." That was Riley's most striking characteristic,
and here it is expressed quaintly and unmistakably. In
these letters we see the real man as he was.

WILLIAM LYON PHELPS.

Yale University, 7 April 1930.

CHAPTER I

Early Struggles

Early friends—Longfellow Encourages—The "Leonainie" hoax—
Early literary struggles—Success in Boston—Technique Formu-
lated.

To Captain Lee O. Harris.

Captain Harris, Riley's school-teacher and first encourager,
diverted him from the "yellow back" to the best literature. (See
"Lee O. Harris," Biographical Edition, V, p. 432; "Three Singing
Friends," *Lockerbie Book*, No. 203, where Benj. S. Parker, an
Indiana poet, mentioned below and also in the next letter, is
eulogized.) The "highly intellectual woman" was Ella Wheeler
Wilcox.

Greenfield, Ind.,
Oct. 26, 1876.

My dear Harris:

Having a few leisure moments to lavish in a dissipation
of thought, I address you.

I have been thinking of you all day, and wondering
were the Muses on good terms with you this "misty-moisty
weather." I've had a perfect nightmare of "fine frenzy"
and erupt occasionally in such hemorrhages, as,

> Rain! Rain! Rain!
> Till the heart is sullen and sad.
> And rain! rain! rain!
> Till I naturally "go to the bad."

And O! to be buried alive—
Resurrected and buried again
Were a fate it were easier far to survive
Than this terrible doom of the rain!

I recently had a letter from Parker asking my opinion with regard to a book of poems for the holidays, in which we three are to constellate in a perfect nebula of poetical luster. I have written him my approval of the scheme and I feel assured, if you have been consulted, it has met with your concurrence—how is it? If it will pay its own way I think we will find ourselves amply repaid in the more substantial notoriety it will afford us. Write me your views regarding it. I have done but little in a literary way since I saw you last, and what I have I will not inflict you with now.

I have a brace of correspondents now that I am more than assured are "worthy of my steel." A highly intellectual woman living in Wisconsin, who writes like a practical angel, and is one I'm inclined to think—for there's nothing she hasn't read, and quotes with more aptness and variety than any one I ever knew—though I only know her through her letters, which are prose poems throughout. The other is Mary Hannah Krout, of Crawfordsville. A poetess of acknowledged ability, and a contributor to such journals as *The Boston Transcript, New York Tribune, Times,* etc. She spoke of you in her last letter, and I have promised to ask you—for her—for "A Dream of Summer" and your "Clover Bloom." Send them to me if you have extra copies—if not, and can loan from individual scraps, I will return after copying. I enclose one of hers that you may judge of her merit for yourself. Her style is always pure and simple, and I admire her very much. Please return MS. when you write. Well, there's nothing more for me to say I guess, so I'll focus here. Write me at your earliest convenience, and tell me what you are doing in the line of rhyme. I have a lecture on "Funny Folks" nearly completed, which I think contains some good things perhaps—would like to have you "bucked and gagged" that I might read it to you. Give my regards to Mrs. H. and the children, and accept my warmest love.

Yours, etc.,
"TROUBLED TOM."*

To Benj. S. Parker.

Greenfield, Ind.,
Dec. 5, 1876.

Dear Parker:

I'm in a perfect hurricane of delight, and must erupt to you, "O gentlest of my friends." I sent you a postal recently stating my intention of addressing Longfellow.— Well, his response to my letter lies open before me, and as it is brief, I will quote it verbatim:—

"Cambridge, Nov. 30, 1876.

"My dear Sir:

"Not being in the habit of criticising the productions of others, I can not enter into any minute discussion of the merits of the poems you send me.

"I can only say in general terms, that I have read them with great pleasure, and think they show the true poetic faculty and insight.

"The only criticism I shall make is on your use of the word *prone* in the thirteenth line of 'Destiny.' Prone

---

*A character he took in a local play given by the dramatic club of which Harris was also a member.

means face-downward. You meant to say *supine* as the context shows.

"I return the printed pieces as you may want them for future use, and am, My Dear Sir,

"With all good wishes,

"Yours very truly,
"HENRY W. LONGFELLOW."

Shake! And let me thank you for the very great encouragement I have received from you, and your genial friendship from our first acquaintance. I am too full to write more, but will copy for your inspection, one of the little songs I sent Longfellow.

IF I KNEW WHAT POETS KNOW*

If I knew what poets know,
  Would I write a rhyme
Of the buds that never blow
  In the summer-time?
Would I sing of golden seeds
Springing up in ironweeds?
And of raindrops turned to snow,
If I knew what poets know?

Did I know what poets do,
  Would I sing a song
Sadder than the pigeon's coo
  When the days are long?
Where I found a heart that bled,
I would make it bloom instead;
And the false should be the true,
Did I know what poets do.

If I knew what poets know,
  I would find a theme

*Lockerbie Book, No. 47.

Sweeter than the placid flow
  Of the fairest dream;
I would sing of love that lives
On the errors it forgives;
And the world would better grow
If I knew what poets know.

I wish you would write me an answer to this; and send me anything you may have written since I saw you last. Oh, yes! I have a genuine poetess for a correspondent, and will enclose a poem of hers which you may return when you answer this. I speak of Miss Mary H. Krout, of Crawfordsville. We have exchanged quite a number of poems, and the one I send you will like I know.

I get an occasional letter from Harris, and they are always tinctured with a wit that makes a mental tonic unexcelled. He also has a letter from Longfellow, and wrote me of its favoring his productions—and so, you see, I'm doubly glad, and so are you, I know, and so are we all, and in the language of Tiny Tim,—"God bless us every one!"

Please write me at your earliest convenience.

With warmest regards to Mrs. P., I am yours

J. W. RILEY.

To the Editor of the "Kokomo Dispatch."

Anderson, Ind.,
July 23, 1877.

Dear Sir:

I write to ask a rather curious favor of you. The dull times worry me, and I yearn for something to stir things from their comatose condition. Trusting to find you of like inclination, I ask your confidence and assistance.

This idea has been haunting me:—I will prepare a poem—carefully imitating the style of some popular American poet deceased, and you may "give it to the world for the first time" through the columns of your paper—asserting in some ingenious manner that the original MS. was found in some old album, in the poet's own handwriting, signature, etc., and that you now have it in your possession.* Something of that sort—you can fix it—only be sure to clinch the story so she'll stick. If we succeed,—and I think sheer audacity and tact sufficient capital to assure that end,—after fooling the folks a little, and smiling o'er the encomiums of the press, you understand, we will "rise up William Riley" and bu'st our literary bladder before a bewildered and enlightened world! ! !

I write you this in all earnestness and confidence, trusting you will help me perfect the project—for should I use the "Democrat" as the medium of its introduction, people would "drop" most likely, and my bloom of hope be "nipped in the bud."—So in my need I come to you, feeling that the benefit—if any may arise—will be mutual. Should you fall in with the plan, write me at once, and I will prepare and send you the poem in time, if possible, for your issue of this week. Hoping for an early and favorable response, I am

Very truly,

J. W. RILEY.

---

*For the Poe imitation and the hoax, see "Leonainie," *Lockerbie Book,* No. 225. Also letter to C. B. Foote, Nov. 22, 1886, p. 63, following.

To John M. Anderson.

Greenfield, Ind.,
October 25, 1877.

Dear Anderson:

I have just received your letter of date October eighth, and this is the twenty-fifth. From exterior appearances your communication has been kicked and cuffed about from one point to another and "moved on" with as direful effect as ever was "Poor Joe" in *Bleak House*. Not less than a half-dozen directions are slashed, drawn and quartered on its erewhile snowy surface, and there are so many office stamps upon it that it now presents the appearance of being in the last agonies of some patent small-pox the government is introducing. Another thing,—it has been ravished as I think by some lawless wretch; for in it you speak of enclosing an article I fail to find. In consequence I am at some loss to translate your full meaning when you say, "It would be like you to do such a thing as this, and yet it scarcely was you, else the poem would have merit, which the article I send you disclaims." I can only guess, dear A., the article referred to is relative to the recent Poe-poem fraud, in which I played the leading rôle. If it is, it is but a segment of the abuse that has been heaped upon it by an irate press throughout the entire country, and only condemned in that it was the means of duping that owl-wise institution almost from A to izzard; the outgrowth simply of an idle scheme of mine to demonstrate the theory I held and hold, that all that is necessary to make a poem successful and popular is to prove its author a genius known to fame. This I accomplished with the assistance of a friend of mine, a journalist, who gave it to the world, with a cock-and-bull story about its being found, in faded ink, on the fly-leaf of some "quaint and curious volume of forgotten lore," for the poem was a "chow chow" imitation of the lamented Poe. Well, it went. "Everybody took it." In fact, it might have been said of it like any other humbug,—"No respectable family should be without it," until I am glad to say, my proposition was most thoroughly established. Not only was it gobbled by the state press, but by the ablest literary journals of the country, not to except William Cullen Bryant's *New York Post*. This latter named oracle, no sooner acquainted with our exposé, wheeled about, as did a hundred others, and heaped upon the poor, puny, baby verses every species of malignity and venom they could coax out of their bile. So mad, in fact, so duped and thistle-whipped, they could but writhe and bite and sting themselves. And let me add a truth patent to the mind of every one who looks with fairness at the case. Whenever the poem has been attacked, the assault has come direct from some poor victim of the fraud. Poor victim— doubly, trebly poor in that he would attempt to shield himself with the poor, vile, rotten barrier of a lie. Don't think from this I claim the poem has any special merit, for I do not, but I claim that while the ninnies thought it Poe's they blindly acknowledged it a "gem of purest ray serene."

Excuse me for so long a ramble o'er the desert of my theme, but hoping I have touched upon the matter of your query, I close myself like a Chinese lantern and blow out the light. Write me at once; your letters are most welcome. Any further inquiry I will be glad to answer, and if the topic I have spoken of is the one referred to by you, let me know and I will send you newspaper comments—as the sideshow "blower" would remark—"From all pawts of the wohld!" By the bye, in a postal weeks ago you spoke of having sent me a sketch of yours. Send it again, for it never reached me. I'd be particularly glad to welcome it just now, for you see, my boy, I'm recreating—that is, I'm out o' work and lying here as the poet says:

> "Like a sun discolored lover
> Stretched at full length on the sand."

Anything in the way of literary caramels I "open my mouth and shut my eyes" for "with languor that no lips could name." So send along your contributions to His Royal Indolence.

Truly your friend,
J. W. RILEY.

To Benj. S. Parker.

Greenfield, Ind.,
March 19, 1878.

Dear Parker:

I write to thank you for your defense of me in last issue. The *Herald* never tires of its attacks; but as they arise, as you discover, out of pure enmity, malice and hatred, and without tincture of judgment or justice, they only nettle me like stinging gnats. Again I thank you most heartily, and will hope to repay your kindness with a more substantial return than this.

Very gratefully yours,
J. W. RILEY.

Regards to family and friends.

To Charles Philips.

Charles Philips, a friend; the father a venerable friend and mentor, a newspaper editor of state-wide influence. (See "T. C. Philips," Biographical Edition, I, p. 263.)

Greenfield, Ind.,
July 8, 1878.

Dear Charles:

I write to offer you my warmest sympathy, and mourn with you in this dark hour. I had hoped to attend your father's funeral but could not. My heart was with you, and is with you now. I enclose a sonnet, which I trust you will accept as tribute of my love for one so far beyond our reach to-day that God smiles at our vain attempts to see him through our tears. I can think of no fit words of consolation; but be brave—act as you feel would best please him—feeling, believing,—aye, and knowing, that

> "Out of the deepest sorrow—
> Out of the darkest night,
> Into the peaceful morrow
> Flows the purest light."

With warm regard and tenderest sympathy to your family and friends,

I am as ever,
J. W. RILEY.

To Eugene Bundy.

Eugene Bundy, an Indiana lawyer; Albert G. Porter, a governor of Indiana.

Greenfield, Ind.,
April 8, 1879.

Dear Friend:

Your good words of the third I received with all gratitude, and believe I appreciate your great kindness. Such compliments, to me at least, are more than gold.

I am encouraged by your good opinion, and the interest you manifest in my welfare, and my hope is that I may never disappoint your expectations. My future is dubious. I know what I'd like to be, but am in great doubt at times as to my cramped condition financially ever allowing me to attain to that ambition. You suggest that my prospects might be advanced by a government position of some kind. Doubtless you are right, but where is the position?

I had a long talk with Albert G. Porter the other day, who was present the night previous at the Indianapolis Literary Club, where in response to an invitation I gave two or three original readings. He was especially pleased, and manifested so great an interest in my future that had your suggestion been before me then I should have turned it over to him as a gentle intimation that any little office running around loose in his jurisdiction would be gratefully accepted by "Yours Truly."

He said he would send me a letter of commendation which might be of service to me in case I desired to approach the august East with any of my literary work.

This I may do before a great while, for it is certainly my desire to excel. Many of the leading men of Indianapolis, as well as eminent men through the country, I am glad to say, have been attracted, and are urging me to "go up higher," etc.

I thank you very warmly for the additional interest you express, and earnestly trust that in some good way the auspicious moment will arrive.

I ask you to remember me kindly to your family, Judge Millet, and other friends, and am,

Very gratefully and truly yours,

J. W. RILEY.

To Theodore C. Steele.

Theodore C. Steele, an Indiana artist.

ROSES*

I dream that you are kisses Allah sent
    In forms material, that all the earth
    May taste of you, and guess of Heaven's worth
Since it can waste such sweetness with content,—
Seeing you showered o'er the battlement—
    By Angel-hands plucked ripe from lips of mirth
    And flung in lavish clusters, yet no dearth
Of rapture for the Anthem! I have bent
    Above you, nestled in some low retreat,
Pressing your velvet mouths against the dust,
    And, ever nurturing this old conceit,
Have lifted up your lips in perfect trust
    Against my own, and found them no less sweet
For having kissed the dust beneath my feet.

J. W. RILEY.

---

*"The Rose-Lady," *Lockerbie Book*, No. 317.

Dear Mr. Steele:

Here is the sonnet—and the sketch. Hope you will enjoy both: Wish you'd illustrate *"Ye Scholar,"** —for in that I can but think is a glorious theme: old interior— bric-à-brac—antique furniture—tapestry—musty tomes of ancient lore—with a Don Quixote-looking chap for central figure—— Ah, my dear Steele, you may paint roses, roses, roses, but *I* would paint the dear old idiots who pursue *ideals* to the death, and chase them into Heaven.

I am half sorry that we were not alone yesterday for I could have talked like a phonograph—fortunate for you perhaps that our surrounding did not permit; but I'll swoop down upon you ere a great while when I can have you completely at my mercy. In the meantime, in the language of the legend on my coat-of-arms,

"Keep on a-inchin'!"

and "God bless us every one!"

J. W. Riley.

To Howard Taylor.

Sept. 4, 1879.

Dear Taylor:

I'm just "dreened" out clean to the dregs. There's been a two-weeks' kink in my usually prolific fancy, and I can't get past it. Been working on my lecture—trying to—but am scarcely over the threshold, and my time is almost up. Wish I could see you, and get lulled again. That's what you do for me, if you want to know—you lull me, and I wish I could be near you always.

Your letter was full of pure good, and I can never

---

*"Ye Scholar," Biographical Edition, II, p. 62.

thank you enough for the love of that warm old heart of you that throbs in every line. I think you must be very happy always, and I hope you are. I don't pray often, but when I do you always come to me hand in hand with those I love;—"And O! The *children* with us—tender lambs!"*

My lecture is on poetry and character, and I think you will like it. It is in layers, you know, fruit-caked together with original poems, dialect and otherwise. My idea is to have it less profound than entertaining, but I think I'll have quite a tang of the former element. I do indeed. Tell you what I need: genial companionship, but I'm clear out of gun-shot of it here. It's getting awful. People all stop talking as I pass along the street, and stare at me like a "sum" in compound interest. Can't get me "fixed"—nor I them, and it's just naturally bearing down, and shuttin' me up like a Chinese lantern or a concertina— that's better—and squeezin' all the music out o' me. I've been trying to rest, but I don't believe I'm doing it. But I don't want to tangle you up in my troubles, and yet I'd give a hatful of my ripest worlds to *talk* with you an hour.

You're busy, too. That's good, for you are doing good all the time, you are at work—only everybody doesn't appreciate you as I do. They don't know how, though, and you mustn't blame them. But it's a glorious thought to me, that some time we'll all be made equal, and *en rapport* each with every other of God's children.

When will you send another poem to the *Tribune?* You have no idea how many friends that made for you among our literary people! You've a reputation to sustain here now, and I want to see you at it.

Tickled me—your description of how you humped your-

*From "Atheos," a poem by the friend addressed.

self up in the corner, and twittered the "Treat Ode"* for the "gudewife." Your conception of how it should be rendered is my very own, and I knew you'd get it right, if you hadn't said a word about it. Just finished a poem to-day that has *some* worth I think—though it's not whole-some. It is called "Delilah,"† with an approach toward the sensuous that I only indulge, believe me, for the ex-ercise of method, etc.,—not for any pleasure found in the contemplation of the theme.

The *Cincinnati Gazette* letter has never appeared, though I still look for it a little—having been "inter-viewed" by two different reporters. Of course you have seen the *Chicago Tribune* letter copied in the *Herald.* I would have sent it to you a week earlier, but didn't get a paper myself till it was a week old. You will find it *verbatim* in many respects, only the "purling brooks" the "warbling birds"—the "gleam of tiny stars" and all that you will recognize I trust, as far beyond my capabilities. You must wait yet a little for the picture. I will have some taken soon. I must—'cause I'm going to sacrifice the mustache before I read this winter, besides it's in my way for other reasons—and it's too big for the little man, and keeps me tilted—like a pair of steelyards, or somepin', and it's red anyhow, and don't match my hair—which is blue, you know.

And, now, Good-by! and if you can, write me sooner than you do generally. It seems ages between your letters.

---

*"The Tree-Toad," *Hoosier Book*, No. 3.

†Later incorporated in "The Flying Islands of the Night." See Krung's speech, p. 608, *Lockerbie Book*, lines beginning:

"I loved her.—Why? I never knew.—Perhaps
Because her face was fair; perhaps because . . ."

As I close I've a bewildering consciousness of having left out the very things I wanted most to say, and incorporated in their stead the unimportant. You will forgive me though, I know.

Write soon and let me know all that you are doing and dreaming for the future and "God bless us every one."

As ever, with all love,

Your friend,

JWR.

To Mrs. Mary Hartwell Catherwood.

Mrs. Catherwood was the author of *Lazarre* and other novels and is referred to in subsequent letters.

Greenfield, Ind.,
Sept. 16, 1879.

Dear Friend:

Seems like ages since I wrote you a *letter*—but it's ages I've been engrossed with a thousand things that prevented. Everything about me is tangled—tangled—tangled. My elder brother is growing well, I think, but is yet quite feeble and oftentimes discouraged over his slow recovery. The old promises for my brilliant future are still promising—they never let up on that, and I'm still believing as of old that I'm goin' to make it. Though just now I'm considerably muddled with a complication of prospects. Of course I don't want to go on a newspaper if the lecture business *will* pan out, but would like to reserve even that in case the lecture *shouldn't* pan out as I'm hoping.

By the ending of this week I hope to have ready for presentation the lecture—then somebody's got to suffer, and they *shan't* dodge it. The probabilities are that should I read at Indianapolis, it will be at the new Park Theater, which I understand will be the place, but it's a venture, you know,—fifty dollars for hall—to say nothing of advertising, tra-la-la-la, etc.

Just got a letter from Charley that is sadder than "a sorrow's crown of sorrow." I haven't written him for a century, and the poor boy's troubled about the dear old Home besides. I can't send a whimper, and it seems no one else can. God help us every one!

Whoop!

My attention has just been called to a "personal" in the *Journal,* stating that a complimentary benefit will be tendered Mr. Riley at Grand Opera House in the near future. And now this letter must be put aside for business. The cold chills and hot flushes are sweeping over me as I write. It seems a great undertaking to me there. "Where shall we land?"

Yours forever and a day,

J.W.R.

How I hope those influential friends of mine in the city are awakened to the true sense of their obligations(?) to your long-suffering, but still hopeful

GRAYGROLE.

Please write me soon. I'm so all alone here I die hourly. Write! write! In God's name, write!

To Mrs. R. E. Jones.

Aug. 4, 1880.

Dear Friend:

I'm 'most afraid you're spoiling me with all your good words, praises and encores, and tincturing me, too, beyond my wont with that delirious flavoring—enthusiasm—that leaps and revels so along your veins that my own twang and tingle as I write.   And I'm going to follow your advice— for this morning at least—and not attempt a line of verse until I shall have answered your best of letters and the soul it held.   "You are glad you are an enthusiast," and I'm glad, too,—'cause even though your lavish praise may stimulate an egotism as alert as mine, still that is just the spirit that needs active exercise, and should by no means lie dormant as you seem to think in your case,—"To write my best, only for the sake of beholding it in print seemed egotistical to me."—"And there are so many writ-ers in the field there doesn't appear to be room for all."— Make room, then, and for yourself—and I do assure you that you can't do that, no matter what your worth, with-out the strongest consciousness of that worth yourself, and the continued emphasis of that fact in your bearing toward the public, and in all you undertake,—and that may doubt-less be called "egotism,"—let 'em call it what they will— the more you possess of it, the sooner you will shake hands with Success is my serious belief.   But, ah! you say—"A man can wave his hat and shout bravo! and a woman she can"—just strike hands with him and climb right on to glory by his side—if she has only strength—as Mrs. Browning—the God-woman—to conquer her own mod-esty and self-disparagement, and let the great strong, towering soul step out and straighten-up among the stars. And what a glorious giant she is then!—I gather from your letters and your poems that it is your desire to reach, at last, *some height,* at least, along the upward path.   And this is why I have spoken, and will speak, most seriously.

More than four years ago I received a letter from J. T. Trowbridge responding to my query as to how I might find market for my verse. I was then, as now you are, writing gratuitously, but hungrier a thousand times, I know, for some crumb of pecuniary help, and recompense for my work.—And Trowbridge said in order to make poetry marketable in this day and age, it must be a part of it—that is, it must possess the qualities of the great Present: dash, brilliancy, strength, originality—and always a marked individuality of its own—a striking something that would stamp it from the ordinary. These are not his words—but the meaning of them as nearly as I can give it after the constant endeavor of years to follow his advice. Then it was not long till some hint of real success came dawning—not in the East, however, where naturally one looks for dawn—but here in the West, where are so many papers seemingly eager to advance and lend assistance to the poor bedrabbled strugglers in the ever-standing army of poets, jingle-ringers, and verse-carpenters. Since then, I have been steadily gaining, until now—with the exception of one magazine and paper of the East—I have more engagements for verse alone here in my western home than I can fill creditably—the pay not much, but still enough to humor some extravagances, and steadily increasing. Another thing I speak of before leaving this modus-operandi outline of how I write for market—and that is: We are writing for to-day, and for the general reader—who, by the bye, is anything but a profound or classical scholar. Therefore, it has been, and is, my effort to avoid all phrases, words or reference of the old-time order of literature; and to avoid, too, the very acquaintance of it—because we are apt to absorb more or less of the peculiar ideas, methods, etc., of those authors we read; and as everything is right in its place—so the old authors are right in the past—while new ones must

≈ Office of ≈

THE ANDERSON DEMOCRAT.

Todisman & Croan,
— PROPRIETORS. —

Anderson, Ind., July 23 1877.

Editor Dispatch — Dear Sir:

I write to ask a rather curious favor of you. The dull times worry me, and I yearn for something to stir things from their comatose condition. Trusting to find you of like inclination, I ~~write~~ ask your confidence and assistance.

This idea has been haunting me: — I will prepare a Poem — carefully imitating the style of some popular American poet deceased, and you may "give it to the world for the first time" thro' the columns of your paper — asserting in some ingenious manner that the original M.S. was found in some old album, in the poet's own handwriting, signature &c and that you now have it in your possession. Something of that sort — You can fix it — only be sure to clinch the story so she'll stick. If we succeed – and I think sheer audacity and tact sufficient capital to assure that end – after fooling the folks a little, and smiling o'er the recommends of the Press, you understand, we will "rise up william Riley" and bust our literary bladder before a bewildered and enlightened world !!!

I write you this in all earnestness and confidence, trusting you will help me perfect the project – for should I use the "Democrat" as the medium of its introduction, people would "drop" most likely, and my bloom of hope be "nipped in the bud": – so in my need I come to you; feeling that the benefit – if any may arise – will be mutual. Should you fall in with the plan, write me at once, and I will propose and send you the poem in time, if possible, for your issue of this week. Hoping an early and favorable response, I am very truly,

J. W. Riley.

be here in the present—see? Whenever I am forced to
say a commonplace thing it is my effort, at least, to say
it as it never has been said before—if such a thing can be
done without an apparent strain.   Then, too, as before
intimated, I exercise just all the egotism at command (not
a small stock, I assure you), and try to believe myself as
smart, or smarter, than anybody else who ever attempted
doing anything; and, as a usual thing, to counteract the
many dangers likely to result from such indulgence, I lay
my work aside, as first perfected, forget it as wholly as I
can, and the next day, perhaps, resurrect it in a mood the
very opposite of that in which it was produced, and coldly,
cruelly and most relentlessly attack and tear it into all
possible shreds,—then when Mr. Public gets it, if the critic
can find meaner treatment to bestow on it than I have
given, he must have a very wicked heart indeed, and I a
very tender one, if what he says of it can sting the least.

As ever,

J. W. RILEY.

To John M. Anderson.

Indianapolis,

Sept. 26, 1830.

Dear Anderson:

I never *"snubbed"* any man on earth—and you mustn't
go thinking yourself so favored,—but I'm no typewriter,
and can't in consequence click on incessantly.

The two sketches* you want I can't send without bustin'
up the file, and they won't have that, you know.   Why

---

*See *Sketches in Prose.*

can't you just be a little patient? I'll publish a volume, before a great while now. Something you can just loll back in, with your heels hooked over the eaves of heaven till that impudent old King of Terrors knocks the book out of your hands.

Yours hurriedly,
J. W. RILEY.

To Mrs. R. E. Jones.

Dec. 22, 1880.

My dear friend:

I'm afraid you're too good to me altogether—that I don't deserve half the praise you bestow upon my careless verse. But I like it all the same, and someway it makes me like you better and better all the time. And you may "scold" me just as much as you like 'cause if you'd only scold me the half that I deserve, as I guess you will, why, I'll forgive you with as much heartiness as you dare put in your attack. I did neglect your ballad, didn't I? But I really didn't mean to,—O my friend, if you only knew how they exasperate me—these people I work for and who pay so little—and how exacting they all are—and how everybody wants theirs to be better than all the others— and how little time they have to wait—and how I have to jump from dirges and dead marches to jingles and jim-cracks, etc., world without end,—you'd begin to think "Where on earth, in that little old hick'ry-nut-head of his does he find enough extra room even safely to stow away my name and address!" That's what you'd think, my friend—indeed!—indeed!—The ballad was good—and is good—or will still be—when I find time to re-read it and take it on my knee and pet and fondle it as I shall. You must not think me more selfish than I really am—for that's enough God knows—and so do I. And if you go to thinking me worse than I really am I'll just climb fences and cross lots toward insanity. There!

The *Independent* I refer to is the New York *Independent,* and while mainly religious is not wholly so,—so that your contribution is not frivolous in any way, but genial and wholesome in character, they'll be sure to consider it kindly, and I hope accept and publish what you offer. If they accept, they'll pay well—no fear. And just here while the idea again occurs,—you must, in writing for our modern market, avoid most vigilantly all methods and mannerisms of the old writers in old words, phrases, etc.,—for instance, such words as *erst, wa'st, Thou'rt*—and the numberless others of that order. Reason is, they can't be used without betraying affectation, strain, superfluity, see?—and then, besides, all the shoals of little minnow poets who write in albums have made that vocabulary peculiarly their own. So avoid that by all means. You will notice that tendency in the verses of our good friend Daniel Deronda Buck—but whatever you do, don't put *him* right—'cause that fellow could really write poetry if he'd only comb those old burs out of his lines. But only hear him!

> "The Home, as erst, *betokens* more
>   Than Eden ere *supplied:*
> And hearts are yearning, as of yore,
>   To grasp the *typi*fied."

There are four of these characteristic words marring the verse—making it sermonish and repellent. Do you see what I mean? But there are rare intervals along his mastery of this defect, where he permits real poetry to intrude—at least in idea—for there may always be found a tincturing of the objectionable element.—Speaking of the heaven, he says:

> "But the initials there transcend
>   The ultimates of this."

There's an idea, at least, and well said—poetically uttered, in fact, but for the old tincturing, as I say, of cold-blooded, graceless, sermonish words. And only listen to him again:

> "Fair home, where needs no *solar ray*
>   To smile away the night;
> Where shines an everlasting day,—
>   *The risen Lamb the light.*"

The first line with *"solar ray"* in it! My God! what has "solar ray" to do with poetry! The second line pure poetry in idea, phrasing, everything; and the next two commonplace—the last one absolutely awful! Kill Mr. Buck for me, please. Gather the reverend gentleman to his fathers.—Crucify him!—for it's an absolute shame that a man who could write poetry, only carpenters at it, and *builds* a poem, as he would a pig-pen, out of unwieldy planks and clap-boards. *Kill* the gentleman I tell you!— tramp on him as you would a bald "woolly worm"! You don't know how glad I am that you said—"I send you the poem because he wished me to, and I said I would not, because I think you would care for it." But you may tell him, should he ever ask you, that I found much to admire in the work, as I do, only don't tell him how the rest of it drove me idiotic. And sometimes there is the vaguest tendency in your poetry in the direction I have so bitterly assaulted, but it is, as I say, vague and faint as yet, but still enough that were it entirely out of it, your work would be vastly improved. Now I am talking cold fact. At least I am talking for an opinion of my own, which may be, after all only a crotchet with me. But I think I'm right, and I'm honest in expressing the opinion, and my views regarding it. That's all. And although I already like your verse, as I have long ago confessed, I want to see you improve it all the time as I want my own verse to improve in like respects, and as I'm always striving, most pitilessly regarding my own feelings, to improve it.

Your last poem, "Stay," is very tender, and in many ways graceful, but there is some effort apparent in it someway. Looks like you tried to write it—and of course you did write it with real effort—only one of the finest attributes of poetry-making is to conceal all effort. It can be done. Read any master to find that out. Longfellow above them all. He writes with the most painstaking care and slowness, and yet his verse all seems as though it made itself. There's the art of it. No matter how long it may take to write a verse—even four lines have been worked on as many weeks—so that when finished it shall seem so simple and natural in utterance as to have just dropped from the lips like a "God bless us!"

I've a thousand other things to say to you, and to talk over—for you must bear in mind that although I may put my ideas somewhat rudely and abruptly, I do not mean to shock or wound you—they're only my ideas and that's all they're worth—for, as I say, they may be entirely erroneous—only *I don't think so*. Now I must say good-by. If there are any things I have omitted speaking of, you will know I have overlooked them unwittingly 'cause

I like you with all sincerity, and want to prove it in all ways. Don't ever apologize for writing me long letters. I can stand that I assure you, and thank you for them miles longer. My only regret is that I can not find time to answer them as they deserve to be—that's the trouble. Yesterday I mailed you another poem—and if you don't like it, why, just say so. You can't hurt me by finding fault with me,—for if what you say doesn't agree with my opinion, I'll keep my own and love it just the same, and if yours is better, I'll not hesitate to cast mine overboard.

As ever,

Fraternally yours
J. W. RILEY.

To Joel Chandler Harris.

See "To 'Uncle Remus,'" *Hoosier Book*, No. 152; "To Joel Chandler Harris," Biographical Edition, V, p. 198.

Indianapolis,
Sept. 14, 1881.

Dear Mr. Harris:

Permit me to thank you for the great pleasure your "Uncle Remus" has given me. I like dialect when managed as you do it,—voiced by true character and genuine nature. The touch of the master is in all you do—in verse as in prose. Of your verse I would like to see more, and will you be kind enough to tell me where it may be found, if in print. If not—when you contemplate a book of it. "Good night, Mr. Kildee, I wish you mighty well!"   JAMES W. RILEY

To George C. Hitt.

George C. Hitt, business manager of the *Indianapolis Journal* and the friend who published the poet's first book. Myron Reed, minister and friend, who wrote one of the letters of introduction mentioned. (See "Our Kind of a Man" and "The Onward Trail," *Lockerbie Book*, Nos. 26 and 248.)

Boston, Mass.
Jan. 1, 1882.

Dear George:

Everything is well, and I guess I am goin' to "make it"—dead sure! I have been very flatteringly rec'd by the Bureau people, and the letters I brought are of much importance. With them yesterday I was "open-sesamed" around to a wonderful extent—meeting not only notables to whom they were addressed, but "boosted" on by the recipients till I knew everybody of the ink—all who were not out of town. The *Transcript* didn't need an introduction—remembering me without, and I'm glad to assure you—with some little enthusiasm. I met "Oliver Optic" yesterday—a very boy-like old man, who already had a ticket to my show. John Boyle O'Reilly was out o' town but is back to-morrow. Am sure of him. Positively assured of an audience of at least two thousand people—the best. Longfellow himself would come, he told me, but that his physicians are just now restricting his gambolings. Dan Macauley went with me yesterday, and we saw the old rhyme-clinker in spite of the doctors who have tried to shut the world away from him. He was very, very gracious, and complimented me beyond all hope of expression. Can't tell you anything now. Wait till I return, with the laurel on me brow,

There are many peculiar features about Boston. Yes, and you may tell Reed that Boston is nothing if not patriotic. Where "Fools come here to show their wit," I read this inscription:—"God bless Old Ireland—but damn the Irish!"

As ever,

J. W. R.

I'd like to send the *Journal* a letter, but can't possibly now, tell Halford.

I have seen Beacon Street—The Old South Church—Boston Common—and "The Bridge" where Longfellow "stood on his head at midnight," when the clocks were givin' the thing away, etc., etc.

To George C. Hitt.

Boston, Mass.
Jan. 3, 1882.

Dear Hitt:

What makes a place lovable is being welcomed to it, and made thoroughly at home. I can't begin to tell you how dear to me old Boston is! It didn't—just at first—seem thoroughly to appreciate the honor I was doing it by taking an engagement here,—but now it is "catching on," and we're mutually looking over each other's shortcomings, knowing each other better day by day.

I met John Boyle O'Reilly to-day, and which was the most delighted it would really be hard to determine. It appears that the Irish instinct in him had long ago singled out the peculiar merits of my verse, and by that he has assured me of a very old acquaintanceship. The prints of his fingers have not yet faded from the hand with which I write. His first request was that I should at once furnish him with a lot of my poems—as he wants to write, in their behalf, a special article. Then came a hearty and most pressing invitation to join his club at their anniversary banquet, Saturday night coming—and I wouldn't dare miss such a chance, you know—and so at once saw the Bureau,* who were equally surprised and delighted, and they have telegraphed, deferring two engagements on account of this most luscious one! I'm destined to meet every literary potentate of the town—and on an equality too. Just think of it! Men are bred and grown up here, through all gradations of development, with no other object than to work their final way into this club—and fail and fade and droop away and die without accomplishing their object.—And here I come and sidle in and don't even try to can't-help-myself! And to-morrow night—— (Now be calm—be calm!) John Boyle O'Reilly,† it is arranged, will introduce me to the Boston public. Dan Macauley has been doing splendid work for me, and if he can get time will write the *Journal* a letter.

As ever,
J. W. R.

To. Mrs. R. E. Jones.

Aug. 1, 1882.

My dear Friend:

Yes. The "Johnson" work is identical with the "Walker."‡ The *Herald* comment was simply meant to joke at a man that never attempted to write a line o' verse in his life,—an utterly practical fellow, but well

---

*The lecture in Boston was made under the auspices of The Redpath Bureau referred to; the club was the Papyrus Club at whose dinner Riley met Howells, Aldrich and others.

†"John Boyle O'Reilly," Biographical Edition, IV, p. 83.

‡Riley's early pseudonyms were "John C. Walker" and "Benj. F. Johnson of Boone," country poets, the latter signator to *The Old Swimmin'-Hole and 'Leven More Poems*.

known, and a great favorite with the newspaper fraternity. Wish I could answer your good letter—but can't now. Soon I will be on the road again, and am trying to patch up a programme—besides having a dozen other irons in the fire.—At work upon the completion of a *Patent*.*— Think of that for a "poet"!—The invention being the most startling matter-of-fact and wholesome contrivance ever heard of. Of course, I'll make a fabulous fortune out of it! Anyway, I'm going to try it.

If you wish to write sonnets, you have only to set about it in serious earnest. Read Mrs. Browning's and be strong—as she is strong. Then study Longfellow's, and be artless and subdued and very tender—yet deep as the love—the hope of any human heart—is deep. You must read Keats, too, and try to lure from his rich store some of the nectar of his language. Oh, he is wonderful! And may I again advise you to select words with greatest care. Avoid rigidly the "ersts"—"erstwhiles"—"Chrisms"— "pellucids"—"brooklets"—"cloudlets," and all that swarm- let of detestlets! There are thousands of these words, once used, but now altogether out of taste—and they oftentimes spoil poems for the modern reader when to save his life he couldn't define what was in the verse that struck him unpleasantly. Observe the first eight lines are, almost universally a proposition.—The concluding six, a sort of rounding up—a result—based upon the figurative mission of the former. The last six, the poetic sequence of the first eight. Then select always such rhymes as there are many of. And now I say hurrah for you, and God speed you in all you undertake.

As ever fraternally,

J. W. RILEY.

---

*The patent, unsuccessful, was a replaceable heel which has become famous since in the form of the rubber heel.

To Miss Elva May Riley.

She was a sister called "May," and the "Maymie" of "Old Home-Folks," *Hoosier Book,* No. 252; later Mrs. Henry Eitel. Reference is made below to a severe illness of Mrs. Mary Hartwell Catherwood.

Indianapolis, Ind.,
Nov. 28, 1882.

Dear M.:

I will write to the Catherwoods—should have done so long-ago (tell 'em) only have been selfishly fretting about personal matters. Even if she die, she will not die! but she must be made and kept brave always. That's the best word in the language. Brave.

As ever
JIM,

Riley on Matthew Arnold to Myron Reed.

Boston, Mass.

I don't know whether you will like Matthew Arnold or not—I know you like some things he has written. Two or three days ago I met him, coming out of New York into Binghampton, and had some opportunity to inspect him—my way.

He is English thoroughly, though quite Scotch in appearance. Until you hear him speak you would say Scotch. A tall strong face, with a basement-story chin, and an eye eager, unconscious, restless; gray and not large. A heavy man physically, though not of extra flesh—simply, a fine manly skeleton properly draped. He is self-sufficient, and yet trying to do better, on his own advice, not at all snobbish, and yet with hardly enough vanity to stand the criticism. He is a marked combination of learning—fancy and matter-of-fact. An hour before we became acquainted I inspected him and saw his colossal mind lost in the lore of the railroad guide same as it were Homer in the original text. I noticed, too, that when he bought a three-cent paper, he took back his two cents change and put it away as carefully as he would a fi'-pound note. He is poor, however, and I don't mention this only as instance of a national characteristic which may perhaps have been inherited—only in these "God-bless-us-every-one" times I could but remark in a mental aside: " 'Tis very good to be American!"

He seemed greatly pleased with all he saw and spoke honestly of his surprise at the country he found here. Was utterly stolid, however, and enjoyed it all like working a sum. Didn't parade himself—and wore arctics, and never forgot his umbrella. Much of the time, too, he was studying his lecture—in printed form—and ignoring the dailies that were having so much to say about him. I think he has no sense of humor whatever. A joke that tackled him, would hide its head in shame, and skulk away and weep.

He is not the genius Irving is. Irving is the one Englishman you will like clean through. You must see and hear them both—but Irving is the boss.

Hastily and heartily,

J. W. RILEY.

To Dr. James Newton Matthews.

See "Three Singing Friends," *Lockerbie Book*, No. 203.

Indianapolis, Ind.,
March 4, 1883.

Dear Matthews:

It's a good letter you send—and the sonnets likewise. The "Current Poetesses" series are good in their way— some lines well worthy to survive in real ambitious efforts, like

"Fan their souls with wings of butterflies . . ."

"Unloose the kisses from their languid eyes . . ."

"And wipe the midnight from their tousled hair," etc., but—even though the poetesses deserve censure for their highly erotic verses, I doubt the taste of any versified attack upon them. Let 'em ferment and effervesce, God bless 'em, as they may. Fate shuts down on 'em, as a rule, soon enough to make us, in the end, always forgiving and utterly compassionate,—save when God turns loose a Mrs. Browning. Then we stand back awed and mutely glorying. Poor Fanny Driscoll! Two or three years ago I met her for just a moment. A slight little girl, she looked not over sixteen. Her face was a perfect prayer of sweetness, and her manners simple as a child's. I had no time to study her, but the impression left upon my mind is as though a lily rested there in purest bloom. So doubtless she was white enough for Heaven. "She sleeps—her breathings are not heard."

Now mind! I didn't mean, because I said "grist of poems," to insinuate that you "ground" yours out, as you have interpreted, but to compliment you, rather, on the ability to produce so readily and rapidly. That means anything but grinding. It means spontaneity—fresh-ness—resource—qualities but very rarely found combined in one lucky-cuss-of-a-poet that supports a dignified and money-making profession besides. So don't you warp my meanings any more! Doubtless you do "grind" some-times—I know I do—but we don't get any poetry that way—and I said "grist of poems," please remember.

In the Poe sonnets, the work is splendid—masterly in parts—only the theme is joyless—and that hurts the success of such an effort, however deserving in all other qualities. It is what hurt Poe, and will always drape his memory with gloomy speculations and unsatisfying con-templations. He was a marvelous intellect perhaps as estranged from himself as from all of his kind. Anyway he seems, always, to me, unhappy, and his influence always cheerless. If I ever get to Heaven I will doubtless love him better there where all "will be unriddled." All melan-choly themes are pets of mine—positively; but I am grow-ing to avoid them as much as possible for I am more and more satisfied of their hurtfulness every new one I indulge, and then, too, I notice the poems we love the best—the poems that really live—have always blood and pulse and heart-warmth in them. There's the thing!—But I must close, and with a feeling, too, that you'll be glad of it—only I hope I'm wrong. I congratulate upon every-thing—not forgetting the "gudewife" that you love. Write me when you can, and always send whatever you have written or are writing in our mag.

As ever fraternally yours,
J. W. RILEY.

I send you with this a patent Spring Poem of mine, a beautiful song of Miles O'Reilly's (Maj. Chas. A. Hal-pine) "Jeannette's Hair." Perhaps you are long ago

familiar with it but I send it, in case you are not, as a
marvelous instance of tenderness in verse. And did you
know that its author blew his dear brains out in a fit of
despondency? God rest him!

To Benj. S. Parker.

Greenfield, Ind.,
June 10, 1883.

Dear friend Parker:

Your letter and poem, received yesterday, have delighted me greatly, and the latter is already on the *Journal*
hook for next Saturday. It's an odd confession you make
regarding your lack of confidence in any poem returned
you by a magazine, and I had to smile, remembering how
I used to be similarly affected,—for in my case I've had so
many returned, the disagreeable effects have entirely dis-
appeared, and now I rather like 'em better when they get
back from such cold-blooded cusses. However, I'm not
"goin' to give it up so, Mr. Brown" till I get one to stick
in every magazine that has ever rejected me! This is as
good as sworn to, and I want you to "hang on" with me,
and we'll "bring 'em" yet!

I can't tell you how really sorry I am at being without
hope of getting up to see you this summer, but maybe
next season the Fates will be kinder. And here, as I'm reviewing your letter, you ask for Mrs. Catherwood's address.—It is Hoopeston, Illinois. And when you write her
you mustn't fail to congratulate her over her marvelous
industry, and the continued and increasing favor her work
is meeting with throughout East and West. I am only
sorry that she seems to have given verse up entirely.

The new magazine you speak of—*The Electra*—I have

not seen yet, but will be on the lookout for it. Your Decoration poem I read with much applause and saw copied in several papers. The "spots" you speak of wherein you think now you could improve it, I suppose every writer finds in his work after seeing it printed and beyond recall—but *the reader,* I fancy, seldom finds a hint of them. I got a copy of the *New Castle Courier,* with your "Whistling Joe," which I think very wholesome and happy everyway. I feel sure, however, that your very best work is in that vein found in your "Vernal Vagaries" and "Birthday Poem" where your ship, "song-wafted, sails away."—That marvelous blending of truth and purity and fancy that is to give your verse endurance beyond your wildest hopes. I feel sure of this. And that poem, "The Darkened Room," is prophetic——

> "Into the peaceful morrow
> *Flows the purest light!*"

and that you "shall be led hereafter out of the darkened room" into the sunshine of your deservings be very sure.

The magazine venture you speak of would be glorious, and I sigh with you that such an enterprise may not be attempted. Wish to God you were at the head of such an institution!—Then I know I could squeeze my verse between covers for once, anyhow!

For the last few weeks I have been quite busy writing, and think, too, that I am doing something better than I have accomplished for a long, long time, if not better than ever in my life—but I will not occupy this remaining space with myself, but fill it instead with saying that Piatt's* book is simply superb. Your "Morning"† is in it,

---

*The friend, Piatt, is "Donn Piatt of Mac-o-Chee," *Lockerbie Book,* No. 159, a soldier, journalist, judge and poet, and the compiler of an anthology.

†Parker's "Morning" is referred to in Riley's last poem, "To Benj. S. Parker," *Lockerbie Book,* No. 408.

and with a lovely illustration stair-stepping down a full page. Harris, too, has been so honored—his "Harvest Days of the Long Ago" handsomely illustrated. I am going to try for a copy of the book, but will not (can not) pay $20 for it—that's the price—so you may know it is very very fine. Harris has a copy, but told me he got it at some discount some way.

Regards to all, and as ever I am Yours——

J. W. RILEY.

To Mrs. Mary J. Cartwright.

Indianapolis, Ind.,
July 3, 1883.

Dear Friend:

You must pardon my long delay in reference to the examination and return of your MSS., since my time has been so occupied I have not until now found proper leisure in which to study their worth and promise.

There is much in your verse to suggest your possession of valuable poetic faculties, but your inexperience, as yet, can not, of course, show them at best advantage—so you can not hope now to find a market for what you write.

You must be, as every writer of poetry must be, possessed of infinite patience and untiring industry. The road is anything but inviting. Even with the very highest deservings you may fail to gain the recognition that is your just due. As to advising you as to what course to take in the matter of the future exercise of your talents, I would say, by all means, continue; but I would not rely upon the results. Even Longfellow dared not do that— but aside from his marvelous genius as a poet—leant first upon a practical basis of support—a sure thing. So I would advise you, or any new beginners in the literary field. Of all followings this is the most precarious. But the talents you already display are worth fostering and developing with the utmost care; and your surroundings, however rich in opportunity, would be of no advantage whatever unless you had the hardihood to labor ceaselessly. Your friends will help you all they can, but you yourself must prove your own high worth—and that's the real work after all. Were I to offer you further advice, in this view, I would say: Study—study—study! Read—read—read! Study to discover the real secret of success in writing, and read—only successful books—to dissect and hunt out the deep-down secret of the beauty of the successful poet's song. Avoid reading the older poets (this is not the usual advice, I know, but the best advice, I believe) and read only the successful modern poets. Longfellow, first of all—not forgetting, as you read, that not the easiest-flowing line of it all but was produced only by oftentimes the most painful effort. Tennyson, the same.—All pure beauty of real verse is only produced by pure effort of real artists: The verse when completed sounds exactly as it should sound,—as though it made itself—but universally such perfection is only reached by genuine and most persistent effort. Some enthusiastic admirers of Tennyson once said to him, pointing out such a perfect utterance,—"Ah! This is so simple—so artless—so graceful in flow of expression—I at once recognize it as having come unbidden, just of itself, in this perfect form!" "But you are entirely wrong," said Mr. Tennyson, "I smoked not less than six cigars in the construction of that line."

Now, Mrs. Cartwright, you see, you have only to work with the rest. If they whose success is proved, set such patterns of patience as these, what may you not hope to accomplish with like patience and endeavor. Believe always I wish you every good thing, and have great belief in your promise. Remember me kindly to our friends, and I am

Very respectfully yours,
J. W. RILEY.

To Joel Chandler Harris.

Greenfield, Ind.,
Aug. 9, 1883.

Dear Mr. Harris:

For a day I am here at home, where I have taken my little sister's* paper (but she is a very generous little girl—with no end of pets—one cat is *Arethusa Huckins* and one is *Dr. Radcliffe*) upon which I hastily imprint my thanks to you for the gentle way in which you accept my book. You are a good man, and the things you say of my work please me more than I can tell you. I like all you have written, because in it you make your characters speak—until there seems no artist anywhere. That is my idea of real art.

What you are doing, I am trying to do.

Why I didn't publish with Osgood of Boston—as you ask,—I felt I couldn't get in gun-shot of 'em. After while I want to tackle 'em—and will.

Your work to me is pure poetry—the finest art—utterly forgetting self. I can't tell you how greatly I enjoy it. Every way believe me your most fraternal friend.

J. W. RILEY.

---

*Mary Elizabeth Riley (Mrs. Mary R. Payne).

CHAPTER II

Name and Fame

Lecturing—His first book—Literary correspondence—The Nye-Riley combination proposed—Letters to Nye—The place of dialect in literature discussed—The book *Afterwhiles*—The Authors' Readings, New York City—The Nye-Riley combination—A dinner in his honor—London publishes a Riley book—The poet meets a public misfortune—His friends rally around him.

To John A. Riley.

John was his older brother, the "Johnty" of "The Old Home-Folks," *Hoosier Book*, No. 252.

Delphi, Ind.,
Aug. 29, 1883.

Dear Brother John:

That was a good letter you wrote about the book, and I should have answered it at once, but—the old excuse,—still absorbed in most exacting restlessness, and deferring everything until I shall have come up to the real breathing-space that has been so "long, long, long on the way." And, I guess, after all, I am really going to "get there"—maybe very soon now—as it seems.

A week ago I came across from Indianapolis to lecture, eight miles from here—at Camden; and it being out of the legitimate season for that work, and having made some particularly warm friends here a year ago, when a party

48

of the same drove over to hear me "argy" and to bring me here, why, of course I came, and have been with them ever since, most thoroughly enjoying the stay and all the rest and benefits involved—among the latter, especially, an entertainment urged by the citizens, in which, at the opera-house, night before last, I raked in a clean fifty dollars, above all expenses, and the applause of the general public in no whit abated. But to-morrow I get down to work again, and, I confess, loathfully indeed. The real lecture season opens soon, and as a bran-span new lecture is advertised by the Bureau, I've got to have it down in both manuscript and memory, and the last day of grace is looming vividly in near outline.

As to the little book,*—it has been signally successful so far, and will go through more than one edition—the second already arranged for—a scheme in which I have no investment but consent to the further publication, receiving for same the very liberal royalty of twenty cents on every volume sold—and if this sort o' thing keeps up, I'll soon be able to work more leisurely, and with less fever and more health evident in all that I produce. Private letters of praise from the literary nabobs of America settle the fact of the quality of the future that awaits—only, I'm tolerably tired already—but guess I'll worry on all right. The Editor of the *Century* writes: "I must say that there is nobody at present writing who seems, to me, to get so much of genuine human nature into a short space, as you

---

*Refers to First Edition, *Old Swimmin'-Hole and 'Leven More Poems.* Its second edition was the first of many books published for Riley by The Bowen-Merrill Company, later The Bobbs-Merrill Company. Throughout his life this firm was his official publisher and its rise and success were coincident with his. The company published some hundred different books or titles for Riley. The relationship between the poet and the entire personnel of the house, especially with Mr. W. C. Bobbs, Mr. Charles W. Merrill, Mr. John J. Curtis, Mr. H. H. Howland and Mr. D. L. Chambers, was intimate and happy throughout, and it may be said that seldom have publishers understood an author better, or an author returned the compliment more happily.—EDITOR.

have." And Joel Chandler Harris says: "You are the only verse-builder within my knowledge who has caught the true American spirit and flavor."

And so, "God bless us every one!" I should like to see you very much.—Some time everything will be right. I feel surer of this each newer day that dawns and dies away.

When last home, all were well. The girls are very lovable, and very brave. I think we are all heroic enough to make God glad—and your goodness and patience, my dear brother, I think must keep Him smiling all the time.* With warmest love and affection for you and yours, I am as always

Your affectionate brother,

JIM.

To Joel Chandler Harris.

Delphi, Ind.,
Aug. 29, 1883.

Dear Mr. Harris:

Your recent good letter, favoring my literary ventures, should have received a prompter reply than this, but I have been skurrying fretfully about the country, with no breathing space till now.

It pleases me greatly to see, what seems, at least, evidence of newer and worthier ambitions in our present writers—many of them: The old classic splints are being loosened and taken off, and the long-cramped mental members are limbering at the joints, as it were, and striking straight out from the shoulder, and I would rather

---

*Mr. Riley here refers to the home made desolate since the death of the beloved mother.

have you call my verse *Nature* and *American* than this
hour to find myself the author of "Queen Mary." While
not a howling dervish in the patriotic line, I can truly
say of the right scream of the Eagle,—"I like it: it has a
soul-stirring sound!" and I believe we are at last coming
upon the proper spirit of this voice in literature. Some
nights ago a reverend friend of mine—a beautiful MAN—
read aloud to me your "Teague Poteets"* sketch; and at
every character-spot in it I wished you there to hear and
see. His minute acquaintance with the real personages—
quality—surroundings—dialect of brain and soul as well
as speech—all wonderful, and wonderfully faithful in interpretation, as I felt, of Nature and your own exquisite
reading of her very heart.

Cordially and gratefully yours,
JAS. W. RILEY.

To Howard Taylor.

Cleveland, O.,
Nov. 2, 1883.

Dear Taylor:

This isn't an answer to your last, but to tell you that I
have just met John Hay, and he doesn't look or act at
all like the man who wrote either "Little Britches" or
"Woman's Love," nor yet "The Whiskey Skin." Very
businesslike he is, and care-worn in appearance—but says
it is occasioned by ill health. He is not the stalwart frame,
I have heretofore fancied him, but rather slight in build,
a fine face, and head, and a keen dark eye—sees clean

---

*The man who read was Myron Reed. (See "Our Kind of a Man,"
Lockerbie Book, No. 26.)

down into the bowels of things. I regret that he is rich, and half-way think he hates it. Says he would like to write more, but business vexations take up all his time. He was very kind and courteous, and has invited me to his Euclid Avenue home. And did you know that he was born in Indiana? At a little old town called Salem, which he laughingly said had never appeared in history till John Morgan and his men swept through there "durin' the Army" and burnt it down. You would like him I am very sure.

I am dodgin' round a good 'eal of country, and only a few nights ago "argied" below Crawfordsville, and your brother John joined and went along. He is a very lovely character, and I think we like each other wholly.

Remember me kindly to the "gude wife and the bairns."

Hastily, but always heartily yours

JAMESY.

To Mrs. Mary Riley Payne.

Mary Elizabeth Riley (now Mrs. Mary Riley Payne) is the youngest of the family, the "baby Lizzie" of "The Old Home-Folks," *Hoosier Book*, No. 252.

Boston, Mass.,*
Jan. 30, 1885.

Dear Mary:

You said I must write you from every place on the road during my absence, but almost any good little girl ought to know that one can not do that, par-tic-u-lar-ly whilst one is trav-e-ling through New England during the Winter Sea-son, for, you should know, that the Winter here is a great deal cold-er than Char-i-ty, and so it is, that you will know bet-ter how cold that re-ally is when you have grown to be a woman as bald and bleak as your brother.

You know at Scranton, Pa., I said the weather had no-wise grown formidable. But I didn't get to stay in Scranton. So it is I am shivering here in Boston, and almost wishing myself on a veritable Greeley polar junketing ex-perience. I sleep now with my arctics on, and am awake at all hours of the night trying to thaw my head loose from the pillow.

Last night, on the rostrum at Peabody I fled shivering from the audience after just exactly forty minutes' ap-pearance. It seemed to me forty years. When I am dead—a very long time—I may be colder, but I can't bring myself to believe it. Peabody is patroned, as you will guess, by the deceased philanthropist who endowed it, among a hundred other such villages here, with some pub-lic library, or educational foundry, and it is quite prob-able, I dare say, he was born there. In that event it's no wonder he's dead. Directly in front of about the one-hundred-fifty-year-old hotel where I stopped, stands an elegant marble statue to the old toot, sixty or eighty feet high—and you've no imagination to portray to you how cold he looks without an overcoat even as thick as mine. Once in a while a cold man rushes into the hotel to warm himself and stamps his feet so hard that his nose jars off and splinters into glittering fragments at me feet— though I positively heard an old Bostoner say this morn-ing, "Seems to be mildin' up considerable. Shouldn't be 'sprised if they wa'n't a slip o' sleddin' by Sat'dy!"

Some two or three more Mass. engagements, then back through Penna. again—one at Phil., care Y. M. C. A., then West, and can't wait for the time. Dates exact not listed yet—so, if any special word, it must be sent care Bureau here, 36 Bromfield Street, as you doubtless know.

To-night I may accept friendly invitation to theater, but seriously think of going to bed about dusk—I'm so utterly fagged out.

Mustn't forget to add that I saw Grover Cleveland at reception at Albany in his honor the other night. Seemed to have a hand on him recently dipped in hive of bees, and a head on him equally swollen, but not with pride. Altogether the impression received I count a very pleasant one. With love to all, and a bone for the dog to roll over, I am as ever,

Your affectionate brother,
JIM.

To Samuel L. Clemens.

Indianapolis, Ind.,
Feb. 25, 1885.

Dear Sir:

Your studies in which real characters and their varied dialects occur have interested and delighted me for many years, and in thanking you as I want to now, I beg you to accept the little book of Hoosier dialect I mail with this.

Very truly yours,
JAMES WHITCOMB RILEY.

Peace kindo' sorto' suits my diet—
    When women does my cookin' fer me,—
They wasn't overly much pie et
    Durin' the Army.

To Alonzo Hilton Davis.

Indianapolis, Ind.,
Apr. 16, 1885.

Davis, Dog-gone it! I'm in bed again! I was glad to get
your letter, however, and will try and build a little one in
reply. I am lying flat o' my gifted back and writing with
my toes. I have seen better days. Guess I'm goin' to
have another bile,—there's a red streak coiled around my
leg now like a boa-constrictor and great grief! how 'turts!
If you never visited Mount Vesuvius during business
hours, come and see my bile when it erupts. I wrote to
Mr. McIntyre and McConnell yesterday, but concealed
my real condition, knowing both would encourage me to
die—one wanting to *funeralize* and the other to *obituarize.*
You ask for my life, but I'd rather give you my money.
I was thirty-one years old last spring.—I am a blonde
of fair complexion, with an almost ungovernable trend
for brunettes. Five feet six in height—though last state
fair I was considerably higher than that—in fact I was
many times taken for old High Lonesome, as I went
about my daily walk. Used to make lots of money but
never had any on hand. It all evaporated in some mys-
terious way. My standard weight is a hundred and thirty-
five, and when I am placed in solitary confinement for life
I will eat onions passionately, bird-seed I never touch.
I whet my twitterer exclusively on fish-bone. My father
is a lawyer, and lured me into his office once for a three-
months sentence. But I made good my escape, and under
cover of the kindly night, I fled up the Pike with a patent-
medicine concert-wagon, and had a good time for two or

three of the happiest years of my life. Next I struck a
country paper and tried to edit, but the proprietor he
wanted to do that, and wouldn't let me, and in about a
year I quit tryin' and let him have his own way, and now
it's the hardest thing in the world for me to acknowledge
that he is still an editor and a most successful one. Later
I went back home to Greenfield, Ind., near Indianapolis,—east, and engaged in almost everything but work
and so became quite prominent. Noted factions and public bodies began to regard me attentively, and no grand
jury was complete without my presence! I wasn't, however, considered wholly lost till I began to publish poetry
brazenly affixing my own name to it. But I couldn't get
any money for it, although stranger editors wrote me
letters of praise regarding it. Then I sent a little of the
best of it to two or three real poets East, and they com-
mended it, and I showed their letters, and have been paid
ever since. Still I am not rich. A skating-rink proprietor who yearns to be a poet should be regarded with
suspicion.

But seriously, my dear friend, I can't write seriously,
the way I feel. It is too solemn a thing. Mainly, however,
the foregoing truthfully outlines my brief career. But
I've been blue over being "downed" again by the blasted
lameness, and I'm trying to keep cheerful. Whenever
you can give me a line, I want you to. I like you and
want you always for my friend.

Sincerely yours,

J. W. RILEY.

To George C. Hitt.

Cleveland, O.,
March 6, 1886.

Dear George:

Last night here we bagged the town—a success not even second to our Indianapolis ovation. Nye* is simply superb on the stage—and no newspaper report can half-way reproduce either the curious charm of his drollery—his improvisations—inspirations, etc., or the, at times, hysterical delight of his auditors. We repeat to-night by especial request of everybody. Newspapers all sent reporters, quite an audience of themselves, as they sat in be-tabled phalanx in the orchestra-pen and laughed and whooped and yelled and cried, wholly oblivious of their duty half the time. Mail with this their result as printed up to date.

As ever,
J. W. R.

To. Mrs. R. E. Jones.

Indianapolis, Ind.,
March 30, 1886.

Dear Friend:

Am just home from a long but very successful trip about the country. With Mr. Nye for company the trials of travel are lessened till now I am almost content with what seems my principal mission here on earth, i.e., to spread over and run all around it like a ringworm.

*Edgar Wilson, "Bill," Nye gave a famous series of readings with Riley in 1886 and continued, at intervals, until January, 1890.

But the beautiful paper you have written in *The Union-Advertiser!* And how "to-day's poets" ought to rise up and call you blessed! *One* I know of does—and asks God to join him—clasp hands with him—clench teeth—and bless—catch breath, and bless and bless and bless with mutual might!

I write with great haste. Know how more than grateful I am.

As ever fraternally yours,
J. W. RILEY.

Will mail with this, New York paper with Nye-Riley sketch.

To Edgar Wilson Nye.

There are several poems to Nye and his family: "Edgar Wilson Nye," *Lockerbie Book*, No. 289; "To Edgar Wilson Nye," *ibid.*, No. 198; "Max and Jim," *Hoosier Book*, No. 81; "The Robins' Other Name," Biographical Edition, III, p. 410.

Major James Pond, the famous lecture manager; Henry Ward Beecher; Amos Walker, Riley's own manager; Hiram Y. Potts,—see "The Artemus of Michigan," Biographical Edition, IV, p. 4.

Indianapolis, Ind.,
April 6, 1886.

Dear Nye:

Pond is in town to-day—with Beecher, who lectures on "Conscience" to-night—Pond, I suppose, plays "bust" in the harangue. Walker had a smiling conference with him this morning; and I fancy, from the way Walker still smiles, that he must have "got back" at the Major very pleasantly.

I'm afraid our *Potts-poem* has spiled the fellow. He writes me a very dubious postal, enclosing us thanks; and

from that—together with a comment in Field's column—
I am led to fear he has misunderstood the kindly intent of
the rhyme. Ain't it too bad?—Pat a man, and he thinks
you're "beefin'" him!

Why don't you write?—or can't you read my first
childish attempt? We're dyin' to hear from you—both of
us. I'm writin' poetry by the yard—The first one of enclosed list* is to my new girl—and you're the only one,
outside of ourselves, that knows it. She says she doesn't
care for just you—if I don't.

Hastily,

J. W. RILEY.

To Edgar Wilson Nye.

Indianapolis, Ind.,
April 7, 1886.

Dear Nye:

Potts is all right after all.—Hurrah! I sent you a letter
just received from him. In his *Courier Journal* comment
he said of the poem simply:—"It will be observed our
name incidentally occurs in it." Just got your letter—and
oh! Sir, how can I ever repay you? To me it bears a
striking resemblance to

"The moan of doves in immemorial elms—
The murmur of innumerable bees."

Walker is not in town to-day, so I can't tell what it
looks like to him. Would that he were indeed here!
Wouldn't be at all surprised if he were out marrying; I've

---

*"Five Poems by James Whitcomb Riley," *Lockerbie Book,* Nos. 56, 146,
214; *Hoosier Book,* No. 120, and "Babe Herrick," Biographical Edition, III,
p. 336.

just telegraphed my last chum before him in congratulation of his nuptials. Oh! my God—my God! As the poet John D. Hopkins might wail:

"The women came running,
   Crying 'Oh! what a time—
James W. Riley not married,
   The sun will not shine!'"

Am mighty glad to hear of your tacklin' our *Railway Guide*.* There's not an hour of the day I'm not thinking of that venture—and more and more convinced that it'll stanch a long-felt want. And we can hustle it into market, too, before any long delay. That's the beauty of it—it really wants to look impromptu—and be so—measurably so, at least.

The dear public here is on the "key-veeve" regarding our next appearance, and oh, my boy, we're going to git their everlastin' pelt on our pitchfork! I haven't yet on tap enough imagination to picture the size of the house that'll greet us—but it'll be positively tremendous. You and I, with our retiring dispositions, would never be able to get into it were it not for our peculiar connections with the proceeds. Therefore let "Come-easy-go-easy!" be ever our watch-word as we press on from ear-to-ear.

Arrange for limited yet lordly audience with me during our next list: Mrs. New† is preparing for one of her receptions for her church. You're to help me there, and

---

Nye and Riley's Railway Guide, containing almost anything but time tables, published 1888, and reissued under various names, as *On the Shoestring Limited with Nye and Riley.*

†Mrs. John C. New, stepmother of ex-Senator and ex-Postmaster General Harry S. New.

then, in return, as per promise already, I'll "speak" for
you any place you want to take or send me.

Hastily yours,

J. W. RILEY.

To Edgar Wilson Nye.

(*Cir.* April 14, 1886.)

Dear young Friend:

Although my time is greatly taken with press of literary engagements, I trust, as now, I shall always have a
cheery word and a kind smile for the timid, though deserving, novice in letters that you prove yourself. My first
duty, as I count it, is to warn you not to be discouraged in
your literary work simply because you find it irksome to
compose and can not at once dash over countless pages
with the grace and ease of the skimming swallow. This
faculty can not be acquired in a day, as I myself recall, in
the far-off youth of my own fame, how sometimes in the
turning of the simplest epic I have wasted whole hours.
Do not you, therefore, hope for the fadeless laurel, in lieu
of the six-and-five-eighths hat which for years yet must
grace your broad and oasisless brow. Think you that
either Cicero or Potts "got there" the first dash out of the
box? Ah, no! a thousand noes! They panted, and they
blowed, and sweat till you could see their suspenders
through the back of their vest, and even then, as Aristotle
tells us, "their copy was little less than most villainously
damnable and vile."

But to business: Walker is effecting some guarantees
that are simply exquisite. Day after day he tears himself
from my side and goes forth into the busy marts of men

and lumps us in for the lowest possible rate. So we have
already cut out for us some very pleasant work. But the
ruling passion is still strong with him, for only yesterday
he came in to say, with ill-concealed and feverish delight,
that he has sold us to another Ohio town, and immediately
immersed himself in his *Railway Guide,* coming to the
surface occasionally to knead his whiskers, and stare off
into limitless Chaos. I doubt very seriously if you will
know him next time you meet. He has grown so gray!
so gray!

It is the lecture agent,
    And he has grown so gray—so gray—
I'd write the cuss a letter,
    And send it right away—
        For if much longer it's deferred
        He'll be too old to read a word.

It is the lecture agent,
    And he has grown so mixed—
You'd ought to send his mental traps,
    Somewhere and have 'em fixed,
        For RR Guides and routes and maps
        Have wrecked him hopelessly, perhaps.

As ever, yours faithfully,
J. W. RILEY.

To Robert Underwood Johnson.
(Editor, The Century Company.)

Indianapolis, Ind.,
Nov. 11, 1886.

Dear Mr. Johnson:

Your note of October twenty-fifth is gladly hailed at
last. Like yourself I've been away; so this loitering answer.

The reason I have sent Magazine nothing in the line you ask after, is—it has had unprinted dialect poem of mine for three years. "Nothin' To Say"* is poem's title. Do you recall it? I've added two stanzas and use it in public readings with effect.

Let me know soon the fate of the poem. And oblige,

Faithfully yours,

J. W. RILEY.

To C. B. Foote.

C. B. Foote, in collecting books, had found the old Ainsworth Dictionary on which Samuel Richards, the artist friend below mentioned, had inscribed "Leonainie" in imitation of Poe's own hand. (See note and letter to *Kokomo Dispatch*, July 23, 1877, p. 14.)

Indianapolis, Ind.,
Nov. 22, 1886.

Dear Sir:

Replying to your recent favor, regarding authorship of the poem "Leonainie," I can claim the poem only—the autographic copy which your letter describes—its original, at least—was executed (at my instigation, and with equally boyish unconsciousness of guilt) by an artist friend of mine, now wearing first honors in the Art Schools of Munich. He did his part well, and was thus the author of the best part of the poem. He worked then as he works now,—straight from the heart. He had only a line or two of Poe-facsimile to "inspire" from, but some way the fellow caught the spirit of the whole vocabulary from it, furnishing a result that many notable and most exacting critics were bewildered by, as I myself saw tested many times.

---

*"Nothin' to Say," *Hoosier Book*, No. 196.

It is but just to all concerned, for the better understanding of the real facts of the case, to speak further, though
with you now I will be as brief as possible: The poem was
written about twelve years ago in the town of Anderson,
Indiana, while I was a very callow writer on the *Democrat*,
of that place; and, being rallied to desperation over the
weekly appearance of my namby-pamby verses, by the
editor of a rival sheet, I devised the Poe-poem fraud
simply to prove, if possible, that critics of verse would
praise from a notable source what they did not hesitate to
condemn from an emanation opposite. By correspondence
(still preserved) the friendly editor of a paper (the Kokomo, Indiana, *Dispatch*—still conducted by same Ed.)
assisted me in foisting the hoax on the public through his
columns—this for reasons obvious; while still further to
conceal the real authorship of the poem, as soon as published with its editorial hurrah, I attacked its claimed
worth and authenticity in my paper. Then every one who
knew me, knew, of course, I didn't write a rhyme of it.
And so it went—and went—and kept on going—till at
last the necessary exposé. Papers everywhere lit into
me—friends read all this, and stood aside—went round
the other way. The paper upon which I gained the
meager living that was mine excused me—and no other
paper wanted such a man—wouldn't even let me print a
card of explanation—not for weeks, while I stood outside
alone, and walked around the Court-House square at
night, and through the drizzle and the rain peered long-
ingly at the dim light in the office where I used to sleep,
with a heart as hard and dark and obdurate as the towel
in the composing-room. All of which is smiling material
now, but then it was pathos from away back.

But pardon all this, and tell me one thing that to me is
quite as singular as any other part of all the "mess."

I am at great loss to account for the book and poem being in your hands—if, indeed, you have the original,—as I myself carried and placed it in the hands of the editor of the Kokomo *Dispatch,* where, until your letter, I still thought my property reposing. There certainly must be a gnarl somewhere. You did not give me the name of your dictionary. The one employed for my purpose was an old, leatherbound Ainsworth's, in fair condition then— not dog's-eared—still compact in binding, unblemished, and other evidence of having been nicely kept.

Let me hear from you soon regarding this. I will be more than grateful. Pardon me for so long occupying your better time, but should you care to see detailed history of the affair, advise me, and—should I answer overture am now considering—I will be glad to send you printed article.

Very truly yours,
J. W. RILEY.

N. B. Would not ask you for prompt response, but that my stay here is brief, and being on the road so much your letter might not overtake me for weeks.

J. W. RILEY.

To Richard Watson Gilder.

(Of the Century Company.)

Greenfield, Ind.,
Dec. 4, 1886.

Dear Mr. Gilder:

Your comment on the bits of dialect makes a very glad man of me and I thank you warmly for your kindness. The meaning of one line you ask after,—

"Like her, too, about *livin'* here,—because *she*
   couldn't stay,"*

refers, as you surmise, to the mother's death; and while it
may seem a harsh reference to so grave a fact, its speaking character seems, to me, to demand it, and later, for
same reason, the reader, I think, wholly forgives, if not,
forgets it.   However, direct me, if I be at fault.

Pardon the delay of this, as it has been out of my power
to write you sooner.   Am on the road, nearly all the
time—and now write at sorto' fatigue trot.   Tell Mr.
Johnson I will soon answer his favor.

Faithfully yours,
J. W. RILEY.

To Eugene V. Debs.

Greenfield, Ind.,
Dec. 6, 1886.

Dear Eugene Debs:

Dr. Hays† has just reminded me, by mail, of my over-
due promise to send you the new and unprinted stanza of
the "Terry Hut" poem.

You must pardon, as I know you do, my seeming
neglect, finding my full love for you in the rhymes.

You would better, I think, get a *printed* copy of the
poem as originally published.   And watch the "proof" by
comparing with this "copy," else, the God-blessed printers'll manage to ring in a cold deck of dialect on us, sure!

Faithfully yours,
J. W. RILEY.

---

*The quotation is from "Nothin' to Say," *Hoosier Book,* No. 196.
†Dr. Franklin W. Hays, one of the poet's most intimate friends.   "Re-
gardin' Terry Hut," *Hoosier Book,* No. 53.   In this poem Riley paid a memorable tribute to Debs's warm heart.

To Colonel D. A. Barrackman.

(*Cir.* 1886.)

My dear old friends: It jes' beats all, the way you write
    a letter
So's ever' last line beats the first, and ever' next-un's
    better!
W'y ever' fool-thing you put down, you make so inter-
    estin',
A feller, readin' of 'em all, can't tell which one's the best-
    un!
It's all so comfortin' and good, 'pears-like I almost hear
    ye,
And git more sociabler, you know, and hitch my cheer up
    near ye,
And jes' smile on ye like the sun across the whole perarries
In April, when the thaw's begun, and country lovers
    marries:

It's all so good-old-fashion'-like to talk jes' like we're
    thinkin',
Without no hidin' back of fans, ner giggle-un an' winkin',
Ner sizin', how each other's dressed—like some is allus
    doin',—
"Is Marthy Ellen's basque ben turned, er shore enough a
    new-un!"—
Er ef Deam's city friends hain't "jes' a little kindo-
    sorto"—
Er ef he wears them eye-glasses jes' cause he hadn't orto—
And so and so, dad-libitum, 'tel all of us feels *some* way
Jes' like our "company" was best when we git up to come
    away!

That's why I like old friends the best—jes' 'cause they're
    so confidin',
Ef I was built to live al-ways, my principal residin'
Would be amongst the folks 'at kep' me kindo' thinkin'
    of 'em,
And sorto wantin', every day, to tell 'em how I love 'em—
Sich folks, you know, I jes' love so I wouldn't live without
    'em,
Er couldn't even drap asleep but what I dreamp about
    'em,
And, ef we minded God, I guess, we'd all love one another
Jes' like one fambly—me and Pap, and Madaline and
    Mother!*

Your old friend,

JAMES WHITCOMB RILEY.

To Benj. S. Parker.

Greenfield, Ind.,
August 29, 1887.

Dear Parker:

Just as your letter came I was called from town, and
so till now I have been kept from answering it.

In many respects I agree with you regarding dialect—
Yankee, Southern, Hoosier and all the rest; still I most
conscientiously believe (outside of all its numberless de-
viations) there is a legitimate use for it, and as honorable
a place for it as for the English, pure and unadulterated.
The only trouble seems to be its misuse—its use by writers who fail wholly to interpret its real spirit and character either through blind ignorance, or malicious perverse-

---

*"Writin' Back to the Home-Folks," Biographical Edition, IV, p. 279.

ness, in what they are about. To range back to the very
Genesis of all speech, we can only righteously conjecture
a dialectic tongue—a deduction as natural as that a babe
must first lisp—the child babble—and the youth and man
gradually educate away all like preceding blemishes. And
I think it is absolutely necessary, in the general illustration of human life and character, to employ the dialect as
the speech refined—its real value, of course, dependent on
the downright wisdom and honesty of the writer who employs it. And my ambition in the use of dialect is simply
as above outlined. That I have few endorsers among the
scholarly I grievedly admit, yet am graciously assured
and compensated by the homely approbation of my class
and grade of fellowmen. Once in a while, however, (and
there's, at last, a discernible growth of the tendency)
some finished critic discriminates and estimates the dialectic purpose exactly. Let me quote from *Art Interchange*
of August thirteenth:

It says of a dialect poem of mine in August *Century**
that it "is an illustration of the only possible excuse for
this sort of work," in that "the tender and touching little
poem does not depend on the dialect"—but that—"The
feeling, the homely pathos of the verse makes it of value,
and the dialect is simply its strongest and most fitting
expression." Now I am very proud of this detailed estimate of the poem. That is the highest praise I seek or
my ambition desires, and I think you will believe me and
approve me there. I want to take advantage of your
kindly invitation to come over to you for a brief visit. For
a long time I have thought of surprising you so anyhow—
for always your kind of welcome, to a cuss like me, is
remembered more pleasantly than any in the world beside.
But I'm hampered and handicapped, even as every other

---

*The poem referred to is "Nothin' to Say."

yearning spirit in the world, and can only do what the Fates allow. Had I not been called on the road I would have seen you here, during our fair, as I learn you were over. Everything I can do, in the way of talk, I am doing for your prospective book; and anything I can do in the way of buying it I will do as gladly. Dr. Matthews, of Illinois, too, is the same inclined—and a lovelier character than he has not been shelled out of the pod of ages! And hosts, and hundreds more of your true friends and admirers will doubtless hail the volume with prolonged delight. Send me your prospectus, price list, etc., in number, and I may be able to distribute same to some effect. With best regards to your good family, and love eternal to yourself,   I am,

Yours as ever,

J. W. RILEY.

To Edgar Wilson Nye.

Indianapolis,
Sep. 23, 1887.

Dear Nye:

It was with no small feeling of delight to have you recount your many happy experiences and ever-accumulating joys in your new home. And now, joined with your family once more, and, haply, housed, with all modern conveniences at beck and call, and a dingus to let the water squirt without no pump to prime er nothin' ever' time you want a drink er rench yer hands! The New York friends of mine I am mighty tickled to hear about—especially that publisher who read you the harelip dialect* poem. I had

---

*Nye's joke refers to "Joney," a poem in Hoosier dialect, about a boy with a harelip,—*Hoosier Book*, No. 46. The publisher in reciting seems here to have overinterpreted it.

almost forgotten it was the reason I never recited it to
you. But, do you intimate, you will perhaps now never
want to hear it again? However I have just completed
a new dialectic study enlarging on the peculiarly interesting characteristics and eccentricities of an old friend of
ours you will, I'm sure, most pleasantly recall. The poem
bears simply his distinguished name, "Doc Sifers,"* and—

Of all the doctors I could cite you to in this-'ere town
Doc Sifers is my favorite—jes' take him up and down!
Count in the Bethel Neighberhood, and Rollins, and Big
   Bear,
And Sifers' standin's jes' as good as ary doctor's there!

He ain't much at his office, er his house, er anywhere
You'd natchurly think certain fer to ketch the feller
   there.—
And—can't blame Doc! he's got all sorts o' cur'ous no-
   tions, as
The feller says, his odd-come-shorts, like smart men
   mostly has.

He'll more'n-like be potter'n' round the Blacksmith Shop;
   er in
Some back lot, spadin' up the ground, er gradin' it ag'in;
Er at the workbench, planin' things; er buildin' little traps
To ketch birds; galvanizin' rings; er graftin' plums, per-
   haps.

Make anything! good as the best!—gun-stock—er a flute;
He whittled out a set o' chesstmen onc't o' laurel-root,
Durin' the Army—got his trade o' surgeon there.—I own
A finger-ring 'at Doc made out of a Secesh bone!

And so the chronicle runs on to the doctor's *medical* excellence and to the very natural final summary of his
being "Jes' a great, big, brainy man!"

---

*"Doc Sifers," *Hoosier Book,* No. 67.

I quit bed here, according to Hays' promise, in five more days, for an Ohio engagement. By the bye I want awfully to come, as you imply, to "show with you," and visit you as well. Will be thrown back for a while by this blasted spell, but once on my pins I'll be ahead of the hounds again in no time. Then invite me again—that's all.

Tell Catalpa* I send her a poem—just ground from the charmed pencil-tip wherewith I write,—couldn't put it in ink—can only sit up long enough to back an envelope and lick it shut and cuss. Remind the children of me, still deluding them in the belief of my being a very pleasant little gentleman. . . . Do you ever see the *Century* folks? Mr. Johnson there has been and is treating me good. If you ever see him tell him of my gratefulness.

Mr. and Mrs. Grover Cleveland's visit here I of course look forward to with no common interest for fear they will find me all tore up. I hear many talk of being at the depot when they come. It will be a very crowded train no doubt and no peace o' yer life on it.—Write soon. Thanks for everything. Don't fail to send me your articles. I miss 'em, and I'll do anything in return.

As always
JAMESIE.

To Edgar Wilson Nye.

Indianapolis, Ind.,
Nov. 4, 1887.

Dear Nye:

Did you get home without a backset, and how are you now? I am filled with remorse at not seeing you for a

*Nye's nickname for his wife was "Catalpa."

longer time and permitting you to do more of the talking. I have ever since been reticent enough, but no one fills the interim, and "Silence aches around me like a strong disease and new," as Polk Baker would say. Have been on the hump, however, fortunately: and waiting for trains, and then getting on the right ones, has done much toward keeping my mind too much employed in one focus of regret— otherwise I would not be thus shoveling you coherent thoughts, but doling and poking you the contrary through the bars of my cell at the Asylum. Mainly on these later excursions I have been fortunate, but stepped in on a poet my last trip whose aroma has not wholly died away in the disinfected past. He was the author of the famous "fly-speck" poem, in which he most ingeniously employs the fly volapuk. This poem he read and recited to me many, many times, deftly wiping his mouth at the conclusion of each stanza.

Have you heard anything further from Walker? I have not and am afraid he's sick again. He had a long spell of it some weeks ago, about which he said nothing, but I heard of incidentally.

Your letter to Mathews pleased the fellow beyond expression, and the lovely man deserves every pleasure, too, that overtakes him. Always say a word to him when you can. Some day he'll make every better-on-him very proud. And he's steadily growing too in his profession, and coming to be regarded by the general brotherhood of his state as a man they want at their head, and he'll be so officially placed in an early convention, I learn from a prominent Champaign (Ill.) physician.

Pardon my brevity, or like me better for it, since it's my best for the present. I have said nothing, and can prove it, but none the less I felt the attempt at saying something would at least be noted by you as a good sign. With warm regards to your family all, I am,

Faithfully yours,

JAMESIE.

To Mrs. R. E. Jones.

Nov. 9, 1887.

Dear Friend:

Your October letter from Chesterville was wonderfully welcome to the then "shaddery" invalid I was. Been ill for months and months, and now anything but a Samson in point of strength—though so much better, the last few weeks, I'm printing, for the Holidays, another poem-book, called *Afterwhiles,* which I'll send you, among first of my friends—see! the very promise, tense and all, is thus down in the poem:—

> Afterwhile—and one intends
> To be gentler to his friends,—
> To walk with them, in the hush
> Of still evenings, o'er the plush
> Of home-leading fields, and stand
> Long at parting, hand in hand:

So you must forgive me for all my devious remisses every way—I'll correct them—*afterwhile*

> Afterwhile—the poet-man
> Will do better—when he can
> He will even fulfill jes'
> Ever'thing he promises!
> Afterwhile, with deep regrets,
> He will even pay his debts;
> And by drayload, cart and hack,
> Will take borrowed volumes back,

Envelope addressed to Mr. J. M. Anderson with a pen sketch by Mr. Riley

That their owners, ages gone,
Haven't had their clutches on
And will gibber, shriek and smile
When he brings 'em—afterwhile!

Only, this stanza is not in the poem but just here for "smiling purposes," as Bill Nye would say. So some one told you I was married, did they? No, I've only just been dying of other "visitations," such as coughs, colds, "rhumatiz," and "every-other-day-ager"—a very popular variety in this locality.

And now will you pardon the brevity and nothingness of this capering page. It seems I'm always out o' breath more and more with each oncoming year. I holler at each day that whizzes past and lifts my hat: "Say! whither dost thou scud—and where's my sere and yellow hair evaporating to?" Am not steadily in lecture-work this season—hope only to fill occasional dates, and do more writing—too much and long neglected, by years. And now at last, can actually make money by it. Only think of it! ! !

Always fraternally yours,

J. W. RILEY.

Address me here. Tell me all you're writing and contemplating, and all success be with you.

To Edgar Wilson Nye.

Indianapolis, Ind.
Nov. 11, 1887.

Dear Nye:

Just now there is an invitation to me, through Mr. Johnson of the *Century,* to come and "say a piece" at "The

Authors' Readings"* in International Copyright League interest, dates November twenty-eighth and twenty-ninth. And upon consulting my intentions about the matter, I find that I can go, and thus hasten to warn you of the fact, so's you can have your chores at home purty well off your hands and the house red up perparitory-like, as the feller says, to receive me with, with corroberatin' eclaw; and, last but not least, to ast you if I hadn't better fetch along a extry shirt, and buy my tobacker here, as I have heard my kind is not to be had there fer love er money. I wish, too, that you and Catalpa and the fambly would meet me at the depot—wherever I git off at, so's I won't git carried past and run on into some other town where I hain't got kith ner kin, I'm the blamedest fool on travelin', I reckon, they is outside o' the durn lunatic asylum—'bout not gittin' trains, er gittin' the wrong one, and all sich aggervations thataway!

In replying to Mr. Johnson's request to name selections, for them to draw from, I gave one only title for program,—"The Educator" which you know as "The Object Lesson."† (New name's better, don't you think?) The rest of titles simply "hedges," you know, such as "Character Study"—"Dialect Sketch"—"Poem," etc. Then told him to see, or get word to you, and you'd know better than I what would stand the best chance of pleasin' 'em, in point o' length, theme, and the rest—not forgetting "motif" of course.

Mr. Johnson mysteriously postscripts invitation, to keep it dark for few days. Wonder why,—and what 'ud be-

---

*"The Author's Readings" were given in Chickering Hall, New York City, November 28, 29, 1887, and the outstanding writers of the nation were invited to appear. Riley's success on this occasion when he was invited to appear on the second program after appearing on the first and was felicitously introduced by Lowell was a stepping-stone to wide national recognition.

†"The Object Lesson," Biographical Edition, VI, p. 188.

come of a feller if he'd take it back, and I'd not get to go there after all? Reckon, though, it's all right, as I bet on his friendship among the first. Write me soon, and allus believe in me henceforerd—'cause 'y God, Bill, I like you! As ever your

JAMESIE.

To Edgar Wilson Nye.

Indianapolis, Ind.,
Nov. 21, 1887.

Dear Nye:

How kind it was of the Bostonians to go and hear you, and how grateful you must indeed be! And did Bronson Alcott express himself *en rapport* with your theme and *motif,* and greet you as greedily as he was wont to hail and boost along young Rufus Choate and Daniel Webster? Did you deftly touch upon the Renaissance—and how did they tumble when you gave "The Fuzz upon the Porcupine" and "Little Orchid Anna"?*

Have just written Mr. Johnson, (who asks that I be there two or three days previous) to say lecture-dates hold me from arriving sooner than Saturday twenty-sixth—then don't know the exact time, but will wire you on the road som'eres. Hope Lowell will not crawfish 'cause I'm goin' to give 'em sompin' new in dialect, and you must assure him that my estimate of some of his is really very generous, but you can tell at the same time that I could see it was all put on, and that I knowed he could spell better if he tried. I got on to that, durin' the Army, when he wrote on the fly-leaf of an old Ainsworth dictionary the prescription:

---

*Nye parodies refer of course to "When the Frost Is on the Punkin" and "Little Orphant Annie."

"Ez fer War I call it murder!—
    There you hev it plain an' flat.—
I don't hev to go no furder
    'N my Testament fer that."

Wish you *could* stroll down to the depot, but if you can't conveniently I'll track you to your lair somehow, though you've been now in captivity so long.

The book is now fitfully dropping from the Press—in paper boards, however, so I'll not send it you till in cloth— then bring it, 'y God! and make you read it! Tell Lowell, and the rest, you think you can work it so's they'll get a copy. And I'd freely give Howells one if he'll turn in and write about two magazine pages regarding its chaste Tolstoian and lubricous purity.

Will telegraph you soon as I know bearings.

So *Adios, Mon Share!*

To Edgar Wilson Nye.

Indianapolis,
Dec. 20, 1887.

Dear Sir—Kind Sir—Oh, Sir: How can I ever repay you for writing those little lines on my new book?—Doggone it, Bill! I can't talk nonsense now! You've just delighted me clean to the bone, and my joyous laughter is actually damp with tears. You have got away under my spareribs, and I'm a-lovin' you about as readily as I did that last hour of our parting, when we stood on the restaurant steps and talked real serious facts and swopped hearts, you might say, till we'd catch up again on our European tour—

"With a terrypallin hat and roundabout so blue,
And pace the quarter-deck like our Daddy ust to do."

All around the office comments have been goin' till your sympathetic soul should tingle clean off there on Staten Island! One says: " 'y God! that's good!" and another: "Dam' if that ain't sense!" and whoever says anything, and whatever he says, just the same as he says it, he means it—and they all laugh over it some and love you more.

You and I must get together some way. I don't travel—don't, some way, seem to get over the ground without you—too much lame-and-halt-and-blind business about my gait. Le's "hee-o'-hee" together once and see if we can't make it.

Pond told me he'd write Walker,* and he evidently hasn't. *He* (Pond) wrote me and I've just sent Amos that. Wanted W.'s address (which of course he's got already) and said he thought he could put him right to work. Now if Pond and Walker would or could work together I'm sure it would benefit me as well, and then I'd feel a hope, at least, of standin' in again with you—even there in N. Y. I believe, we could open to a marvelous business, workin' it up as we could do if all our heads were shuffled up together on the scheme. Encourage Pond, if you will, in the matter. Did you get Mrs. Nye's book and the Rain-poem all right? First edition all gone—second issued and half exhausted—and there's no end o' promise for the darn thing! And it's sellin' the other two books again—and "it all beats Sheol." As always   Affectionately yours,

                                        JAMESIE.

---

*Major Pond, the famous lecture agent, and Amos Walker, Riley's manager, shortly consummated this Nye-Riley combination which Riley here proposed.

To Richard Watson Gilder.
(Editor, *Century* Magazine.)

Indianapolis,
Apr. 23, 1888.

My dear Mr. Gilder:

This is to make you acquainted with Mrs. Mary Hart-well Catherwood, whose prose I regard, in point of pure narrative, force, fidelity to life and character, as second to no writer's out of the West.   She is visiting the East,* and would advise with best editors and publishers regarding unprinted matter in hand; and this I would urge you to examine, assured of your interest.   In any way you can further her desires you will find just reward be sure.

Faithfully your friend,
JAMES WHITCOMB RILEY.

To Richard Watson Gilder.

Indianapolis, Ind.,
May 3, 1888.

Dear Mr. Gilder:

Quite recently I sent a western lady—Mrs. Mary Hart-well Catherwood, of Illinois—a letter of introduction to you.   I have known and admired her high gifts and womanly character for years.   Endowed natively in a very superior way, she is a trained writer, as well, as her finished and most wholesome juvenile serials in *The Wide Awake* magazine have for years attested—not to the children alone, but the "youths of larger growth."

---

*It was after this visit that Mrs. Catherwood had accepted by *Century* her first novel, *The Romance of Dollard,* this being published serially in the magazine.

Particularly I would like you to know her, and examine, too, any manuscript of hers, should she present it, as I feel certain her maturer work is worthy of the highest and best audience of our present.

With all sincerity your friend,

J. W. RILEY.

Again I must thank you for your great kindness to the "Little Wesley"* poem. The artist adorns and drapes it in a gentler pathos than its own,—and the vain author forgets himself and grows *kindo'* moist and glimmering around the eyes. Kemble is certainly *our kind*. My best to the staff entire.

JWR.

To Richard Watson Gilder.

(*Cir.* May 7, 1888.)

Dear Mr. Gilder:

With your last letter came one from Mrs. Catherwood— both a delight to me, since you each express a like satisfaction in the acquaintance I was blest in bringing about. She was, and is henceforward, yours gratefully you may depend. If all applicants for editorial favor were as deserving every way as she, what a pleasant office you would have to fill, and how envious would I be! My best regards to all the friends, not forgetting your good wife, and Mrs. Johnson.

JWR.

---

*"The Absence of Little Wesley," *Hoosier Book,* No. 197.

To *Alonzo Hilton Rice.*

Indianapolis,
May 18, 1888.

Dear Sir:

As you request, I return the poems which I have read with interest and pleasure, and for which I thank you most heartily. You have a talent for verse that is certainly worth cultivating. Do not wrap it up in a napkin. I would not advise a too close application to the sonnet form. Poets who have gained wide recognition on this form alone are indeed few. A conformity to its strict rules results more often in obscurity and failure than otherwise. Your "Mulberry Tree" is a pretty pastoral with a lilting measure in true keeping with the subject. As to directing you in regard to a publisher, you can only seek them with your wares. Rarely, however, do they encourage any author, however excellent his work, unless the market absolutely demands it. Then they will not "fatten" him by any means. Every author should have some certain means aside from his literary work whereby to "put money in his purse." All successful ones have so provided. Longfellow, Bryant, Stoddard, Stedman, Twain—all. And that's what I'm trying to do and must. I wish you every good thing.

Sincerely yours,

J. W. RILEY.

To *Edward Eggleston.*

Indianapolis, Ind.,
May 26, 1888.

Dear Doctor Eggleston:

For an hour or more I have struggled to copy something on the vellum to look, as well as read, "neat." If, as I fear, I have only succeeded in spoiling the sheet, frankly say so, and give me another chance, with your forgiveness.

Very truly yours,
J. W. RILEY.

To William Carey:
(Of the *Century*.)

Indianapolis,
July 5, 1888.

Dear Friend:

Tell me who wrote that beautiful, tender, honest-sounding little poem to me in last *Century*. It's as good as a great big cup of coffee creamed with the milk of human kindness. And thank the Eds. too, and the blessed institution from "turret to foundation-stones" and if you don't send me your picture—and the rest of 'em there—and the Keats masque, I am goin' to come over there and git 'em. Nobody needn't ever lie thataway to me! With all heartiness remember me to Miss Hutchinson and God bless us every one! As ever the best of friends—ain't us, "Pip"?

JAMES HOOSIER RILEY,
The Whitcomb Poet.

To Edgar Wilson Nye.

Indianapolis, Ind.,
Sep. 1, 1888.

Dear Nye:

Just mailed letter in which I forgot to ask about

"proof" of *Guide*.* Will I get to see it? Think I should if at all possible—especially the dialect. Hope Pubs are so instructed, as one "get" for "git" would prove fatal to me, as you know. By consulting Pond you could tell 'em where proof would reach me promptly at any time, and with like promptness I'll review and return. Did you know Vanzile's† a poet, or does he "let concealment like a worm i' the bud——"? Anyway tell him *I've* told *you* he's to write me a Pome that gits there with the full complement of feet. And now if he doesn't let up, I'm goin' to print the news here that he's a rabid writer of Campaign songs, and contemplates changing his department's Caption to "People Lied About." Give him my best.

As ever
JAMESIE.

To Joel Chandler Harris.

Indianapolis, Ind.
Sept. 18, 1888.

You mos' sho'ly did, Uncle Remus,—and I bleeged to 'low I done run out o' 'propriatin' thankys evah sence!

Very seriously, your estimate of any success of my effort is more gratifying to me than could be that of any critic living. From the first, your work has struck me as just the kind of literary fabric needed, since so honorably stamped with the profound neglect of Scholars!

Your work is Nature's—exactingly honest—purely human—wholly artless. In fact, you really seem to think

---

*The *Nye and Riley's Railway Guide* is again referred to.
†Edward Van Zile, of the *New York World,* to which Nye contributed his famous sketches.

that anything in material of scene and character that is good enough for God is good enough for

Always His grateful Servant and your own,

J. W. RILEY.

To Edgar Wilson Nye.

Indianapolis, Ind.,
Oct. 3, 1888.

Dear Nye:

Your last goes very well for a letter despite your apologies regarding its shortcomings in that regard; and I am sure it will prove worthier in that line than my present effort. The main trouble with my present mental condition is—I've been trying to answer all the orders for Christmas poems that have rained in for months, and are still at it in sharp spiteful showers—and my intellect with no umbrellar and no hole to crawl in till the thing blows over.

As to *The Guide*—as fast as proof comes, my tire-women sponge me off and prop me back against fresh-pounded pillows, then administering revivifying draughts, they again give me good pencil to me keeping whilst I ransack through the pages till me brain reels.

Well, mainly, I like the book, and in all events think it'll go; but—I may be supersensitive about the artist's true mission and position with the authors. You remember we discussed before the same tendency on his part—the artist's? I don't mind his frolicking some—but I do urge that he should, at least, deport himself on a level of gentility with the author—not *below* it, and thereby drag the innocent down into his de-basement-story. Therefore two of my poems I've asked the publisher to excuse from being seen in public with the artist's idea of my depraved condition, which condition, I need not remind you, is really not a wholly lost one. But I don't like to criticize, for fear pubs will think I'm knockin' just because I can. Though in all sincerity, I think the book would be improved by the loss of many of the pictures—the material otherwise made none the less attractive—in appearance—page-form, and the rest. If you vest me with the power, I'll not spare the artists, who, as I understand, were instructed to furnish suitable designs, and in perfect taste and keeping with the matter to be illustrated. I just pray for the success of that book; and if it does succeed—we've got a little jersey mine, and one of the very pleasantest ones to work in the world.

Yess sirr!—Your old man that milched on his boots'll make a splendid number, I think:—and The Old Man and photograph sketch, too, I think would get there very firmly. Lord! I just eech to be out now facing the clamorous, and dear, at the same time, Public! Yes, I consider your handwriting fair, but it will improve, you will find, upon hanging about a joint more of your tongue out on left side when you are writing letters. I've got some new numbers that I think'll go—"At The Capital"*—and "Little Johnts's Christmus."† My book here is with printers now, and goin' to be a winner I feel certain. About size of "Boss Girl," but far pleasanter arrangement of matter, five prose sketches, intervened with four books of poems. The title,—*Pipes o' Pan at Zekesbury*. With love as ever.

JAMESIE.

---

*"Down to the Capital," *Hoosier Book*, No. 199.
†"Little Johnts's Chris'mus," *Hoosier Book*, No. 88.

Reply to An Invitation of the Western Association of Writers for a Surprise Dinner, October 18, 1888. *

Indianapolis,
Oct. 15, 1888.

Secretary Western Writers' Association,

My Dear Mrs. Andrews:

Some damp, dank, dismal morning like one confronting me, I fancy Master Shakespeare's morning-face all suddenly illumined,—as he forebodingly sorts out such letters in his mail as may predict his breaking into duns, and submitted manuscripts and requests for autographs with no stamps for return,—all suddenly, I say, in fancy I behold the grim face brighten as the inspired gentleman turns hastily to his private Secretary, with the remark:

"Gad Zooks! me dainty lady typewriter,
Some here do send me bidding to a feast
Who little recks the appetite they roused;
So! nimbly now let dance thy finger-tips
Athwart the chattering keys that bind me love
And fullest service to them, with huge thanks.
And prithee answer quickly—dost thou mark?—
Else may they have most cunningly contrived
A string attached the subtile invitation
Wherewith to jerk it back by ere my most
And fullest acquiescence clinches them."

But very seriously, I find no fitting thanks to offer you. Simply, my friends are too good, and myself too otherwise that such an honor should come to me from your most generous hands and hearts. Certainly one good must

*See letter from S. L. Clemens, Appendix, p. 329.

come of it to me—a higher sense of what my duty is to my first and best friends in the world. And God bless us every one!

Faithfully and fraternally,
James Whitcomb Riley.

To Charles A. Dana.

Buffalo, N. Y.,
Oct. 22, 1888.

Dear sir and friend:

A recent letter from you to literary friends* at home did me such honor that I am at utter loss to thank you fittingly. Your good comment I would rather have than fine gold; so it is that, although a very wealthy man is now addressing you, he still remains too poor in speech to pay you a tithe part of his gratitude. Simply you must know that your expressed confidence and interest in my effort strengthens and makes better my resolve righteously to deserve it. Steadily ahead, too, will I move in quest always of the way wherein I hope to find your approbation.

Faithfully and gratefully yours,
James Whitcomb Riley.

To Edgar Wilson Nye.

Buffalo, N. Y.,
Oct. 23, 1888.

O Sir!

How exasperantly propinquent art thou, and yet, indeed, remote! I am swearing sotto voce as I write.

---

*The "literary friends" to whom the poet refers were gathered at a dinner in his honor given by the Western Association of Writers, the Denison Hotel, Indianapolis, October, 1888.

Vaguely I trust yet to get on to you this trip, but fear I'm yet to hang fire. I want to see and thank you personally for that letter of yours to "The Strayed Revelers," on the occasion of my recent banquet.* Of course I was knocked indisputably out; but none the less you should have been there to observe my *porte* and *bonhomme,* and other mental and literary sundries. It was a merry gathering, and my hair stood up and pulsated like a telegraph pole. (You will note, by this figure, that I am not wholly bald yet—by one hair, at least.) Your letter easily took the gate money, and with great great applause that jarred the plastern loose and uncapped hell, as Milton would blindly but commensurately grope through and permeate the appropriate way to put it.

Will not, dare not, now attempt any details of the affair,—but they're interesting to even an outsider who is forced to *work* for "bread to eat." Soon hope to open up entire budget and hear your well-beloved chortle of delight. What you tell me of Edwards is appetizing in the extreme, and certainly I will hail his coming in our midst either locally or for all time. Simply, what suits you will suit me, I'm dead certain—only, I'm oh, so impatient to be in the hands of those who will protect me from myself. I wouldn't travel a mile and three-quarters, alone, in any direction, either in or out of a railway guide, for any money on earth, were I not compelled to. Soon, I spit on my hands and pray, I will be utterly abolished from all the ache and cark and care of the one-man-show business! Then only will I be supremely blest, and at full peace with God and man.

Just leaving home, the English book† arrived. My

---

*Nye's humorous tribute on the occasion of the dinner mentioned in the previous letter.

†The "English book" is *Old-Fashioned Roses,* published in London, by Longmans Green and Co., 1888.

eyes! and eke "Odds-bobbs!" quoth I! It is simply exquisite—never anywhere have I seen its beauty, taste and
elegance surpassed. It looks like a Classic! Tell Catalpa
I'm reserving a copy for her, soon as I can devise a worthy
enough inscription to set inside the opening cover. Saw
yesterday's *World,* where Van Zile quotes London
Academy regarding it. If it only does "catch on" there
as implied!—well, old man, we're made, that's all! With
no uncertain gratitude nor laxity of affection I remain
steadfastly yours.

JAMESIE.

To Edgar Wilson Nye.

Indianapolis, Ind.,
Aug. 5, 1889.

> *"It's home, boys, home, and it's home you better be;*
> *It's blithe you'll return to your own counti-ree:*
> *The oak and the ash and the bonny willow-tree*
> *They're all agrowing green in your North Ameri-kee!"*

Dear Nye:
  By yesterday's paper I very joyously note that you've
embarked for home. Much as I've enjoyed your Parisian
letters, direct from the Champs Elysées, I uncomplain-
ingly exchange 'em all for you, confident that when I see
you you'll put me on to the French tongue "as she is spoke,"
with a Staten Island accent. Someway, from your summer work, I recognize that you've been feeling first-rate,
which is a condition I have but very recently attained.
Three days ago, in fact, was the first time I've put a pen

to paper since our divorce: So now I am attending night school and learning to write again, with fair prospects, as you see. All of your sojourn I've been with you, in fancy, and shared your sorrows and your joys; with you I have talked many different tongues with a strong national impediment, and secretly marveled why the foreigner, wherever found, seemed so unfittingly endowed with clothes; high over your vessel's careening yet majestic poop have I peered, with you, into the bosom of the deep, when perhaps I should have looked elsewhere. The gales that buffeted your sails blew blithely also through my whiskers, whilst the oft-recurring Porpoise humped himself out of the briney just long enough to spit on his fins, and, hastily excusing himself, go down again; and when you struck the farther shore, life also was a summer's day to me though I didn't know a soul in the town, or even where the barber shop was. Recently—for many weeks—I've been medicating at some of Indiana's amateur health resorts. At Martinsville I've found a genuine humorist, and you must see and hear him. Already he's a stump orator; perfectly modest, and, in real fact, a wonderfully funny and original type. Jap (Jasper) Miller is his name, and I've just written him a poem* which outlines him very fairly, so I enclose it. Soon as you are rested enough give me a line or so. My best remembrances to the wife, Miss Mitchell and the children, and to Miss Mitchell say I'll have a letter for her and literary friend just as soon as my handwriting is recovered.

As ever with affection yours.

JAMESIE.

Your old friends here daily ask after you, George Hitt and the rest, and all want to be remembered.

---

*"Jap Miller," *Hoosier Book*, No. 113.

To Eugene V. Debs.

In appreciation of flowers sent the author when ill.

Indianapolis,
Feb. 18, 1890.

My dear Debs:

Do you think I've entirely forgotten all I owe you? *No:* that query is gratuitous, and knowledge of your loyalty throughout the past forbids all affectation of questioning it now. But I've been anything but a well man for a long, long time, and in consequence I've simply been deprived of the pleasure of expressing to you, until now, my ripest, richest gratitude for your recent floral remembrance. As Tom Moore sings in effect,

> You may break—you may shatter the little
>   bench-legg'd poet if you will,
> But the scent of Debs' basket of roses
>   will cling round him still!

May this find you as glad at heart as your gift made me and may your gentle interest in all human kind never wax nor wane though all the stars of heaven keep up their speciality. My love to you—your brother, and all friends—particularly Ben Cox.

Affectionately as always yours,

J. W. RILEY.

To Mrs. Neal.

The occasion of the following letter, when Riley's good friends rallied about him, is difficult to describe briefly. Suffice it to say that the strain of the heavy lecture schedule and what for Riley were the woes of the road, together with a clash with his shrewd and hard-driving manager, ended in Riley's failure to appear on the platform, and the Nye-Riley tours came to an end. The said manager assisted the press to report the incident elaborately, and days of mortification for the poet followed. This critical moment in his career was made memorable by the action of his friends of the Indianapolis Literary Club who gave him a reception to express their faith and tender regard. The publicity at this time fixed in the minds of many that Riley drank frequently to excess and even composed his verse under the influence of liquor. The poet very seldom drank to excess and did not compose his verse with a mind confused by alcohol. His reaction to his accusers in the following letter is therefore cutting and without patience.

Indianapolis, Feb. 24,
—1890—

Dear Mrs. Neal:

Not only do I accuse you of being very, very good, but I can prove it by this last letter you have written me, in which you so ingenuously talk of everything but my "sad failing"—"my weaknesses"—(as though I'd made a speciality of them for years and doubtless had gathered together the largest, rarest and most comprehensive collection of them in the world!) And again, too, your real generosity and kindliness is emphasized by your not sending me a wild appeal—a surcharged supplication, in red ink, to "In Heaven's name desist!" as "there is, even yet, hope for you,—yea, has He not said, the vilest of all sinners," etc. God bless you, I therefore say, for writing just as you did—thereby implying your unshaken con-

fidence in your friend's unwavering best effort, under any
stress to do the best he could, however badly he might
find himself "stove up" as the result of his intrepid and
heroic venture. Simply, you should see some of the mail
that has been poured in—pumped in upon me, all of which
I must read and attend, though sometimes my heart just
squeals like a little sandy shoat that has been imperfectly
run over by a dray in the street. But you should see the
good letters that, like your own, were considerate—worthy
of their mission of doing real good; enlivening, not kickin'
out a fellow's last scrap of vitality with the hob-nails of
unprovoked commiseration. It is not pleasant, really, to
have some practical drunkard, in the best running order,
for instance, write, advising me—his *"dear brother"*—to
"restrain my damning appetite for rum." He controls his—
that's exactly why he wrote me, and lied when he wrote
so—drinking more whisky in a month than I in a year,
only it affects him differently, that's all; and I'm selfish
enough to be just a trifle proud of the difference. It don't
"show on" him *externally* at all—it only rots his conscience, and sozzles his honor and integrity, makes of his
human sympathies a sort of clotted fungus that we want
to poke at with a wet umbrella and go wagh!—But pardon
me—pardon me—pardon me! I didn't mean to refer to
one unpleasant thing in this—and beg you to take oath
right here that you'll, at least, never divulge a single word
of the fact that I have therein failed, to the amount of a
page of such unpleasantness.

Speaking of the prospective visit to H.*—for indeed
I'm coming,—George Smith suggested last Saturday, and
I'd have come then, but for the sudden change in the
weather—so had to wire him I must defer till probably the

---

*Hamilton, Ohio, where Mrs. Neal, George Smith and other friends lived.

coming Saturday. Am weak physically now almost as I've always been mentally,—so you readily see that my condition is in reality somewhat serious, if not necessarily fatal. Sorry to have been absent during the discussion of the oysters of Thursday; but assure you that I could, if again advised, eat quite a few of them upon almost any other day in the week. You see, we men on the road have to adapt ourselves to all sorts of conditions—so that even upon Sunday, to be frank, I've been known to slip around to the back door of an oyster saloon, to come reeling forth again under the influence of a reeking stew or fry that I had wantonly "put into my mouth to steal away my brains"—thus purchasing oblivion, for a few brief hours, from the hell hound of R-r-remorse that ever howls and bellows on me track!!

As ever,

Sincerely and gratefully yours,

J. W. RILEY.

This is a nawful raggedy letter—ain't it?

To Mrs. R. E. Jones.

Feb. 27, 1890.

My dear friend:

It is very particularly good of you to write me the extra letter, and I thank you with very particularly extra thanks. Physically, I am gaining slowly. It will be some time before I regain the real health I've been robbed of by my managers—God save the mark! Mentally, never felt primer in my life—nor happier. I apologize for my enemies. In good time they will want to do so, but it will not be required of them. All was written at the Beginning. God's hand's on the helm and His breath in the sails!

Your unanswered letter, with the poems and all received, though some time you must send me your scrapbook. Am now contemplating New York Publishers' long expressed desire to bring out a book of mine* in best possible way, and am about deciding I'll be well enough in two weeks more to set about it. Have not lost a friend I had, and evidently (from my mail) have gained hundreds. Demands for both writings and *readings* advanced to an extreme as astounding as gratifyingly surprising and bewilderingly unaccountable, etc. For years I've been on a dead run, and now I'm to pause a while and catch breath. After a while I may be able to see and appreciate the great magnitude of the blessing your influence, and the influence of like friends, have been to me. Here it has been raining for days and days, and likewise some other days and days—kind of a serial rain, the author of which seems to be trying to produce something longer and more tedious than *Middlemarch;* and so last night I began, as I thought, entirely to succumb to its dread influence, and sat down to write a melancholy poem—with what result? Why, bless you that little poem just laid back and laughed and laughed as if somebody was ticklin' its feet! and I was so jollied up by it that I laughed with it, and the pair of us purt' nigh raised the neighbors!†

Some weeks ago saw Mr. Jones for just about a second at the station. Would have liked to stop and talk, but, as usual, was racing to catch a train. Remember me heartily to him—and by the by, I must assure you both that recent reports suggesting Mr. Nye's disloyalty are

---

*Probably *Poems Here at Home,* published three years later by The Century Company.
†"The Little-Red-Apple Tree," *Lockerbie Book,* No. 94.

without foundation. Never have I known a kinder, more considerate or loyal friend and chum. He said no ill thing of me. If you saw first reports of the affair you could not have failed to notice in between the lines, the evident malice and malignity of a most cunning managerial Mephistopheles. Well, that was not Mr. Nye. Mr. Nye is my real friend—the paste friend, of course, never was; and he it was who finally drove me to my last resort. It had to be and it *has* been; and the result, in its just sequence, leaves me nothing to regret with bitterness, but its being so late accomplished. I should have done it years ago—forbearance was my greater fault.

As ever, gratefully your friend,

J. W. RILEY.

CHAPTER III

LITERARY FRIENDS

Discovers Kipling—Much attention to publishing—S. Weir
Mitchell—Charles Warren Stoddard—Mark Twain—Rudyard
Kipling—Howells—Trip to England and the Burns country—
Sir Henry Irving—Ellen Terry—Joseph Knight.

To Dr. James Newton Matthews.

Indianapolis, Ind.
April, 8, 1890.

Dear Matthews:

Got your picture, and sketch by McIntyre. Good—
both of 'em. Gave the last to Miss Nicholas for the
Journal, and sent you copies. Did you get 'em all right?
Are you sound again in health? Hope you are, and
"writing like any clark!" See Longfellow's Chaucer Sonnet—the best one that I know of on earth.

Have you struck anything of "Yussuf's" verse or prose?
England has just punched him out from under the wood-
pile. His real name is Rudyard Kipling, and he's only
twenty-four years of age. His work is great—with the
East in it—the Indians—the frontier—British soldiers—
barracks—camps—courage—fire and tow;

"Four things greater than all things are:—
Women, and horses, and power, and war.
And since we know not how war may prove,
Heart of my heart, let us talk of love."

98

Then there's a new singer in the South here: Madison Julius Cawein, of Louisville, Ky. He is bang-up; and you'll be charmed, if not already. His book is *Lyrics and Idyls*—brought out at home in very pleasant form. He is young—his verse full-rich, though masterly, and the promise very high. He does interior country bits exquisitely. "The Bridle-Path," "The Old Farm," with its old orchard—"In the bee-boom and the bloom," and Oriental, opulent vocabulary—chivalric flight, and romantic clean up to concert pitch! Best, though, kindo' potterin' round the place. Them's my idees, anyhow; and, ef I had my druthers, I druther have him thataway jes' stiddy all the time. Write and swap books with him; and I'm writing him a poem which I hope won't hurt his prospects.

Give me a line when you can, and never mind my desultory responses. Every chance that sneaks by me I grab hold of and say something. You do the same. How is McIntyre now, and where? My love to him. Heard he'd lost his voice. Wish I'd find it.

Don't forget my best regards to Tyner, our artistic friend. He wrote me a very kindly letter—and I bet he's jes' a-cussin' 'cause I never answered it. Lord! if he only knew the hundred others that I just had helplessly to give over trying to, he'd find no shade of fault with me, I'm sure.

With best love to the boys and their gentle mother, I am, as always yours faithfully,

JAMESIE.

I enclose one Kipling poem—not in his best vein at all—though you'll catch some of his savor.

To the Honorable W. H. Calkins.

Indianapolis,
April 28, 1890.

Dear Friend:

How can I send you a book of mine when there isn't a single copy to be had in the market! For once a-poor-devil-of-a-poet's books have indeed "gone off like hot cakes."—They were in the Bowen-Merrill Company Publishers' big fire, and there's not a smell of 'em left.

Hence!

I do not send you a book: I congratulate you.

As ever your friend,
J. W. RILEY.

To Madison Cawein.

Indianapolis, Ind.,
May 11, 1890.

Dear Mr. Cawein:

Have you seen any of the work of the new-found English Poet, "Yussuf"—otherwise Rudyard Kipling? Whee! but he's a humper!—

"With the mouth of a bell and heart of hell and the head
    of the gallows-tree!"

as he describes another blooded hoss. In very truth, though, he's doing some gallant things. Look out for him—he's an arriver, dead sure! Also I mark poem of Miss Evaleen Stein, of Lafayette, Ind. We think here her work is of great promise, as well as now unusually excellent. She's an artist, as well—painting beautiful things—things beautiful, in fact, almost as herself. Is about eighteen, and with such eyes as would inspire you to attempt to try to begin to describe the marvelous, lustrous, loveliness of. Is just visiting here; and I met her this afternoon.

Yours fraternally and hastily,
J. W. RILEY.

To Madison Cawein.

Indianapolis,
July 3, 1890.

My dear Cawein:

You mustn't think me purposely neglectful of your last favor, together with the book; for since I left your royal group at Louisville I've been back into the complexities of business eyebrow-deep, and with scarcely a moment to call my own—only to loll back and rest in—pantingly recuperating for "the endless toil and endeavor" of "to-morrow and to-morrow and to-morrow!" At such unworthy interludes as these only have I been permitted to look into your new (to me) volume, *Accolon* and attendant poems. And I do wish you could be made aware of my real expressions of applause at your evident genius, when you hold the blooded thing curbed and reined just right—its master—not it yours; and how I tremble for you when sometimes it seems in Mastery of you. God help you hold the upper hand steadfastly—as I think *is* the divine intent. Oh, but you do many, many great things; and your capabilities are greater than you know. But I want you here on the present, palpable earth more—in *to-day,* and among to-day's virginal material— its woods, hills, mountains, rivers, lakes and skies; and,

above all, its people and their lacks and loves and yearn-
ings and possessions all touched into the just divinity your
art certainly commands and has proved in instances as
rare as they can and should be made numberless. Do you
understand me fully? I mean, then, that the simplest
thing God ever made is worthy of celebration. You can't
toss a pebble in any quarter of any back township in Kentucky and not hit a poem spang on the top o' the head—a
poem that no one has ever heretofore dreamed was in
incipient existence. Write me about "The Old Farm,"
as you do—and of "The Bridle-Path," etc., etc., *ad
libitum,* not forgetting "The Jellico-Spur," nor "Her
Grace! her Grace! her Grace!" Then keep 'em all sunny
and sweet and wholesome clean to the core; or, if ever
tragic, with sound hopes ultimate, if pathetic, my God!
with your own tears baptized and made good as mirth.
Think how earnestly I mean everything I say. Nothing
to encourage falsely. Go among all kinds of people and
love 'em whether you want to or not. Get rightly acquainted and the boor's even a gentleman. God gets
along with him, it seems. He listens.

Before a very long time, now, I shall send you a new
book*—a Child's book it's to be, though some o' the poems
are written to please if possible, those who are children
no more. You must write to me when you can. I like you
and your work. You and I have more to make us happy
than millionaires. Let's don't trade with 'em either.—
We'll be kind to 'em and help 'em all we can—only we
mustn't trade—it would leave us so very, very poor!

Affectionately yours,

J. W. RILEY.

Best love to all our friends.

Rhymes of Childhood.

To Edgar Wilson Nye.

Indianapolis, Ind.,
August 16, 1890.

Dear Nye:

Since your last greatly overestimated letter I have been trying to regain my shattered average at several summer resorts in flattering propinquity to our flourishing city here. All Indiana is now sporadically measled over with health resorts, and our mortality, which spares not even such men as Colonel ——, is in consequence making a great hit every now and then. Our mortality, in fact, if it keeps up its recent lick, will be given a public benefit by a grateful people who most earnestly desire to show their appreciation, and express in some substantial way, their heartfelt gratitude and pride in an institution that occasionally rolls up its sleeves and reaches out and gits the right man. The Colonel's last words (composed largely of an eructation of about eight octaves) were, "Whilst at Havre, don't you know"—So peace, at last, fell on—his friends—together with the administration at Washington.

Maurice Perkins is still here—too in love with this country and its people such as they are—ever to wander away again, and despite even the blandishments of Louisville or Chicago. You should see the cuss—he's a plum' dude—

With the airs and all
Of Berry Wall!

He reports health good for the *Sun,* and is deep in other schemes—special work—letters and the like for other papers. Maurice and I often convene, and talk about you over late rarebits and other curios of a gustatory and strictly incombustible nature.

Doctor Hays contemplates a brief trip to Europe, and I'd like to make the trip with him, but for various reasons can't hope to—at least, this year. And I'm not *swearin'* either. Simply I've quit *worryin'*.

Have latterly returned from a brief visit to Debs, at Terre Haute, who wants me to remind you of him in a taking way. Mind, I say a brief visit—for, first dash out of box, he must drive out to that blessed little vineyard where they serve you, out under the trellis, with such tantalizing lunch, one needs must handcuff one's appetite, else plunge headlong into their seductive native wines—made while you wait, by the gifted old man, who readily accomplishes his hellish purpose with one hand tied behind him. Need I dwell on the picture? I deem not by a dam sight. Well—abruptly I must close. Perkins is just here, and our rarebit is savoring the immediate future. Will do better next time. In meanwhile will trust that ere many moons we may haply meet, where and when we can talk to the proper purpose. Hope you'll find time to write, between your very bunkum-squintum public utterances, which, be sure, I never fail to see and applaud.

As ever, with "Perk's" love thrown in,
Your faithful
JAMESIE.

To Mrs. R. E. Jones.

Sep. 17, 1890.

My dear friend:

The sad news of your mother's death is here, and I can say nothing to you of any service. For many weeks a poem has been shaping itself in my mind—but only in fragmental lines. There is, as yet, but one completed stanza—evidently to be the closing one. The title is—

THE WATCHES OF THE NIGHT*

ONE leads us through the watches of the night—
By the endless intercession of our loved ones lost to
    sight
He is with us through all trials, in His mercy and His
    might;—
    With our Mothers there about Him, all our sorrow
        disappears,
    Till the silence of our sobbing is the prayer the
        Master hears;
    And His hand is laid upon us with the tenderness of
        tears
      In the waning of the watches of the night.

As ever your friend,
J. W. RILEY.

To William Carey.

Indianapolis,
Sept. 21, 1890.

My dear Carey:

With you I am greatly pleased with the Child-group; and, without a bit of vanity in the world, as it seems, I jest lean back and enjoy it, and applaud it till I'm hoarse! Never shall I be able to thank you all enough for your

---

Lockerbie Book, No. 164.

kindness toward, and presentation of it; and I hope and believe its public acceptance will occasion you no regret.

In the matter of dropping the reiterated *"Raggedy! Raggedy! Raggedy Man!"** line—I would not. It is, in appearance, I admit, trivial and superfluous, but none the less it is, perhaps, the most telling child characteristic in the entire series, and as it is distinctive in the series, I'd retain it by all means. It's the little chap's own invention, you see, and he favors it all through and never tires of admiringly mouthing it over and over again. Change it if you like and I'll not murmur—only I do hope you'll see that I've a real reason for advising otherwise and not merely stickling over a trifle.

In title *"Uncle Sidney's Boy,"*† I think, should be in quotation, as it's the little fellow's affected name—for in reality "Uncle Sidney," in the author's fancy, is a bachelor, and has to pirate the children he loves; and this particular little fellow is his nephew. Other child rhymes introduce, and refer affectionately, in the boy's character, to his "Uncle Sidney" again and again. So I've marked that, and two or three little other typical flecks. And I do hope you'll let me have some extra proofs, as you did before, God bless you! And know, too, that I'm steadfastly reserving my best poems for my book with you—which we never get to—but Lordy! It'll be *a corker when we do reach it!* With best love, appreciation and gratitude to you all.

J AMESIE.

---

*"The Raggedy Man," *Hoosier Book,* No. 104; the other five poems printed in this group were: "A Boy's Mother," No. 105; "The Runaway Boy," No. 108; "The Fishing Party," No. 106; "Our Hired Girl," No. 109; "The Boy Lives on Our Farm," No. 107.

†"Uncle Sidney," *ibid.,* No. 72.

To Edward W. Bok.

Indianapolis, Ind.,
Oct. 23, 1890

Dear Mr. Bok.

Answering your kindly inquiry: am, just now, going to press with two Holiday books; the first, for grown-up children; the last, for the happily otherwise. The former, in dialect verse, which Kemble's pictures make twice-over better than the poet can—is *A Chris'mus story, unconciously dramatic in spots, and in my best vein, since another fellow tells it.** The other, entitled *Rhymes of Childhood,* is a book of nearly two hundred pages, and a hundred and one poems, dialect and serious equally. Getting it together has been great fun, and I'm the happiest boy in it, for literally therein the enthused writer goes scampering barefoot from page to page, with no more sense of dignity than socks, and the like wholesome rapture in heels and heart. The serious studies have, of course, their place—only, I can not conceive the type-divine of the real boy ever desecrating his lovely personality with good grammar. I think of what a child *Lincoln*† must have been—and the same child-heart at home within his breast when death came by. It's all in the line of Fact; that's the stuff only that good fiction, romance, poetry, can be made of. I digress to say this, but I glory in the crime. Thanking you with all heartiness I remain as ever,

Very truly yours,

J. W. Riley.

---

*"What Chris'mas Fetched the Wigginses," *Hoosier Book,* No. 125.
†See "Lincoln—The Boy," *Lockerbie Book,* No. 340.

To Dr. S. Weir Mitchell.

Buffalo, N. Y.,
Oct. 30, 1890.

Dear friend:

Your recent hail has just reached here, to cheer me in my pilgrimage out in the awful world,—for I'm again on the road—a sort of a literary François,—as cheerily and featly capering as my wits and often faint heart will permit. The book has been received at home, but since my absence, so as yet I've been denied the studious and contemplative enjoyment of rereading the delectable and wholly novel performance. As I write I recall (among a long list·of invariably applausive reviews of it) at least two in this city's papers of this morning—the which I will clip out and here enclose to you, with just indorsement of their very highest praises, together with my best congratulations. When you speak of journeying away from home again I am made still more wistful of the desire and hope of seeing you and talking with you; and now, moving in an orbit which ere many weeks must encompass your near vicinity, I have been visioning my very meeting with you and the tangible delight that should be mine in that event, however brief an audience you might accord me. But whenever and wherever you go, know that my halest thoughts and wishes are meeting every train you may select and taking passage with you on any boat!

As ever gratefully and truly yours,
JAMES WHITCOMB RILEY.

To Will S. Otwell.

Indianapolis, Ind.,
Nov. 17, 1890.

My dear Otwell:

Your letter was just purt' nigh as good as old home-
made pie 'at squashes when you bite into it and won't eat
it with a fork-ner-knife uther! Specially your description
of your landlady—"And blessings on her kindly voice and
on her silvery hair!"—and the general gentle group about
the table which she graces. God bless you every one! I'm
with you many times right there, listening to things as
good as the coffee on crisp mornings! No matter where
you are or what you are, every one of us ought to be just
a little happier and more thankful than he ever was before
this thought occurs to him. As for myself—every day I'm
a-gittin' a little riper and mellerer till, first thing I know,
some blame boy'll climb over the orchard-fence and steal
me! Am awful' busy, but put up with prosperity with appropriate resignation. The Flower Mission Charity here
is preparing again to tilt up its horn of plenty, and among
some new schemes for eradicating largess from the most
delicate apparels of the rich, will issue a little volume of
poems (the same copyrighted) contributed especially by
some six several Hoosier Poets—"among whom I am
which." But I digress. What I was just leading up to,
was the explanation of the enclosed poem. It is a proof-
sheet of my contribution to the above-referred-to brochure, as we say in domestic French—so it's for your own
personal regalement—not for publication, obviously,
please note.

And now, sir, do you know how late at night it is with

me?—Just a quarter past three in the morning. Rain the whole day through! And so I've associated with the weather very little, but stayed in and slept, occasionally waking up to stare out and still find the universe bathed in tears—the day still weeping like a runaway bride on the second floor of a railroad hotel, and Herbert, with the tragedy all knocked out of him, trying to build up a mollifying letter to her folks.

But, unlike the rain, I'm going to let up right here and now—so good night and God love you!

As ever your old friend,

J. W. RILEY.

To George C. Hitt.

This letter, written from the *Journal* office, Indianapolis, was addressed to Mr. Hitt at London, England, where he was serving as Vice Consul-General of the United States, under Colonel John C. New who was Consul-General.

Indianapolis,
Dec. 22, 1890.

Dear George:

Very hastily I write to say that just now I mail you new Child's Book, with three other copies in your care,— one for the News, as you'll find written—the other two for you to get some way, if possible, to Andrew Lang and Rudyard Kipling, with author's admiration, etc. Later, I hope to send you other and better copies, as our publishers here have a way of getting them perfected "as the years of Ee-ter-ni-tee roll!" Hope you'll be surprised and pleased with one poem* in the volume anyhow, God bless you!

---

*See "The Whitheraways," written at the time of the departure of Mr. and Mrs. Hitt and family for England.—*Lockerbie Book,* No. 124.

You'd be delighted to see the rush for this venture—it leads 'em all!—Moreover, I've not a dissenting nor a timid comment as to the audacity of a part of the book. First and most exacting of the literary highlights are daily thumping my shoulders through the mail. Simply all is well, and very well—can't begin to supply the demand. Actual fact.

We're all industriously missing you here at the office. . . . My very best to the friends, The Colonel and Mrs. New, and the Misses. Soon as my next breathin'-spell occurs I mean to write you all.

As ever your affectionate

JAMESIE.

To Charles Warren Stoddard.

See "Your Height Is Ours," *Lockerbie Book*, No. 230.

Indianapolis, Ind.,
Dec. 23, 1890.

My dear Friend:

My! but you do bear down on what you say of me and what I've tried to write and sing for just such lovely men as you for all these years! To every word you put down I have listened with both eyes, and I thank you with both hands. Over and over I've heard of you—in all parts of the States, and outside. At groaning boards innumerable I've heard you praised and your wit flashed with the wine, and as quotable too, both for tang and sparkle: But steadfastly still you have ever eluded me as a tangible thing upon which my hungry grasp had fain been laid a hundred times. Now—at last—I seem to be nearing your blessed whereabouts, and I hail you joyfully. Young Meredith Nicholson gave me your present address—so to him I am indebted for more good things than even his poetry. By this you doubtless have his first book of verse—wherein he says such things as though God some new hymn had writ and whispered it from star to star!— or to that effect. Well—it is such things as these breaking out through his work that made me expectant of a very desirable altitude for the young man later on. But will you let me hear from and of you occasionally? I know of your limitations: All good men have 'em—therefore thank God you're not without. Think of the many poor devils there are without a limitation to their back, as we might say. One is right here this holy minute with me,—the last fag-end of my time as well as paper. But write when you can if you will, and know always of the abiding esteem and gratitude of your friend and

tempestuous applauder,
J. W. RILEY.

To Charles Warren Stoddard.

Indianapolis,
Dec. 30, 1890.

My dear Man:

The friend-poem you make to recoil back on me so joyously has a pathetic significance, no less, since it was written in most sensitive fear and foreboding, bravely concealed, however, as I fancied, under its buoyant front and most wholesomely intended spirit. It was addressed to the saddest young friend of a day I shall doubtless ever know,—gifted in a wonderful way—for I had known the

sweetness of his verse and the ache and yearning of it for
some years before. He came to me in Boston, where O'-
Reilly had told me of him, and gravely praised his too
serious singing. Just what all was bearing down upon
him I never knew—but that everything from his very
childhood had "marked him for its own." At least, it was
like that. His father long dead—the mother left with
children—all proud—fine-brained and—stricken, one
sister, as I recall the sad history, dumb from birth; one,
blind—both otherwise most lovely of person and of soul.
My God! And so the poet sang his best and hungered
more—and when I saw him, at twenty-six years of age,
his young head was bowed and bald and bleak as his life.
And about five years ago he flashed the falchion of his
voice for the last time and thrust it waveringly back into
its scabbard, and lit out, as I fancy, straight for God, personally to inquire of Him what it all meant anyhow. That
was James Berry Bensel—his fate: and his lifetime friend,
I think Oscar Fay Adams, printed, after his death, a book
of his verse, with biography, though I've never seen the
volume—something then jostling me out of conference.
All that I know was seeing, at the time, his death (sudden
and of heart trouble) announced at New York and his
burial there, as I recall it—though his home was Lynn,
Mass., where he had invited me, at our only personal meeting.

> . . . And so I sing to-day.—
> So may I sing alway!
> Though waving grasses grow
> Between, and lilies blow
> Their trills of perfume clear——

The fellow of this line you have failed to-quote, so I can

not.* Can your memory supply it? If so oblige me—
then it shall have a home—the best my next book can
afford. I can find no copy of the poem anywhere among
all scraps: So you must favor me if possible, as I would
have the missing line exact with the original, and that my
own memory utterly fails to yield up. So—I've been
tedious—but you've occasioned it all by your praise of
what I am now convinced is indeed a worthy poem. God
bless you, therefore—and the poem—and the dear dead
singer, though I'm certain he's already blessed to that degree a human prayer might almost prejudice so good a
God against the boy. Therefore I withhold that petition
and will work it into my own far graver needs, or haply,
better than all else, offer no advice to Deity whatever.

Has your Christmas been to your exact liking? I suspect not—or are you as old now as you used to think, as a
boy, your father was? That, I find, obtruding now among
all considerations looking to positive childish enjoyment—
when once, to possess the mere label of a bunch of Chinese
firecrackers, shot several miles above the altitude of delight so rarely attained to-day by the sole proprietorship
of a fifty dollar check. Truly, "God gives unto those who
have no teeth"—also, firecrackers to those whose phizz-
snap-bangs of perfect rapture haven't a smell of it left
when half a long life after we begin to realize what glory
once was ours!—Dad-burn-the-luck! So you don't agree
with Civilization and think of "herding with narrow fore-
heads" and all that? And where is the tangle we're all in,
and why, and what the cure? As quick as I find out, then
I'll tell you, so you can tell me again—for by that time it

*As laughter to the ear,
Let each mute measure end
With "Still he is thy friend."
"My Friend," *Lockerbie Book,* No. 165.

will have been found out not the cure at all, rest peace-fully assured. As far as I've prospected, all has been meant just as it is; and the thing to do is to accept it, not because it pleases us, but because it most certainly does please the Master Intelligence.—And to know that some day we are to be made a friend and confidant of That, ought to make an ordinary little mortal's hat-band snap and pop with ever-widening pride. So let's content us very cheerily indeed.—And right here I'm goin' to let up on both of us, and go out with a prowling, midnight pie-eating friend who paces at my door and will not rest until I join him in our customary unholy feast, which we al-ways relish the more for being assured that we ought not positively to eat such things at such hours.

As ever and straight on into ——?

Your abiding friend,

J. W. RILEY.

To Samuel L. Clemens.

Indianapolis, Ind.,
Dec. 31, 1890.

My dear friend:

Uncle Mart was a printer, and when I set up pi for him I was also old enough to read some, and then read the funniest piece and the best (because of its absolute life and character plausibility or veracity) I'd ever seen put down in type: and yet I so consider it.* Well, you wrote it, and I've loved you ever since—the more so since my rare for-tune of meeting you and knowing you even for the briefest two or three times we have glimpsed by each other on our

---

*"The Jumping Frog."

common pilgrimage to—what or where we'll cheerily discuss, no doubt, when we get there.

Your comment on the Child's book is the prize gift to me of all this uncommonly considerate Christmas; and I hasten to assure you that, with your own indorsement of the general grade of children and child-character the book so affectionately embraces, all like discriminating judges and critics accept in the same commendatory spirit—so that it would seem you had all combined to make me the happiest dad-burn' boy o' the whole gang!

Anyway, know how glad you've made me, and how much I owe you that can never be collected and in lieu thereof accept my full invoice of gratitude.

Your faithful friend as ever,
J. W. RILEY.

To Edgar Wilson Nye.

Indianapolis,
Jan. 22, 1891.

My dear Nye:

Oh, sir! it is a sad blow to go forth alone, as it now seems it needs must be: but I will take comfort in the thought—thou, too, art pilgriming to and fro companionless—grim, pulseless comfort though it be.

Very cheerily, however, let us grapple with the possibilities. Things might be worse, a durn' sight, to us both. We might, for one thing, have managers. As Walker would say, "Jevver have any of those?"

Have just been forced to decline a New York banquet-date—the sixth of February—by prior booking, may I put it?, for the West. Am sorry I can't get your way, if

only for a few days, as I've been bull-headedly hoping to
for months.   However, when we do meet-up, it'll be all the
gala-er a day for the long intermission.

Need I say your letter was a great boon in every way?
Such thoughts as your mind has at tongue's-end it is beautiful to see.   Over and over, as I perused your lines, my
delight would burst forth in both laughter and "heart-ren-
dering" tears of joy and merriment and mirth and jollity,
as well as rapture and high glee.   No one but you knows
as well as you do how to sweep the trembling strings of my
risibles as they swing slack and attenuated and run-down
in the desolated "corridors of time," as Longfellow got
off once in a poem he had one spring.   All shall be even
as you will it, by all the silken ties that bind friend to
friend!   Even so have I vowed to Allah.

Just now we have organized our first Press Club here,
and she is starting off in great shape.   I'm to be a delegate
from it to International P. C. Association at Pittsburgh
the coming twenty-ninth.   As I was never a delegate before, I bate my breath for fear.—Dang' if they's any dang'
press club in Ameriky'll ketch me.

Minute ago our president, Mr. William Fortune, stuck
his head in here to say you and Mark Twain are to be
wired (or are) to be with us in some joint affair for Club
benefit.   As God hears me, I take occasion to say right
here, I did not suggest this measure to the boys—but, if
it could be made to work—Indianapolis will have never
seen such an outpouring of enthusiastic people—and all
as much in your behalf as in Twain's behalf, and in fact
in *all* our behalf as the press club's behalf, which is indeed
very popular—composed of elegant, fine fellows—no finer
in the land, for either manly dignity and soundness or
mental symmetry and motif.   And I do hope you can

close with 'em,—and take me in like a hostage som'ers with you. This is a great literary center, don't forgit! The press club will build, right away, on Circle. The Literary Women are just to dedicate their own building—superb structure now completed—and every dollar of it contributed and paid by the women of the organization. Oh, Mr. Man! They're great people out here, and universally, the residents are all "up and a-comin'."

As ever yours,

JAMESIE.

To an Unidentified Editor.

(Date unknown, estimated 1891.)

Mr. Editor—"Why in thunder don't you answer my letter?" says you. 'Cause, b'Gawd, your "letter" was a demand for a poem, and I hain't got one to my back, nor the time to write one! That's what you want to cuss about, and how can I help myself! I can't begin to write poems as fast as I'm asked for 'em; if I could, you'd get one instead of this apology to go on cussin' about. I'm sorry, but it's just that way—so what's a fellow to do? "Every man stretches his legs according to the length of his coverlet," says good Chispa, so be very lenient with the little bench-legg'd poet who has the audacity to sign himself,

Your friend,

JAMES WHITCOMB RILEY.

Lines written on fly leaf of copy of "Afterwhiles" by author for presentation to John Burroughs.

Indianapolis, Ind.,
1891.

Mild and gentle, as he was brave,—
When the sweetest love of his life he gave

To simple things:—Where the violets grew
Pure as the eyes they were likened to,

The touches of his hands have strayed
As reverently as his lips have prayed;

When the little brown thrush that harshly chirred
Was dear to him as the mocking-bird.*

Gratefully and faithfully,
JAMES WHITCOMB RILEY.

To Edmund Clarence Stedman.†

January 6, 1891.

My dear Mr. Stedman:

Your beautiful consideration of the Child's book‡ I've ventured to put forth, reaches a sensibility of gratitude I can not hope to express to you in any voice. All I can do is to say I am grateful and with closed eyes blindly hope some vibrant volts of it may tingle to and through you, as through the poet's morning heart:

---

*"Away," *Lockerbie Book,* No. 3.

†As printed in *Life and Letters of Edmund Clarence Stedman,* copyright, 1910. Used by permission of Laura Stedman Gold.

‡*Rhymes of Childhood.*

"There palpitations wild and sweet—
  The thrills of many an old delight,
With dimpled hands that lightly meet,
And hearts that tremble to unite,—
Arise upon that rosy morn,
  Pass down the lovely vales and stand,
The picture of a memory born,
  The mirage of a lotus land—
The land where first we trolled the song,
  'Tis morning and the days are long!"*

In so many unspeakable ways am I made your debtor I
seem whelmed about with tumultuous silences,—so you've
secured yourself beyond all corresponding hail of cheer
or blithe ahoy of mine. That's something like the situation
anyhow, and thus, for my own sake, I am grieved even as
I exult. But God bless you for your generous words to
me—and if too generous your good heart is, as half I
fear—God keep it so and humor you and anchor me along-
side for all time!

For the fine presentation of my homely home-spun
verses in your recently completed compilation with Miss
Hutchinson accept my thanks, forgetting not whatever
growth of finer worth they have, or may betray is the
result, in part direct, of your interest and influence. To
Miss Hutchinson, as well, my praise and thanks. Your
mutual effort seems to me the best grounded, the most
carefully elaborated and perfected work of the character
in my knowledge.

Yet, with you, I half-way sigh and wonder when they,
or we, who keep you a slave to prose, will give you gracious
pause in which to give us another book of verse. Ah! my
dear, dear friend, lift voice again and sing! That is your
truest glory—and the world's. And there is such vast

---

*"Morning," by Benj. S. Parker.

Self-caricature by Mr. Riley on fragment of a letter to George Smith

need, too, for the deep voice, and the sound enduring tones that fail not as the chirps and trills and twitter of our junketers of singers nowadays.   Therefore, surely you are to sing again—for lo, where fare thy lordly fellows and where fail their footsteps in the neighboring shades? Again God bless and keep you still for ever young of heart and soul.

May I be remembered most kindly to my very gentle friends, your wife and boy.

Your grateful, faithful friend always,
JAMES WHITCOMB RILEY.

To Frank Dempster Sherman.

Indianapolis,
Jan. 8, 1891.

My dear friend:

Your gentle, genial letter is as kind and indulgent to me as a favorite relative, and my thanks in return are many and most fervid.   Such words as you have written to me seem almost as beautiful as the exquisite beauty of your verse—and that, with steadfast delicacy, is blooming, even as a dewy primrose, before one's very eyes.   It is a very deft touch you have, dear *poemer,* and I think, too, your heart is swung in you about plumb; and that's the clapper, after all, that pulses out the song the whole world wants.— And now, sir, you're *a primrose* and a *"Big Ben" bell* all in a sonnet's space!

So keep you always sweet and all-pervasive through all time and all eternity.

Your grateful friend,
J. W. RILEY.

To Madison Cawein.

Indianapolis,
Jan. 13, 1891.

My dear Cawein:

Have you vast patience and abiding faith? Then, dear man, bear with me yet a little. Just in a perfect vortex of conflicting duties all the time or I should long ago have written you. . . .

Have just got hold of Kipling's *Departmental Ditties* (what a waxy mouthful o' cumbersome title that is!) & *Barrack-Room Ballads* (Oouh! rest your jaws at the ache-end of the title entire!) He's a queer cuss. Some of him's wonderful—and there's a spoor of genius strung clean through whatever he does. But he is not ripe yet, or planted next field to the punkins:—His "plunk's" all right, but his "meat's" too "pethy" and too pale a pink! Lo, he must lie yet a while in the dew and gasp with his pores and suck in sweeter juices, and more of the mellowing brand—not the maddening kind. He's so near being perfect, it would be bad as Chatterton should he fail now—and he won't. As ever, your friend,

J. W. RILEY.

*To Mark Twain.**

Pittsburgh, Pa.,
Jan. 30, 1891.

"I'll have to git you to excuse me!"—Tom Quartz.
Dear Mark Twain:

While it is a matter of the gravest doubt with me that

---

*See letter of Feb. 2, 1891, from Samuel L. Clemens, Appendix, p. 329.

you could so honor any kind of verse, still I should like to hear you, in some deep, reposeful state of satirical exasperation, very deliberately and mildly recite the following heartfelt tribute to our mutual friend,—

Honest Old Sam Hungerford

I hain't none of yer lofty breed!—ner don't p'tend to be
Much posted-up on books you read on Love and Poertry:
But ef the gift of Song jes' poured like music from my
  pen,
I'd write of old Sam Hungerford, the prince of honest
  men!

I'd jes' raise up and call a halt on heroes made of dudes,
And hero-ines, without a fault, in heavenly attitudes;
I'd pick my hero from the ways of "them that waits and
  serves,"
And give Sam Hungerford the praise his honesty de-
  serves;—

Sam Hungerford was natchurly jes' *ornry*—drat his
  melts!—
He couldn't pound sand!—ner be learnt how—ner nothin'
  else!
And yet, no man was honester to jes' fess-up, like Sam,—
He never earnt a dollar, ner he didn't give a dam!

As Nye would say, Sam was indeed a lovely character!
As ever, gratefully and faithfully yours,
J. W. RILEY.

Pardon me too, for the real tribute in print which I enclose. The subject is just such a rare, sane, sound, lovable man as you would delight and revel in, every possible way; and all I've said in his praise is not the tenth part strong enough. Wish you could see and know him.

To Rudyard Kipling.

Denver, Colo.,
Feb. 16, 1891.

Dear Mr. Kipling:

Your fine, strong, tender poem* in answer to the Child's book sent you in care of Mr. Hitt, has been forwarded me here where I'm just packing to return to Indianapolis; and I ought perhaps to stay my reply to you till back in the serenity of home but I can not. So I hope you will look upon this with all the leniency you can.

J. W. R.

To George C. Hitt.

Indianapolis, Ind.,
Feb. 21, 1891.

My dear George:

Your letter barely holds itself together now, I have reread it so many times and passed it round among your many friends—all of whom, like myself, are coming, at last, really to appreciate your inim'utable worthiness—"if I may coin a phrase!"

But I didn't mean to occasion you the trouble that I have, in the personal delivery of the books—though I dare say, as you English have it, you enjoyed the bother given, since its reward—in the first instance—was your hand-to-

---

*"To J. W. R.", by Rudyard Kipling, Biographical Edition, IV, p. 513.

hand encounter with Kipling The King.—All hail! Nor can I scratch another line until I copy for you his delicious poem in answer for the Child's book*—named by you, old fellow, and therefore blessed and sanctified. In token, mark this poem alone:†

And this is what I said back to the man with all promptness, as I felt impelled:

Denver, Col.,
Feb. 16, '91.

To—R. K.

To do some worthy deed of charity
   In secret and then have it found out by
Sheer accident, held gentle Elia—
   That—that was the best thing beneath the sky!
Confirmed in part, yet somewhat differing—
   (Grant that his gracious wraith will pardon me
If impious!)—I think a better thing
   Is: being found out when one strives to be.

So, Poet, and Romancer—old as young,
   And wise as artless—masterful as mild,—
If there be sweet in any song I've sung,
   'Twas savored for thy palate, O my Child!—
For thee the lisping of the children all—
   For thee the youthful voices of old years—
For thee all chords untamed or musical—
   For thee the laughter, and for thee the tears.

Rhymes of Childhood.
  †Here Riley quoted thē poem written by Kipling "To J. W. R.," dated November 20, 1890.
  A later letter from Kipling is given in the Appendix, p. 333.

And thus, borne to me o'er the seas between
  Thy land and mine, thy Song of certain wing
Circles above me in the "pure serene"
  Of our high Heaven's vast o'er-welcoming;
While, packeted with joy and thankfulness,
  And fair hopes many as the stars that shine,
And bearing all love's loyal messages,
  Mine own goes homing back to thee and thine.

J. W. R.

This was from Denver, where Mr. K.'s poem was forwarded, and first read with our dear old Myron* at my shoulder. "Just think of it!" I said rapturously,—"men at our time o' life as tickled as two boys over our first sweetheart's valentine!" And you should see Reed now.— Stronger than ever and reliant and reposeful as the boss-pyramid of old man Cathay's justly celebrated collection, as Nye would say. Will enclose in this, one of his war sermons—"Sherman"—wherein you'll observe the old galvanic volts that ever characterize his word. Had a whole week with him, and the halest, wholesomest session of 'em all. Gave two nights in his church, and his club—The Glenarm—just loaded four hundred dollars, clear into my coyest, most retiring pocket. And right here in confidence—I think you may look for a pair of us your way this summer. Will sail about June, as now about agreed upon. Reed is going sure, and I guess I jes' got to take and turn in and pack up and go too. But law me! I don't see how I can drap all now and leave the place to go to rack—and stock and all—like times is now, you know— and go philanderin' off, from pillar to post a-knockin' round amongst my betters and follerin' them 'at kin go—

*Myron Reed.

bein' pervided, and a not a-keerin' fer the constant dreen-
age and expense 'at keeps the pore man with his nose
ag'inst the grindstone all the days of his life.*

Mostly I don't use around here much my self any more,
and am even eating less midnight pie than has been my
wont for years. And I'm even entertaining some proposi-
tions looking to the road again—though I shall avoid being "managed" for quite a time yet I've no doubt. Can
get any price I ask—and calls from all parts of the United
States. It doesn't seem possible, but it's fact; and so I say
now's the time to be deliberate and not git overhet. Ain't
that right? And there's a thousand other things I want to
ask you about, and kindo' pirate your advice, as always
in the past.—So guess I really will have to go over to you
purty soon.

It's good to hear and know of all the growth of good in
your own prospects and the children. Ah, George!
They're the fellers for a man to anchor by! 'F I had just
one, even with the scallhead, or warts—I'd be a happier
and I know a durn' sight better citizen. Am just now in
the midst of preparation for our Press Club Benefit.
Burdette† is to be with me, and to be crowned lord of all
by the united fervor of the town, as he deserves. Write
me when you can, and all of Kipling you come to know.
Glad you're friends at start—that means always. God
bless you. Best to the wife, the children, the News, every
one. As ever,

Affectionately yours,

JAMESIE.

---

*Here Riley assumes the vernacular of the farmer, pretending he himself
is weighed down with the cares of a farm.

†Robert Burdette, the preacher and humorist, and one of the poet's
most loved friends.

To Miss Katherine Parks.

April 21, 1891.

Dear Miss Parks:

Your letter of request is very good to me—so good, indeed, I smile childishly and think I'd like to go to school to you, with all the happy other little children. Tell them that, for me, so that they may know what a nawful good teacher they have and how grateful and happy they should feel. You may tell them, too, that my first teacher was not by any means a crisp young lady with glad eyes and quick bright ways: but, instead, was a "Little Dame Crump" old woman, fat, and round and wabbly as a ruddy dome of jelly when "Company's come!"—Yes, and as sweet, too, she was, and is this minute, in my memory! But she was not young—oh, no! Why, bless you! she wore a cap, and the "part" in her hair beneath it was broad, and rosily bald, in fact, as it showed through the thin gray hair; and there was a mole on her face—right spang where Abraham Lincoln wore his, only, a little boy once said, "they was *eye-winkers* in that mole of hers, 'cause sometimes when she kissed him they tickled his nose!" Yes; she was a very old woman—and a very *dear* old woman to all of us who were little children then in her school.—So old she was that she died one afternoon—just like falling asleep. She was so tired—so worn and old. Now, who knows? she may be rested now, and Somewhere waiting yet for all of the little boys and girls she loved to come romping in again. She used to stand in the door, waving her big silk handkerchief and cheerily calling "Books! Books!

Books!" Next time I see her and hear her, I often think, how I will run to greet her!

As ever gratefully your friend and the children's.

J. W. RILEY.

To William Dean Howells.

Indianapolis, Ind.
May 2, 1891.

Dear sir:

For many days I have been thinking how to thank you for your recent great kindness in receiving my book of Child rhymes. While I was made very glad and proud of your consideration, I was no less touched by the gentleness of your comment. And its heartening influence is to endure with me—the assurance of which simple fact, I venture to surmise, will be better thanks to you than words! words! words!

Sincerely and faithfully yours,
JAMES WHITCOMB RILEY.

To George Smith.

New York City,
May 26, 1891.

My dear George:

Must write you—or, rather, hastily and heartily waft you—one last lingering, loitering, wistful farewell. At seven in morning we go aboard—an hour later we will doubtless stand—our little cluster of three—very near one another—very compactly together, waving our farewells with the general tender storm of them—just as though our own beloved were of the throng on shore, and we glimmeringly caught again the sunlight of their smiling and the bright dews of their tears. But we'll not weaken. Not a bit of that. Mr. Fishback will clear his throat and in a very incisive tone of voice call attention to some ridiculous phase or scene or proposition; Mr. Reed will unreef his hat-rim to the full breath of the breeze and stand stoically looking as though it were a drop or two of spray that flecked his cheek; while the little bench-leg'd poet will, with alternating admiration, gaze on both, and not say a dam' word—only jest "chaw" on. But my dear, honest, old, decrepit pensioner of the Mexican War, I will think very lovingly of you—both for the dear past's sake and the dearer future on ahead. And steadfastly on this latter do I mean to fix my spiritual eye:—when I shall have returned to tell you gleefully of my personal interview with Shakespeare's old haunts—every one of 'em—the little old home of Anne Hathaway, and every sweetheart-memory that still ghosts it in that old time that could not be told in prose, else William Black had written *Will* and *Anne's* Youth and love instead of *Judith Shakespeare*. By the bye, if you've not read it, turn at once and read this most idyllic of all Black's novels.—Which reminds me, we've a letter to Black, and may smoke a pipe with him. Of course I'd like to hear from you and word of all our many friends—what you are all doing—when and where and why—and that through all the changes you are not sitting idly by, suffering me to be forgotten utterly! 'F you *do* permit that, dam' 'f I'll read for your church! Sit down, therefore, and write me promptly all about everything—'cause it will so aid, comfort and further a *foreigner*—as I'll soon be—to hear from the old home place. Can't, of course, give you yet *explicit* address, but letter addressed care Consul General John C. New, London, will reach me, as our mutual friend George Hitt there with him will promptly forward my mail to any quarter of the Old World in which the curse of the wandering foot may take me. Will write him immediately upon arrival, as we may in all probability leave London till last of our pilgrimage. In meantime go and see my brother and sisters—where you are liked, I am very proud to know, almost as well as John likes you, or I, myself. Love also to all the Hamilton friends. Keep their general reliance in me propped up in all the saggy places. Same, too, with Indianapolis friends—yes, and Columbus and Dayton.—Ah! Miss Callahan! who has said ne'er-the-divil-a-word o' my poetry to her, regarding you're hoggin' up the major part of the candy popcorn she sent us *ekal!* And see, perhaps, what she may miss by way of some Classic Souvenir garnered from some odd corner of the world by my veteran and victorious hand—for I mean, this voyage, to "ransack the ages" and "spoil the climes"— nothing short!—to poke, as it were, both the ivory beak of me gallant barque and my nose into manifold strange realms and goodly Kingdoms—where Lotus-Eaters bide in endless bliss in isles enchanted—wherein it seemeth always afternoon; and where

> "The Queen of the Orkney Islands
>   She rides on a sea-green whale;
> And he takes her a mile, with an elegant smile,
>   At every flip of his tail!"

—Just tell Miss C. there is no way of estimating what list of curios might not have been her possible possession but for her abrupt termination of our correspondence. Enlist Mrs. Holstein also in my behalf and help me all you mutually can to make Cory Callahan regret the sad day she ever "fixed a vacant stare" on Jemmy O'Reilly and "slew him wid her noble birrrth! !"

So, very cheerily indeed, and with a trust that passeth understanding, "I commit myself," as the Robinson Crusoe hero always does, "to the Great Father, both of the Sea and land!"

As ever yours,
J. W. RILEY.

To Henry Eitel.

Husband of the poet's sister, Elva May Riley, a banker and his business adviser.

Dumfries, Scotland,
June 9, 1891.

Dear Eitel:

Have brief time only for a few silly and serious remarks. To some this may, perhaps, be fitly referred to as the Old World, but to me it's a little the newest world I have yet struck. New people—new customs—new costumes—new tongues—new countries—every ten steps of each other;—new *weathers,* even, and with far more loyalty in them to the inclement types than anything in America anywhere! For instance, since landing, yesterday produced the first hour of sunshine, constant rain and cold prior—save to residents—their comment, and indeed their actions suggest to us, however, that the climate is exquisitely, radiantly dulcet and divine. Yet as God hears me, I have three shirts now upon me back—and if me waistcoat, etc., would permit, I'd hasten to sheathe myself in about three more!

In fact, here in the city where Burns died so prematurely, I fully realize the reason of such an act on his part
and most heartily indorse it. Have to-day visited the
house he first occupied upon his coming here, and also
house in which he died—something better than the first,
I was glad to note,—this latter bearing newly printed
placard above the door, "Burns' House—To Rent." I could
have cried. Some time later we were persistently fortunate
enough to find the young man who seemed to have the
house in charge, and by him were admitted and shown
through it. I think all three of us did quite a quantity of
hard breathing and thinking as we reverently moved from
room to room—main room and kitchen parallel below—
then at back of narrow, winding, stone stairway above,
and—the room in which the last work of the great poet's
pen was done,—most exquisite, tender, loving, human
songs, that clamber still and twine and bloom about all
hearts; and, no less, the prose appeals, wrenched from
him for a pitiful pound or so of loan, to provide against
the commonest household necessities! But let us again
talk about the weather: Just *now*, at least, there is
virtually no night here. Until half past nine of evenings
one can see to read at the open window—indeed it is a
more preferable light to read by than the thin white greasy
ghosts of it that stalk in later in the shape of candles.

The candle, here throughout the United Kingdoms,
seems to attain a priceless value. Were I addicted to a
solitaire bosom-pin I would gladly, proudly discard it for a
candle! . . . From our different rooms the three of us sit
on in the loitering gloom of night, covertly listening for
the stealthy scratch of the match that signals the lighting
of the first candle—sometimes Reed's, sometimes Fishback's, and sometimes even mine. Ha! how the waiting

twain swoop then upon the glare! With bated breath and cushion-footed tread how they burst in upon their fellow to spend a social hour—or two with him—with him! And as at last the final guttering—the supreme death-rattle of his candle "aches on the senses"—how low and tender are the good-nights to him, as his guests severally depart, each in the barred security of his own room trimming his virgin taper and lolling back for the luxury of a long hour's midnight read in bed, and to note drowsily through the window-slats the singular phenomenon of the actual twilight yet merge into actual dawn.

Shipboard I was a nautical ass enough to wear a nautical shirt, with a low collar and sailor tie. Even as I put it on and gazed raptly at myself in the glass, there ominously flitted through my Waterbury mind the words of A. Ward, "Good-by, my gay sailor boy." But vain!—I wore it bravely forth upon the deck. In consequence I have lingering with me still the lung-rattlingest cough that ever jarred the quaint little window-sash of the *King's Arms Inn*—our present quarters. Still every day am improving. With love to all as always affectionately

JIM.

To Sir Henry Irving.

London,
June 29, 1891.

Dear Mr. Irving:

Very pleasantly remembering my good fortune in making your acquaintance in New York, at the Brunswick, an evening later repeating for you a little sketch of a character you fancied, I would like now to come and pay you my respects. Have passed your Lyceum two or three times, yearning to enter and inquire for you, but appreciating fully how much your time is taken up, I write instead first to ask if I may come, and if so at what hour of the day, and for however brief a time, I may call.

Very truly yours,
JAMES WHITCOMB RILEY.

To Sir Henry Irving.

London,
July 1, 1891.

Dear Mr. Irving:

It is very kind of you to ask me to come to the Theater (as I certainly shall) on Thursday evening, July second eleven-thirty o'clock, as you direct.

So most gratefully I muse—

> When Shakespeare's voice was heard of old—
>   When Shakespeare's voice was heard—
> What matter if the "house" were "cold"
>   And no applause occurred!
> For more, to me, persuasively
>   Comes thy full courteous word
> Than, in the days of chivalry,
>   When Shakespeare's voice was heard.

Very truly yours,
J. W. RILEY.

To Miss Ellen Terry.

London,
July 16, 1891.

Dear Miss Terry:

Won't you please remember me and permit me to present you (as I now venture to) a much better edition of my poems than that you once thanked me for sending to you from America. Begin, therefore, by remembering America,—then New York, then your and Mr. Irving's delectable series of public triumphs, at Delmonico's, the Brunswick, etc. Then remember Mark Twain, then General Sherman ("God rest his bier!"), and then the very frightened little man he called up, away across the table and opposite to you, who tried to read a homely bit of German-English pathos—by request—and, finally, remember your telling him later that he *made you cry*. What he then said, all under-breath, so you could not hear it possibly, he now says aloud in ink, is, "God bless you!"

Is it simply coincidence or what? First I saw you—in midmost America—you made me cry; next in New York, where I actually sobbed; then last night, when I burst into tears again, almost at sight of you. However, I laughed enough, and was glad almost, as "Alexandre" could have been, seeing the fine appreciation and affection of your people.

Sincerely and gratefully yours,

JAMES WHITCOMB RILEY.

To George C. Hitt.

Indianapolis,
Aug. 25, 1891.

Dear George:

If you happen at all to remember the book-package you charged me not to lose, as we rode about in the cab in search of the ever-vanishing Kipling, why, then you will at once understand the meaning of the enclosed *Lost*

Property notification, which same I beg you to answer in my stead, taking unto yourself, to have, hold and possess, the two unemasculated copies of my new English book, the contents of said package as aforesaid—providing, strictly, that you at all consider them worth the attendant trouble and expense, for which latter I can think of no way of reimbursing you, as I haven't but one English coin to my back, and what that is in value, I affirm, I've not the vaguest idea in the world.

Or turn the paper over to Doctor Hays, who may be with you by the receipt of this.

Your friends all asking after you. The *Journal* folks are all well, joyous and "holdin' fast to the horns of the altar." My best to Mr. and Mrs. New, and to Harry, Mr. Moffitt *et al.*

JAMESIE.

To Sir Henry Irving.

Indianapolis, Ind.
Sept., 1891 (?)

Dear Mr. Irving:

I venture to inclose to you a bit of prose of mine—a Dickens imitation, the principal character of which (Mr. Twiggs) my pleased fancy sees you in the rôle of constantly.* Read and see if theme, situation and characters have really a dramatic possibility in them, as I some way feel they have. In such event, a little play might be wrought out of the sketch. And now I'm going to ask you in this way what I had not the courage to when I took my leave of you that memorable night at the Savoy:

---

*"Twiggs and Tudens," Biographical Edition, VI, p. 58.

Won't you write on a copy of some favorite portrait of yourself and send it to me? God bless you.

As ever, gratefully and faithfully yours,

JAMES WHITCOMB RILEY.

To Madison Cawein.

Indianapolis,
Sept. 16, 1891.

Dear Cawein:

It's all right. I know the reference of which you speak. It very evidently is one made recently in the wild and woolly West by a man with an edged newspaper in his deadly hand, who thinks he is my friend, and therefore, semi-occasion'ly, cleaves me from chin to pelvis with his fatal kindness. He gets everything wrong.—Was born that way. His father had him—or the hired man.—He was not born of woman, God forfend! I shudder when I think of his upas-tree solicitude in my welfare. Haply he even prays for me and prejudices God against me. On second thought I don't send this as a postal. I fear it is not elegantly couched enough for that. All well every-way. Have been very carefully studying your last book. It grows, as does its author. He is destined to topmost niche in American letters—and the world shall applaud his great achievements.

JWR.

To Joseph Knight.

Joseph Knight was editor of *Notes & Queries*, dramatic critic of the *Globe* (London), biographer of Dante Gabriel Rossetti, author of *Life of David Garrick*, etc.

Indianapolis,
Sept. 18, 1891.

Dear Mr. Knight:

Your very considerate remembrance of me, by copy of your *Life of Rossetti*, affords me a pleasure the range of which no words of mine may rightly estimate. In fancy, only, can I grasp your hand again and thank you through that sense of palm-to-palm and face-to-face that errs not anyway.

What you have written of this master gives me also better knowledge, indirectly, of your own sound heart and soul and brain, together with the wholesome, robust greatness of the three combined. Away back here, in the core of the New World, my old friends find me warmer welcome home because away there in the Old World I met you. Surely my debt to you is great as my gratitude is unbounded. Your influence, too, continues to help and hearten me. God bless you and steadfastly keep you happy.

Gratefully and faithfully yours,
JAMES WHITCOMB RILEY.

To Mr. A. A. Dooley.

(Of the Kansas City *Star.*)

Sept. 18, 1891.

Dear Mr. Dooley:

In any event, I can take but limited number of engagements, and those only on conditions of such monetary blandishment as I'm really abashed to think of being persuaded to accept. God knows I've tried to keep myself cheap and within the reach of all, but the perverse fiat, in spite of me, seems to have gone forth and squared its jaws and spit on its hands in the resolve to make me a grasping, grinding, grinning Money-Grabber. . . . As to last book you ask after—it has been out some weeks, but gobbled as instalments from binders come till—I've heard publishers say—they've not been able to supply other demands yet, but will soon. Then of course the *Star* will not be overlooked.

To Madison Cawein.

Indianapolis, Ind.,
Sept. 19, 1891.

Ah! you lucky devil! Just see your belated reward swoopin' down on you at last—and then dare ever to chirp a melancholy note for all futurity! Oh, it's just superb! And so they'll keep it up—your faction, however they may be waspishly opposed. No fear further now, my boy. Let 'em damn and be damned! for just the same they can't hurt you now. Your friends are altogether too many, and like myself, growing more emphatically so, the more they read

and study what you've done and what you show a steady
growth of excellence in in every newer poem born of you.
To my own appreciative consciousness, even, some newer,
deeper worth of yours is borne in, as I review and wallow-
ingly bask me in your poems. Some things, of course, I
don't like, 'cause I know you could have done 'em better—
and will perfect 'em yet, some perfect hour of universal
triumph.—And just here and now I'm goin' to rattle
down a thing or two about your blessed ears. Don't—
don't—*Don't* ever becloud your beautiful ideas by too
intricate—too long, or too involved sentences. Pure
poetry must be pure—star-clear, or lucid as its reflex in
the pool. And don't—don't—*Don't* invert! No matter
though every classic master whose winy verse you ever
jabbed your beak in has inverted, don't you do it. You
improve on them by getting there directly. You can improve on their work, and you certainly will when you
escape that awful defect—the more awful when you sit
down quietly and try to find out why, in the name of God,
they were ever guilty of it—much less their continued and
unending indulgence of the crime. They didn't have to do
it, any more than you don't have to. Poetry should be as
direct in statement as prose. You say "The hornet sucked
gaunt o' the apricot." I say he didn't—he sucked sap.
Of course I readily surmise your meaning, but none the
less your sentence is contorted—humped, knuckled, and
you'd no right to mistreat an otherwise natural, and therefore wholly beautiful speech. And don't you go on forgiving yourself for it because of the same defect in any old
master or the whole pot-shot of 'em combined. For it is a
defect, and all the greater because of its absolute lack of
excuse. And I call you, too, to note the gropings at least,
toward its just banishment in our best masters modern.—

Notably Longfellow—Rossetti as well. The cure for it simply is to do it another way even should the composition of the poem take a thousand times as long. (It won't take *twice*.) To illustrate (further) a special hurt of this method, I quote from just before me this almost perfectly beautiful bit:

> "Red-winding from the sleepy town,
>   One takes the lone, forgotten lane
> Straight through the hills. A brush bird *brown*"
> etc.

Well—right here you virtually say to me, and to all other workmen, or intelligent readers, "See how I haul that rhyme in by its damned ears! Of course, it doesn't naturally belong there, but it serves, and by Gaud! I don't 'low no rhyme to run me!" Wonder how long the master wrought on such simple perfect utterances as:

> "Such songs have power to quiet
>   The restless pulse of care,
> And fall like the benediction
>   That follows after prayer."

Now, give me a line to say I'm understood and that you know I mean it with all kindliness and interest—same as I always strive to arraign and correct, if possible, my own multitudinous shortcomings. As ever

Your affectionate

JAMESIE.

Just got "life" and critical review of Rossetti, with author's "friendliest regards," and he being no less a master of letters than the English Joseph Knight, I'm rendered about as proud and swell-headed as my hat-band'll stand the pressure of!

To Miss Evaleen Stein.

Indianapolis,
September 27, 1891.

Dear Miss Stein:

Your poem this morning is as sacredly beautiful as the day, and shows, I think, both human heart and *art* in simplest—therefore most perfect—unison.   You are of the Elect. Be assured of that. The first book, too, you print will prove as much to the literary world, I honestly believe and pray.

While this last poem is "Impatient," it is very sweetly so, and most wholesomely. So must you abide in selfsame spirit yet a little till the great day comes, as certainly it will.

Do you read and study all the Our-kind poets—they who "belong," as Kipling says?—Keats, Mrs. Browning, Rossetti,—and his sister Christina—Herrick, the peerless, and Longfellow, the divinely pure and artless.

As ever, with all faith and proud acclaims,
Your grateful friend,
J. W. RILEY.

To Madison Cawein.

Indianapolis,
Oct. 23, 1891.

My dear Cawein:

What's come of ye 'at you don't never let a feller hear nothin' of ye any more? Have waited and waited till I'm plum' wore out a-waitin'! Work! Well, my head *whirls* with it. Got some good things, though, and you'd indorse in parts anyway. Is it so, you're contemplating going East to work? Oh, don't do that, I beg. You're right in the country you belong in—so, at least, stay loyal to it, and let 'em send their work to you.—You'll be the better for it every way. Then, every once in a while, we can go East together, as we flourish; and they'll only welcome you the heartier and honor you the more. Indeed, indeed, no money could tempt me ever to quit my home and people. I used to think different, but I was wrong, and am sorry that ever, even in youthful thought, I was ever disloyal to my own. So don't you ever go away. It will, in the end, hurt not help you. God bless you and keep you very brave and steadfast. Yours may be the first and best fame of any of America's own singers. As ever affectionately

JAMESIE.

To John Patterson.

Indianapolis, Ind.,
Oct. 24, 1891.

Dear Sir:

Answering your inquiry of date twenty-first, I must acknowledge the correctness of your impression regarding the real author of the poem "Leonainie"—and theme-coinage, story of "original" manuscript's discovery—all, in fact, but the really clever imitation of Poe's chirography, I grieve to confess the very brazen work of my profane hand and scheming brain.* But I was a boy then, and deserve some little charity. The fraud was not maliciously designed, but simply to prove that a school of

---

*See letter to *Kokomo Dispatch,* July 23, 1877, p. 14; also letter from John Patterson, Appendix, p. 330.

critics innumerable did not know nearly so much as either themselves or the public has been complacently and most persistently persuaded to believe. In other words, my poetry wouldn't go, Poe's would. So we gave 'em the latter variety, through the medium of the *Kokomo Dispatch,* (Howard County, Ind.). Address Editor Oscar Henderson, Esq., for particulars, if desired. As to the opinion of the author of the Edgar Allan Poe article in the October number of *The American Catholic Quarterly Review,* which you quote, his generous estimate of the poem is to me more a rebuke than a tribute. So, too, all like gracious tributes which steadfastly now for years have been appearing. Even the manuscript of the poem (with no complicity of mine, however) has long since passed into the possession of a New York collector, who was wont to exhibit it with much pride till he wrote to me, saying he had bought the poem as Poe's, and inquiring if there was any foundation for the rumor that had loiteringly reached him that it was a base invention of mine. Therefore, as you see my only just share of the poem's fortunings is the ignominy constantly accruing and out-cropping as result of my offense. But, as the man under a tree said, as the lightning struck it, "It must mean me—so I'll jest git out in the clearin' and hump myself, take a few perfunctory volts and have it over with!"

Very truly and gratefully yours,

J. W. RILEY.

CHAPTER IV

Books and Friends and Letters

Stoddard—*The Flying Islands*—Sends his photograph to a friend—John Hay—Thomas Wentworth Higginson—Nye—Howells—John Burroughs—Eugene F. Ware—Joseph Knight—Thomas Nast—Lecturing woes and triumphs—Paul Laurence Dunbar.

To Charles Warren Stoddard.

Indianapolis, Ind.,
November 19, 1891.

My dear friend:

Yes, indeed, I am home, and as glad to get back as I am to get your letter. Be very certain, too, that through all my alien wanderings you were steadfastly kept in mind and longed for many many times. And I would have written you, but that all the time I supposed you, like myself, a wayward pilgrim, with the curse of the wandering foot heavy upon you.*

There! though I didn't mean to quote the whole poem, I've went and gone and done it anyhow, though, maybe, reading it, you can tell me if it's worth the utterance and where its proper place is—either in enduring type or rag-tag-and-bobtail MS., as up to present date.

But I did no work of consequence abroad. Was advised not to even tamper with it. So, in the main, I slighted all inclination even of the kind. Hence two or

---

*Here Riley quoted his "The Curse of the Wandering Foot," *Lockerbie Book,* No. 187.

146

three several times was on the verge of insanity. My God! that Old World! It did so weigh down upon me sometimes—till my heart was squashed flat—like a fly in some monster tome!! Some great things, though, were mine—that I could realize. Among the very first— Henry Irving. His welcome to me was both generous and gentle in excess. Like poor Jo, I have only one meager phrase by which to express my vast gratitude to that loveliest of men. "He was werry good to me." At his hands, too, I met many other Genii, in art, letters and the like. Joseph Knight, the hale old master of us, of the almost stormy aspect, of both brow and voice (the latter like a wounded lion's with a defective "mute" on it)—but withal the gentlest heart and soul that ever welled up and out o' the eyes in tears. And that's exactly what they did, at some of our poor, limping, groping, halting, whole-some American dialect. Oh, and how proud was I! And he wanted a book I'd written. And here on the stand is one of his own he has sent to me, inscribed with his own pen. Who says what's wrong with anything on Earth!

To-day mailed you my last book—*The Flying Islands of the Night*—a fantastic drama in verse. Tell me quick what's the matter with it and what, in God's name, have I done! As ever your faithful friend,

J. W. RILEY.

To Charles Warren Stoddard.

Indianapolis,
Dec. 1, 1891.

My dear Stoddard:
Some time ago I think you asked me for my portrait. With this I therefore mail to you my last, being reminded

of your request by coming on the picture all abruptly in my yet unpacked steamer trunk. Of course I don't look like you've doubtless fancied me all out,—dark, rolling eyes, bleak Shakespearian brow and tumbling mane blent with a hell-to-pay-and-no-pitch-hot cast o' countenance, peculiar to our New World brand óf bard, to whom, I Gawd! you will listen, er wisht you had! No; not at all, I trust. In fact, in subjecting ourselves to the photographer, I rather hold that, as Chispa mildy observed to the serenaders, "our object is not to arouse and terrify, but to soothe and bring lulling dreams." Possibly in this example I have even permeated the opposite extreme and show altogether too meek and gruel-y.—Indeed I fear so, yet am forced to admit that one exacting friend has said of it " 'twas wonderfully faithful to the life, only, it did flatter just a trifle."—To which I was glad to say it was a joy to know 'twas really flatter than the original.

Vastly have I enjoyed your late letters, and the benefit therefrom accrued I count most valuable. Everybody's learning all the time. Are we ever anything but amateurs? Never any venture of my life was more than a trial at some attainment—and experiment—not a forecast certainly of accomplishment. And, fact is, it keeps us duly humble—or ought to. Whatever good is wrought is not our doing—it is through us, not of us, thank God: And that's what He wants to beat into us, and when we just won't have it beat in, why, then He lets loose of us, that we may see, and the whole united populace as well, that here's another weighed-and-found-wanting candidate for enduring glory.—Like Byron, or like Tilton, of our time, Conklin, Proctor *et al.;* or like Shelley, or like Poe, many of the great list absolutely pouting at high heaven, as though God didn't appreciate their real worth, or in all probability was just a little jealous of their high accomplishments and possibilities in the Jehovah line; or Joseph Cook, of whom I am loiteringly reminded. But God bless you! and pardon me for all this useless interjection I've been afflicting you with. What you've "spotted" in the wandering foot* shall be religiously righted. I've felt something was wrong, but on my life, I couldn't ferret it out! So, first opportunity, I'll tackle the thing again.

And now won't you, my dear friend, send me the picture of you? From our dear Nicholson I get some idea, but the photograph will lead all words and skill of speech however deft of any master old or young. So bless me with a copy next you write, and should you write at once, so much the better for

Yours
Gratefully, faithfully and every way,
J. W. RILEY.

To Colonel John Hay.

Indianapolis, Ind.,
Dec. 2, 1891.

My dear friend:

Your generous and most wholesome comment on *The Flying Islands of the Night* is at once a delight and serious solace to me. While writing the somewhat capricious and misguided poem was, as you surmise, a pleasure, I have suffered no little apprehension since venturing to put it in a book. Know, then, how great is my relief and reassurance when you write in sanction of it, and in hale praise, as well. Others, too, and many are joining in the

---

*See letter to Stoddard, November 19, 1891, p. 146.

"pleased applause"—so that about this blessed minute I stand heartened and equipped for anything of counter estimate the deadly cobra critic of the Press may have in wait for me. In fact, I even stickle not to utilize your kindly word both as a good omen and—its own eloquent and sufficient blessing.

Very gratefully and faithfully yours,
JAMES WHITCOMB RILEY.

To Thomas Wentworth Higginson.

Dec. 9, 1891.

Dear Mr. Higginson:

You were so very good to me, writing so considerate a letter and saying such altogether pleasant things of my honest efforts in the singing way, that, with the fever of delight still on me, I dispatched to you at once—another book! What you will think of such a dubious expression of my gratitude I have been wondering ever since. Therefore, in this my first appropriate leisure since let me more deliberately hasten to express to you my serious thanks for your great kindness to me and mine.

Good as it is to have you speak approvingly of my verse, dialect or otherwise, no less do I count it a gracious thing to feel that your demand is absolute clearness and fidelity of utterance. Especially in the dialect of my native region and people this has been and is, my conscientious effort always; though perhaps I have not so often as I should have done printed with the dialect notes of the why and wherefore of the same. As in the case you mention wherein the child-dialect of this locality gives "thist" for "just"—obtaining back into my own remotest child-

hood memories. And it would furnish a curious study to
any one to trace—or try to—the Genesis of such an example as the foregoing. One little bit of a ragamuffin
boy, with this kink in his tongue, will infect an entire
neighborhood, long after "jus" or "dis" seems universally
established. No tangible explanation of it—simply it's
"catching." Perhaps the novelty first strikes the youthful ear—the crisp quip of the sound—something—and it
comes in and has its day, as hundreds of other errors like
it,—notably, at least is this so of our children of the country towns. . . . But you must pardon my own exasperating speech—far more so than the children's.

Very proud and glad would Indianapolis be to welcome
you; and I'm going steadfastly to hope that we may yet
have the great good fortune and delight of hearing you
lecture—and upon your "Old School-days with Lowell,"
if I might name the theme.

Gratefully and faithfully yours,
J. W. RILEY.

To William Carey.

Indianapolis,
Dec. 13, 1891.

Dear Carey:

It is a very lovely thing to get your letter though I
don't believe at all that I deserve it, since never a blessed
chirp have I sent you for long loitering ages! Steadfastly, however, have I thought of you both beyond-seas
and home again—but some way—some way—I have pre-
sumed upon how well you knew my procrastinative way;
and your own great kindness and forbearance with it

time out o' mind that I felt you'd still humor it, and haply even come to thank me for it. The fact is for months now I've not been fit company, even by post, for any one, much less my best of friends.

As Nye—God bless him—would remark, I have been trying to think thoughts for the masses, which effort has so involved my pseudo mind, it has wisely abstained from any possible chance of deflecting disease on the very heads I needs must guard most sacredly. Indeed but I've been at work as never before on earth! and though showing little or no sign of it physically, my reporting *dingus* is all out of whack. So that socially half the time I am trying to explain to friends why I fail to keep my appointments with them, the other half the time I agree to do anything I designate and then promptly forget all about it—or I'll write it down so I can't possibly forget it—evidently to no other purpose than designate the fact that I can possibly forget it! But enough of this! Here with a wave of me magic pen let me describe the enraptured trip to London. There in that great, vast colossal world of a city I was brought to feel my own abject self-insignificance.

Mr. Irving I knew, and hoped he might remember me— but a note and he *did* remember me and asked me to come down with him and meet a coterie of his friends—and Coquelin*—and for him he wanted me to read something he himself had particularly enjoyed in New York. Of course I read, and Coquelin applauded and Irving again and again, and the entire table, till it almost seemed that God was liable to come down any minute to inquire what was up now in the Old Beef-steak Room in the Lyceum.

Through Mr. Irving too, I met (at the Savoy) the vet-

---

*See reference to this in Introduction.

eran dramatic critic and Shakespearean scholar, Joseph Knight, at once the sternest, bluffest-looking yet gentlest gentleman that ever laid his two approving hands upon my two shoulders, for I read again for him at Mr. Irving's instigation, and I simply had to do better than ever in my life before, and I did—and I know I did, 'cause Joseph Knight cried—and coming to thank me cried again, so that he could not speak for quite a while, and finally tried but failed again and sobbed outright.

Well, I was steadfastly kept boring them from about ten o'clock till four in the morning, was even after this invited to the Garrick Theatre by Mr. Knight though, most unfortunately for me, I was to sail the day of the night of their meeting. Pardon all this length of space and nothing said. Would like to see you and talk—but when I'm to be your way again I've not the vaguest idea. Wish I could be with you next Watch night, but remember me to all there just the same.

Yours, gratefully and affectionately,

J. W. RILEY.

To Colonel Richard Malcolm Johnston.

Pittsburgh, Pa.,
Dec. 29, 1891.

My dear friend:

Will you ever forgive my long silence—or has it, indeed, seemed long to you? Work and travel, both have determinedly held me away from all other considerations for ages. But you are good, and infinitely patient with all such thoughtless children as myself, and "while my head's hot" I shan't forget my gratitude to you and warmest love, whether I get to write it down or not as often as I ought to. As to the "Flying Islands," of course it comes out with our usual lot of exasperating errors—my own as well as the printer's; but it's "going," and the gods are good to it. Our first literary lights have written me— in every instance more for than against it—so that, in truth, the consensus places it in the line of a distinctive creation, and with the gracious promise of enduring for more than a day. Straight in with these your comment nestles and abides, leaving me more and more your impoverished debtor.—In fact if there were now a debtor's prison, nothing short of a life-term would acquit me of my just obligations to you, "O gentlest of my friends!"

Your own book, as all mine in some way do, was not done justice to by binders. Otherwise, as far as I can see, it seems press-worthy. As to its contents, you know that delights me, even as Irving, or Ik Marvel, or John Burroughs; or any of that rare, delicious list of those who "bear, without abuse, the grand old name of Gentleman." But our better and more perfect day, in print and ink and binding, is not far off, thank God! when we may utterly depend on that point of excellence in our publishers as on their liberality and honest growth of honor as we find it now. You are continually asked after by the friends you made in Indianapolis—the most loyal and enduring in the whole wide world. They want again to see you and to hear you—as I do. When shall it be? As to myself, I am accepting but very few platform engagements, and always those I do accept I go to with most positive reluctance—as here to-night.—Ten times over I would rather write, when I can select my own theme, and time, and space to put it down in. My holiest tinker's damn on all work writ to order!

Remember me with all kindness to your good family, and like friends of mine wherever you may hit upon them—and God bless us every one!

Your affectionate and always grateful friend,

J. W. RILEY.

To Edgar Wilson Nye.

Indianapolis,
Jan. 18, 1892.

Dear Nye:

Are you at Asheville er whur? As I write I'm still smiling over your last letter to the Press, comforted by that, that wherever you are you're in robust mental health and spirits. Have for a very long time been expecting a word from you personally, in answer to letter and book to you at St. Louis, but this morning's mail bringing books back, care Publishers, I infer 'at neither them nor the letter ever came to your hand. By hokeys! I was mad, and am a big notion to turn in and write Harrison a few lines about my opinion of that-air "Moneymaker," as I heard a comical feller call his P. O. General t'other day. Hell's full o' sich "Generals," says I! Also Mr. Burbank's copy of "Flying Islands" is back with yours—so that I gather your St. Louis date was give' the go-by—though you told me you'd be there.

Again I am a prophet: First news of your accident I ventured to outline the very natural probabilities and give bird's-eye views of the general quail-trap architecture of our modern stage as it is sown throughout the length and breadth of our otherwise stable and undefective republic; and, as God hears me, I said, in all likelihood some stairway had been taken down at dead of night, and the stair-door baited and set, and the lock hair-triggered and the hinges greased!* Judge, therefore, how your account of it has encouraged my superstitious tendency. And I am glad, with thousands of other friends, that the outcome of the accident was not worse, God bless you. See in yester-day's *Herald* a beautiful Nye history—told strongly and with just dignity and seriousness, with all bearings, in fact, set down with proper grace and courtliness. Every way I congratulate you and applaud. You will leave, in my "jour"-judgment, the best and gentlest record of any humorist of our time.

My heartiest cheer for the children all, with all kind remembrances to their mother.

As ever your affectionate
JAMESIE.

As to my late work, I can not refrain from telling you it seems to be fastening on—both at home and abroad.— Aside from dozens of approving letters from Eastern crit-ics, I'm now receiving same from overseas,—the last from no less a literary and dramatic authority than Joseph Knight, the eminent scholar, author and the rest. And "blessings on his kindly face and on his silvery hair!"

---

*The theater in question had an outside balcony where Nye and Riley spent their intermissions during one of their readings. This balcony had been removed but the door leading to it left as before.

To William Dean Howells.

Indianapolis, Ind.,
Jan. 19, 1892.

Dear Mr. Howells:

With all heart and soul my thanks are yours for the good you do me by both word and deed. In any way I am yours to command, and soon as leisure from public readings will permit I will set about the poems you ask me to submit for the *Cosmopolitan.* But do you want dialect—or serious work—or both? And be assured I shall not be "mad at you" if you should not, upon receiving them, choose any. Your verdict, either for or against, I shall gratefully applaud, certain of its kindliest intent toward me and mine.

Uniting with my publishers in the desire to send a complete list of my books to you, we have been delayed from so doing by binding-style suitable running out of stock, necessitating special order to bindery—now being attended, as per direction before leaving the city some weeks ago, as my engagements compelled.

Of my last book venture I want to keep still but I can't.—*The Flying Islands of the Night.* Some first literary people write me in strong praise of it and full indorsement—others cry aloud and spare not. Of course you know which of these extreme factions I naturally desire to be biased by. Which would you suggest? Some time can't you glance the proposition through and tell me? One of last best letters I venture to inclose for your inspection, if you will so accept the confidence—even as from a kinsman who has nowhere else to turn.

Gratefully and faithfully your friend,
J. W. RILEY.

To John Burroughs.

Indianapolis, Ind.,
Feb. 9, 1892.

Dear John Burroughs:

When you tell me that you take my poems Sunday nights over the apples and the nuts, the unconscious poetry of your tribute is, in my liking, a peg higher than *"Across the walnuts and the wine,"* of England's laureate. Aye!

"Across the walnuts and the wine"—
Granting the verse almost divine,—
In sooth, my fancy fondlier shuts
Over the apples and the nuts! !"

Gratefully and faithfully yours,
JAMES WHITCOMB RILEY.

(Am enclosing poem "Right Here at Home.")*

To Eugene F. Ware.

Indianapolis,
Feb. 9, 1892.

My dear Ironquill:

Good for your wholesome and most heartening size-up of "The Flying Islands!" *Good! good! good!* I chortle in dee-lisciousmous reiteration. Things is a-comin' my way shore enough when you plank down your vigorous approval. And I hasten to assure you that your estimate is filed along with numberless others of like high caste and bearing—the last of these received from even overseas, and from no less a literary and dramatic critic and scholar than Joseph Knight, God wot! who hath lifted, in good

---

*Hoosier Book, No. 119.

sooth, in younger days, the lint out of the literary pelt of Mr. Victor Hugo; and, by "The long, low wash of Australasian Seas," perfunctorily mopped off the weltering beach with Mr. Tennyson.

Therefore, it is with no ordinary pride that I find myself enabled to convey to my friends here in "the grand old Commonwealth of Indiany" the gratifying fact that Joseph Knight's opinion of my truly marvelous creation coincides most happily with •my own—and he does not hesitate to designate it even as *"a tour de force!"** But as you observe, "It is not always what an author says, but what he suggests that makes a good," etc. This characteristic of the performance—the very basis of the poem necessarily—is mainly now occasioning the *jour*-critic's adverse comment, as I think. Later on he may come round our way, or else not monkey with the dad-burn thing prematurely—never a-gain no more! Again and again I thank you for what I believe to be as sound an estimate—and certainly as gratifying—as any yet paid the book.

Very gratefully and faithfully yours,
J. W. RILEY.

*To Joseph Knight.**

Indianapolis, Ind.,
Feb. 11, 1892.

My dear Mr. Knight:

If any gracious letter was ever welcomed with the combined spirit and emotions of a just appreciation, your letter has so fared in my regard. To me the earnest, honest voice of it is sacred—throughout every line and word and

---

*See letter of Dec. 26, 1891, from Joseph Knight, Appendix, p. 331.

syllable: That my book—*mine*—*The Flying Islands of the Night*—for whose fate I have been for years fore-trembling, should be so generously accepted and approved by you—were of itself glory enough though all other critics of the Old World and the New leveled their lances and bore down upon me.

When you say the volume is "as much of a puzzle as of a delight"—that you have "read it again and again with augmenting pleasure"—that "it is a *tour de force*"—but that you "need more illumination than you possess from within"—I have nothing (beyond my vast gratitude) left me but to confess the work as simply and entirely a fabrication of the fancy, purposely and defiantly avoiding, if possible, any reference to any former venture or accomplishment of any writer, dead or living, though in this acknowledgment I hasten to assure you that no spirit of irreverence as I wrote was either in possession of or parcel of my thought. It was all bred of an innocent desire to do a new thing. I argued, simply, in this wise: Some mind some time invented Fairies—and their realm. So with mermaids, and their kingdom!—and so I went on with the illimitable list till I found "The earth, and the air, and the sea, And the infinite spaces"—all—all occupied or let or spoken for. So, obviously, I had in my crying dilemma, to put up with flying islands, together with such inhabitants, thereon, as I might (likewise) hope tangibly to suggest, if not create. Then, since I found myself without stable base or space to rest foot on, as I wrought, I was persuaded that the success of such an undertaking must rest entirely upon suggestion—so that the reader (even as the writer) must fancy out the completed thing. Hence the word-coinage—in as temperate monotony as deemed feasible—and so on with every detail of the work, imperfect as it is and must remain. But I am glad and

proud to assure you, as I thank for your own most gratifying tribute, that—at home here many of our first literary men have written me in hearty praise and indorsement
of the work. Of course there are other opinions, and with
edges to the voices of the same with nicks in 'em, that rasp
and saw into a fellow's "feelinks" most indelicate! But, as
intimated—equipped with your approval, and that of my
first countrymen of the writing craft, upon all others—
they who fizz and fizzle and erupt and disembogue—I
bend a commiserative eye, with a latent smile in the tail
of it. With ever continued thanks for the honor you
have done me, I am as ever

Gratefully and faithfully yours,

JAMES WHITCOMB RILEY.

To the Editor of the "Inter-Ocean."

Indianapolis
March 8, 1892.

Dear Sir:

Answering your request regarding my opinion of Mr.
Whitman's poetry and his just place in the world's literature, I am left to confess that, in the main, his poetry has
positively refused, and still refuses, my applause. With
all patience reading it and striving with it, the conclusion
invariably reached is, that the curiously gifted man is more
of a poet at soul than at heart; that at all too infrequent intervals, despite the trammelings of any earthly vanity,—
ingenious finesse of method or intent, the soul breaks all
restraint and sings out naturally, nobly and divinely,—as
notably in his heart tribute to the martyred Lincoln. The
time he sung that, the true poet only held rapt reign.
Walt Whitman was for the nonce forgotten utterly.

JAMES WHITCOMB RILEY.

To Mr. and Mrs. Early.

Washington, D. C.,
April 5, 1892.

Dear Mr. and Mrs. Early:

In to-day's *New York World* I have been reading and rereading the strange, pathetic history of the fortunes and misfortunes of the composer of "Kathleen Mavourneen,"* now resident of Baltimore, and, as this article sets forth, in sore need of human help. Can we not bless this old singer in some smallest measure now for the immortal blessing that his peerless song has rendered unto all humanity? At once, then (as the need seems great) my services may be commanded for dates on till eighth, this coming week,—or, if not available to your committee will gladly arrange later date, upon my return home, as obliged. This event, however, leaves later date an indefinite one to fix; therefore, knowing myself free to arrange any date in next four days, I will be overjoyed to find you can accept same and unite with me in the proposed public entertainment in which I ask such musical assistance, vocal or otherwise, as I feel assured the high talent of your city could and would promptly and cheerfully and most fittingly supply.

Surely we could in such a cause, however hurriedly organized and carried out, raise a handsome sum of money for the dear old man. Telegraph me at once, care Riggs House and do, if at all possible let me know that you accept.

As ever gratefully yours,
J. W. RILEY.

*See "Kathleen Mavourneen," *Lockerbie Book,* No. 283.

To Edgar Wilson Nye.

Duluth, Minn.,
May 12, 1892.

Dear Nye:

As I've just returned from my morning walk and first cursory glimpse of Duluth, I add another hasty page to yesterday's letter to say that the main street here, in point of length, fully meets my demands. In fact, I can conceive of nothing longer than Superior Street, unless possibly, a lecture by Brer Talmage or a Pseudo-humorous monologue by Eli Perkins. Also I send this to enclose some newspaper notices which since yesterday I have been vainly striving to overlook—together with programs of entertainment, by means of which you will observe that I am not only "A Natural Poet," but "The Greatest Born Actor," in all probability, outside o' Hell at the present day. Also I am, through same authentic sources, Ever Thine,

"THE POOR MAN'S FRIEND."

To Miss Helen Carter.

June 3, 1892.

Dear Miss Carter:

Yes, the poem "Leonainie,"* a youthful effort of fifteen years ago, I am forced to acknowledge my invention—name, theme, everything save the certain *twirl* of rhyme and cadence, introduced, designedly, of course, to further conspire in decoying and deceiving that ever-present class

---

*See letter to *Kokomo Dispatch*, July 23, 1877, p. 14.

of critical assailants (who praise established poets only), eternally insisting that anything with a young poet's name to it is not a poem.   Therefore my endeavor was to produce something they would pronounce a poem, thereby demonstrating the fact that they were wholly self-constituted and unfit judges of the merits of any poet, dead or living.   The ruse succeeded—not only then, but is still fitfully at work upon its righteous mission.

Thanking you for your query and the kindly interest you express, I am

Very truly yours,
J. W. RILEY.

To Thomas Nast.

Indianapolis, Ind.,
Sept. 5, 1892.

Dear Mr. Nast:

Since the arrival, two days ago, of your Puritanic masterpiece, "The Landing of a Father," with the typical Boston gentlemen, Philips and Butler, in the foreground (though not so far in it as this just landed contemporary!) I've been too proudly and delightedly busy showing the picture to immediate friends and the general public to express my special thanks to you.   Though attempting such a feat—even at the thought I feel I should fail utterly.   Too much is involved; for I should necessarily go back before the War—even as the magic little sketch transports me—and begin my own youthful hopes and ambitions over again, even as when roused and quickened into newer, brighter, better spirit, and more daring mettle by your pictures.   Nor would I neglect the acknowledgment of a certain art influence of yours that has not only been a constant source of pleasure to me since that far-off time, but has helped and blessed my own efforts in a somewhat kindred line. But I spare you all detail, certain that this mere suggestion will be far more gratefully received, rounded and perfected by you than pages of my pen's best work.

Wishing for you and your art every measure of success, clean on to the rapturous attainment of the most intrepid fancy of your genius, I remain,

Ever gratefully and faithfully yours,
JAMES WHITCOMB RILEY.

To Mr. and Mrs. Charles L. Holstein.

Riley was living on Lockerbie Street at the home of Major Charles L. Holstein and his wife's parents, Mr. and Mrs. John Nickum.

Iowa City, Iowa,
Nov. 17, 1892.

Dear Lockerbies:

This letter-head must be taken only as characteristic of the country out here—not as indicative of my exact whereabouts as I write,—for I'm now just arrived in Des Moines—promptly met by a Ladies' Committee, which has very kindly consented not to entertain me this afternoon, owing to the fact that I really couldn't be there.

Of course, as I argue complacently to myself, the old home there without me is simply glutted with vacancy and desolation! So I hasten this line to allay, in part, at least, your very natural suspense and apprehension. Know, therefore, I am extremely well, and at every town, absolutely dogged with good fortune,—save an experience of yesterday, when for nearly four hours, that seemed almost as many months, we rode in the caboose of a freight train a distance of about thirty miles. Then it was I regretted not having along some standard good authors that I never have been able to read in the past: Scott or Bulwer, for instance. Then I could easily have read the complete works of either. As it was, I in a measure contented myself by memorizing "Nada the Lily," between whiles listening to my fragile manager, Mr. Glass, whose N-Yo'k pronunciation has not quite yet worn away by western attrition. He's a very likable fellow, and I'm more taken with him every day; and doubtless by the time he can say *Omaha,* instead of *Omahor,* I'll be wanting him to come back home and live with me.

This is little enough, but all I can say now. Not worth an answer from you, but yet should you respond in briefest way I'll be elaborately grateful. And you can make my Thanksgiving Day a real one by so doing. At that time I'll be at Coates House, Kansas City,

As ever yours,

Jimpsy.

Best love to ever'body—specially your parents—bless 'em!

To George Smith.

Lincoln, Neb.,
Nov. 21, 1892.

Dear Grandpa:*

Am worryin' on West slow as old molasses; but none the less my interminable "show" seems to bore nobody but

---

*A facetious title.

James W. Riley,

THE HOOSIER POET,

HUMORIST AND DIALECTIC READER,

IN HIS

ORIGINAL IMPERSONATIONS, CHARACTER SKETCHES AND
STUDIES FROM REAL LIFE.

ADDRESS REDPATH LYCEUM BUREAU, SOLE MANAGERS,
36 Bromfield St., Boston;
Tribune Building, Chicago.

Indianapolis Journal, June 6, 1881.

Dear friend Parker:

Brief as your letter is, I am delighted with it, and gladder yet to know that your prospects are so full of soul-reposing promise. I envy and congratulate you in the same breath. And I shall certainly accept your invitation to come and see you if the vaguest opportunity ever offers. But I am — have been, and will be closely — almost painfully — working. My future, like your own, promises to be summery, though I must labor hard to win and wear its golden weather.

We will be more than pleased with any contributions you may be able to furnish the Journal, and Mr. Halford said last night to tell you so, and that, in return, your request for the paper would be eagerly answered.

I am now trying to write prose — hoping to get a book of sketches together before a great while — though I still write an occasional poem, and itch to be at verse all the time.

The coming lecture season looms with most glorious promises. The Bureau thinks I am destined to become a general favorite. So I am at work in that view, and have many irons in the fire beside them — they come. May all good things come to you, and may you write me of them — they come. My best regards to your good wife and family, and let me hear from you often. As Ever,

J. W. Riley

myself. Even my fragile manager, Mr. Glass, is not
wholly shattered yet, though my program is as monoto-
nous as the menu of a two-kinds-of-meat restaurant. Glass
is a fine fellow, and grows more companionable to me
every day—as I'm striving to grow to him. There's no
dam' R. R! Schedule can awe him for a holy minute! and
he does it all, too, just as *e-a-s-y!* He takes me along with
him just like I take an umbrella along with me. It's
simply natural to him; it's a gift—that's what! In fact, I
look upon Glass as a positive "attraction." I bet I don't
begin to "draw" like Glass would if he were managed half
as well as I am! He can even do my meditating for me,
and lets me sleep whole hours at a time, with never anybody's card on earth sent up only when I'm really at
righteous leisure,—ner nobody offended, nyther! So far,
we've missed all the bad weather now ravaging this section,
as I read of in the dailies. Glass also manages that, I suppose. First week out filled five consecutive nights, and
never missed a meal or late night lunch. Sunday in
Omaha—good hotel, and never out o' my good-ole-snug-
gledy-woolly-worm-wrapper, only to go down to dinner
and supper.—Glass had my breakfast sent up to me so I
simply englutted that like a boa constrictor, and rolled
over in a comatose condition again.

Lincoln here is Phil Igoe's* old town. I got on to that,
tell him, 'fore I got here. Here, of course, they say nothing about it—evidently trying to live it down. Otherwise
it seems a really worthy little city, and wakening to a new
prosperity since his absence. The clerk here at the hotel
told me, confidentially, that the community here, in his
opinion, was unjust to Igoe—that they didn't half-way

---

*Igoe was a good-natured neighbor with whom Riley loved to exchange
banter.

appreciate what he'd done to advance the prospects of this town—by going away from it. Glass just now isn't at hand, so ask Eitel where I'm at, and write. Only date I've memorized is Kansas City, Thanksgivin'-Day, "Coates House," Mo. My best to all the friends, as ever,

JAMESIE.

To Paul Laurence Dunbar.

"I was the first to recognize Paul Laurence Dunbar."— J. W. R.

Denver, Colo.,
Nov. 27, 1892.

Paul Dunbar, Esq.:

See how your name is traveling, my chirping friend! And it's a good, sound name, too, that seems to imply the brave, fine spirit of a singer who should command wide and serious attention. Certainly your gift—as evidenced by this "Drowsy-Day" poem alone—is a superior one, and therefore its fortunate possessor should bear it with a becoming sense of gratitude, and meekness,—always feeling that for any resultant good, *God's* is the glory—the singer but His very humble instrument. Already you have many friends, and can have thousands more, being simply honest, unaffected, and just to yourself and the high source of your endowment.

Very earnestly I wish you every good thing.

Your friend,
JAMES WHITCOMB RILEY.

To John A. Riley.

Visalia, Cal.,
Dec. 7, 1892.

Dear John:

The enclosed clipping from the *Times* here will give you still another and very important view of your justly celebrated brother—who, by the way, is gittin' jes' a little hotter all the time at the attitude of the people out here regarding his obvious lack of beauty. They might, I think, be at least as thoughtful in their personal expressions of their views in this regard as the good old negro aunty in the presence of the hippopotamus: She simply said, "My sakes! how *plain* he is!"

Don't forget, writing home, a long letter to Mary.* I don't think she is ever well in health.

Hastily,

○   JIM.

To Mrs. Charles L. Holstein.

San Francisco, Cal.,
Dec. 15, 1892.

Dear friend:

Whatever shall I say in such an awful crowd o' things? My head—such as the poor travesty is—whirls, spins and whizzes! I've been, and still am, trying gratefully to answer all the kindnesses of this overwhelmingly courteous region, and the result is I'm just about laid out. Lord! for a gracious rest from it all in dear Old Idyllic Lockerbie!—Such as your letter wafts me hints of, despite all

_____
*The sister Mrs. Mary Riley Payne.

its piques and slurs and double "intenders." But, for all o' that, rest perfectly assured you can't make me quarrel, or indeed, be anything but smilingly affable and grateful. Ever steadfastly I go straight on, thinking you only gentle, mild and dulcet as a velvety old ballad poured from the mellow throat of old Theocritus. (Pa, who'z old Theockertus, an' what wuz the *matter* wiv his throat?) Papers and reporters, for the most part, keep me busy all hours of the day and night—then, intermittently, the long unbroken file of my first discoverers, pauses personally to call my attention to the fact. "O God!" I sometimes needs must sob out, "What did you let 'em ever find me fer in the first place—let alone this last time?" This morning I got away long enough to order John R. and Lottie Nickum a box of native fruits, nuts, etc., which were to be promptly expressed. Tell me at Portland—er somers—if you got 'em time fer Chris'mas. Dealer said they'd surely reach you. Wisht I was packed in wiv 'em an' ud keep all nice tel Johnnie knicked the lid off an' I come a-tumblin' out wite on the kitchen-floor! Maybe nen I'd git all et up wiv the brownies—an' nen I'd ist choke em ef they don't spit the hulls out—won't I? Whyn't Charles answer my letter? Sent him, also, paper notices. Bored him with them, too, I'm 'fraid. Best love to everybody. As ever yours,

JIMPSY.

To George Smith.

San Francisco, Cal.,
Dec. 17, 1892.

Dear Grandpa:

I hate to write letters to you—have to bear down so hard to make you hear. Glad enough to get word from you and the boys around the table, and wish this minute you were here, as I've my first day off, and 'ud like to show you round town. Last night filled third consec'-engage' to biggest house of the three, and seined in over the foot-lights a big floral tablet—the size of a table-top, which dropped the bloomin' remark, "Good-bye, Jim; Take keer of yourself!"* so that the whole house overheard it with their eyes and cheered and cheered till I was forced to come forward and again wonder what in the name o' God I was ever goin' to do with it. My manager, how-ever, and a picked nine, filed up and escorted it, with martial tread, round through stage entrance and thence on to the floral morgue, where it now lies in state, and, it is needless to add, jest naturally leans back and "smells to heaven!" Popular excitement over me is at last dying down, and the burning passion for my poetry is giving way to the loftier allurements of football, and to-night the great expert, Walter Camp, has magnanimously con-sented to my being entertained along with him at a public banquet, at which affair I've no doubt I'll happily be taught to know my place. But seriously, Mr. Camp is a fine man, sound, decorous, gentle and loved of everybody fortunate enough to meet him. I dined with him at Stan-ford University last Saturday, where we were guests of President Jordan, together with members of his faculty.

---

*Refrain from "The Old Man and Jim," *Hoosier Book,* No. 200.

Would like here to tell you something of this superb college and its certainly assured great future—its enchanted grounds of location—scholastic landscape, scope and atmosphere—its impressive architecture, etc., etc., but must abruptly turn to other engagements due. Thanks for your enclosures, which with this I return to you. Best word to all the friends—and every other blessed Indianapolis ally and compatriot.   As ever,

JAMESIE.

To Mr. Elvin.

(Of the Bowen-Merrill Company, his publishers.)

Merry Xmas! To You All—
and The Boys! ! ! ! !

Portland, Oregon,
Dec. 24, 1892.

Dear Elvin:

Your good letter of thirteenth just here, and I've grinned through it several times.

Yes—*sir,*—send *Madison Cawein, Louisville, Ky.,* autographic *Green Fields* at once.

And you're right, too, about shuttin' off the autographic industry of old Pontius Pilate down to Crawfordsville:—

Ponchus Pilut, Dam his melts!
He's got gall ef nothin' else! !
See him roast in hell's hot core
'Fore I'd write him one k-yard more! ! !

By the author of "There Little Girl, Don't Cry!"*
Hastily, heartily, everyway—
JWR.

*"A Life-Lesson," *Lockerbie Book,* No. 4.

To ———

Portland, Oregon,
Dec. 25, 1892.

Dear Miss ———:

Your poem here seems to be an unconscious echo of Tennyson's "Break, Break, Break."* The comparison of the two poems, I doubt not, will startle you—in almost every line. To compare only your last lines with his last lines.†

His are:

"But the tender grace of a day that is dead
 Will never come back to me."

If, therefore, this is an "average specimen" of your verse, for me to "frankly judge its worth by," I would not advise you to "write for publication." Though Mr. Tennyson is dead now, he has still a belated friend or two yet in the earth-life who might wittily get back at you by removing other effects of his from your temptation.

Very truly your friend—and also Mr. Tennyson's,
JAMES WHITCOMB RILEY.

---

*The verses sent by Miss ——— began:

"Drift, drift, drift,
Over thy pale, blue sky O cloud.
But, oh, for the clasp of her gentle hand
Stilled under its solemn shroud."

†The last lines Riley refers to are:

"But the tender joys of days that are gone
Will never drift back from eternity."

To George Smith.

Helena, Montana,
Jan. 6, 1893.

Dear Grandpa:

Just got your Chicago letter, with like brief one from Mrs. Holstein in which you both say just as little as possible. Have every reason to believe I can write just such a one myself, right here and now, and so tackle it. Of course I'm feeling pretty tolerably fair, seeing I'm home-bound, with now no more than ten dates to fill ere I'm once more on my native sod—(or have you any sod yet visible through the snow? 'Spect hardly.) But your letters—brief as they are—lay over all of interest this whole vast, stupendous territory has afforded, or can possibly afford me. A great many Indianans are here—meet 'em everywhere—and most loyal, too, they are. Still they, like myself, are not at home and therefore very materially lack in dearness. When I do get back, what shall we do? Take a solid week or two off the road and le's have a real Christmas—for I sorto' gather that your Holidays, like mine, were largely fictitious, and could and should be supplanted soon now with something worthier, both for celebration and enduring remembrance. Glad you all seem well, excepting our dear H.,* who is growing weller every day she's home again, and where I hope to find her utterly restored when I return. Then we'll all swoop down upon her in a sort of cherubic swarm, and she'll just have to be restored. *God!* I made a drop-curtain picture of it all that glows with all the roseate hues and tintings of my high and rarely sumptuous, house-painting nature. In fact, I picture her eating things again, tell her,—flourish-

---

*Mrs. Charles L. Holstein.

ing her glittering appetite above her head like a Turkish scimitar once more, and honing it on a Russia-leather sandwich, or prune pie. . . .

Also inform Mrs. H. that I'm patronizing, nurturing, and looking to my own wan appetite,—so have not smoked a cigar since leaving home—taken a club drink of any kind—even *coffee* (the worst drink to be found in any club on earth, by the way!) Indeed, I've simply become a lovely character—one, in fact, that challenges my admiration. But this country, mild and lovely as it is, is not home. Another homesick Hoosier told me yesterday the same. Among other things he said: "All seasons here are just promises. They allus act like they're just goin' to play hell in the way o' fine weather and crop-yield, but you can't raise an umbrella on the dam' land! And the finest spring I've ever seen here, it 'ud take two pee-wees to sing one song—one 'ud sing 'pee'—and the other one 'wee'!"

Yours affectionately,
JAMESIE.

CHAPTER V

AT HOME IN LOCKERBIE STREET, AND AWAY

Riley as critic—Lucy S. Furman—Joaquin Miller—Homesickness—Kipling—The poet's faith—Success on the platform—Longing to be home—Louise Chandler Moulton—Debs—Sonnet on Eugene Field's Death—Death of Nye.

To Miss Evaleen Stein.

Indianapolis,
Jan. 30, 1893.

Dear Miss Stein:

Beautiful! beautiful! both your letter and poem! And how shall I thank you, in the hurry and worry maelstroming about me, always, as it seems, the further I dip into the world. You don't ask me to criticize your ever better-growing verse, yet I like it so well, and want it so perfect, I must say some few small things about it—which you needn't agree with, but *think* over very deliberately. Your artlessness of phrase, cadence and rhyme, is almost perfect—beyond any other of our singing clan;—only very rarely I yet see an inverted phrase. And I too am as guilty of that crime. But yet I hope and pray I may be spared some day to overcome it utterly. Then, shorter (and therefore clearer) sentences. About three periods where now is only one. Watch, too, certain words which seem to prejudice the reading world. (I don't know why—nobody does, but there are just such words, and "fraught" is one of the swarm.) Keep always, in all you write, one eye and ear on the audience. Never for an

176

instant forget that it's their pleasure and approval, as well as your own, that is desired, and most necessary, in fact. Be wholly patient, too, and assured, as I am, that your ultimate success is certain. And may God continue to bless you and perfect you, mind and soul, as surely now He is doing.

Gratefully and truly your friend.
J. W. RILEY.

To Mrs. Harry S. New.

Indianapolis,
Feb. 6, 1893.

Dear Mrs. New:

With all thanks to you for your kindly invitation, I eagerly herewith write my acceptance. Mr. New had priorly intimated that I might be called to find your home, so I've been practising on localities and where they are concealed, and shall strive my utmost to ferret out and successfully invade No. 476 North Tennessee Street, by Wednesday evening. Failing in my own effort, I'm going to throw myself upon the mercy of the Hayses, and beg them to hand me over to you personally.

Very gratefully yours,
JAMES WHITCOMB RILEY.

To Miss Lucy S. Furman.

Indianapolis,
Feb. 14, 1893.

Dear Miss Furman:

Your sketches,* herewith returned, are certainly interesting to me, and I think, too, they indicate decided

---

*These sketches were no doubt among those published three years later in *Stories of a Sanctified Town.*

strength of talent in the author. As they now stand, however, they are of just such excellence as demands of your assured ability still better treatment—more exacting—in *detail* as well as rounded finish. Each sketch is worthy of such effort, and I'm certain, should you patiently bestow the labor, the perfect victory will be yours.

The field you have found is splendid, and your sincerity in recognizing in it the real worth of such simple, homely material is a splendid sign as well. Therefore, do not glean it carelessly, but with elaborate pains. In dialect be as conscientious as in your purest English—seeing to it always, with most vigilant minuteness, that your unlettered characters are themselves in thought, word and deed. In your lettered introductions, descriptions and interludes use all the masterly arts at your command, but in their thought, action, language and the rest, remember no vaguest betrayal of the author's presence must be seen or felt. So, first look that your theme be sound and hale, and worth the performance—that it has a natural ending as well as beginning. Then, let it hold nothing but in some way bears on its general symmetry—its essential entirety. In this effort, rest perfectly assured that the details dare not be neglected. If anything be not plausible as Nature, reject it—scratch it out. The work must appear positively veracious—in the true artist's mind it is fact, whatever he may fashion of the material. And no matter *who* the master—dead or living—he or she wrought, or now does, with laborious and prolonged trial and stress. So must we all take heart to do—nor falter anyway. Be of high purpose, but meek enough to meet the lowliest principle involved. Thus, from the Genesis of our art straight on up to the blessed Day of Judgment thereof.

Reading your sketches I could but note the natural oversight of many dialect writers—namely lack of vigilance in the detail of speech, pronunciation and the rest. Then, too, the (natural, again) failure to consist in all details. Never—on penalty *of death!*—must any word not in the vocabulary of the unlettered be used. Their vocabulary must do their speaking, in its place—just as yours must in its place. Hastily, in this particular, reviewing your pages, I note these violations: (They are mere nothings, individually, but they aggregate into a great defect, which I know you were unconscious of, and therefore blameless, though now, with little pains, may avoid in future.) *Do not* write "for," "or," "nor,"—but "fer," "er," "ner"; nor "get," but "git"; nor "heard," but "heerd"; nor "recollect," but "ri"- or "ree"-collect; nor "always," but "allus" or "alluz"; nor "children," but "child*ern*"; nor "potatoes," but "p'taters"; nor "tobacco," but "tobacker"; nor "shares," but "sheers"; nor "across," but "acrost"; nor "jointed," but "j'inted"; nor "yellow," but "yaller" or "yeller"; nor "chest," but "chist"; nor "window," but "winder"; nor "chair," but "cheer"; nor "early," but "airly"; nor "far," but "fur"; nor "broken," but "broke"; nor "helped," but "hepped" or "holped"; nor "self," but "se'f"; nor "every," but "ever"—(as "ever'-body"); nor "till," but "tel"; nor "yesterday," but "yisterd'y"; nor "if," but "ef"; nor "bountifully," but bountiful' "; nor "been," but "b'en"; nor "before," but "afore" or " 'fore"; nor "poor," but "pore"; nor "further," but "furder"; nor "pretty," but "purty"; nor "ought," but "ort"; nor "took," but "tuck"; nor "close," but "clos't"; nor "dose," but dos't"; nor "held," but "helt"; nor "learned," but "learnt"; nor "woke," but "waked"; nor "printed"—(unless repetition of word require) but

"struck off"; nor "sang," but "sung"; nor "once," but
"onc't"; nor "that way" and "this way," but "thataway"
and "thisaway"; nor "afraid," but "afeared"; nor "again,"
but "ag'in" (and "ag'inst"); nor "sown," but "sowed";
nor "watered," but "wortered"; nor "shut," but "shet";
nor "such," but "sich"; nor "drew off" for "drawed off"—
or "drew" never; nor "forgotten," but "forgot"; nor
"haven't," but "hain't" or "ain't"; nor "askin'," but
"astin'"; nor "gather," but "gether"; nor "reached," but
"retch"; nor "sudden" or "suddenly," but "suddent" and
"suddently," etc. Pardon my listing all this, but, mind,
I'm only looking at these trifling defects as you ought to
look at them when you write dialect. Therefore conscientiously you must proceed, as in all truth I feel you
can succeed, and so afford a more than common luster to
the glory of the world about us in old Hoosierdom and in
amongst——

The Poems here at home!—Who'll write 'em down,
Jes' as they air—in Country and in Town?
Sowed thick as clods is 'crost the fields and lanes,
Er these-'ere little hop-toads when it rains!—
Who'll "voice" 'em? as I heerd a feller say
'At speechified on Freedom, t'other day,
And soared the Eagle tel, it 'peared to me,
She wasn't bigger'n a bumble-bee!*

Very truly your friend,
J. W. RILEY.

*"The Poems Here at Home," *Hoosier Book*, No. 195.

To Mrs. Charles L. Holstein.

Toledo, Ohio.
March 2, 1893.

Dear friend:

Overjoyed to get your cheery, cheering words. And lots o' words, too, from other sources; but yours the best. To-day's mail brought a characteristic page and picture of our bewildering and all-divine Joaquin Miller. (Think I told you I'd written to ask him for a portrait.) Both letter and picture I herewith give into your keeping till my return—knowing you will enjoy the almost saint-like face and mien of this strange man and master. And what other letter have I here in front of me that just now I won't send to you? But it'll take no long time to copy it, word for word, and it is this: "Dear Mr. Riley: All thanks. They come from under the quilt of a double headed blizzard as it were, but they are loud and sincere. I am as you know a huge admirer of all your poems, and these make me even more that way. Children, and loafing, and home life are mighty good things. They are all three of 'em pretty new to a Gipsy like myself, and I love to hear them sung as they should be.

"As the children say at the end of a tale 'Now tell us some more, please.'
"Feb. 27, '93

"Sincerely,
"Rudyard Kipling."

Got in here purty tired-like at half past two to-day. Tried to sleep, but didn't fool myself a bit. Nor can I sleep yet—at 'way after midnight. "Showed" here for the Press Club—packed house—cleared 'em half a thousand dollars anyway.—Then Reception at Club rooms later.—A first rate spread—a *coal* (*d*) *ation,* but with coffee that was hot—and got—to the spot. Only secured three cups of it, having thoughtlessly gone without a bucket, water-pitcher, or even sprinklin'-can.

All day to-day have been thinking this town was Detroit, and wondering where the Carharts were secreting themselves. Got letter from 'em as leaving Indianapolis, to which I hastily responded, referring 'em to Mr. Glass. Therefore they're yet to be encountered. *Fi donc!*

As to future prospects of this tour—it's to be a success, though a galloping one—all work, and mighty few naps promised. Though four days in New York, it only means to skurry in on one train and hustle out on the next—for some other "dead as Chelsea" suburb! . . . In fact, I live only back there at home: Only when the long pilgrimage is over and I'm on my native heath will I be truly at rest. But I've a stout heart, no less, and mean to hold the banner up'ards from a-trailin' in the dust, with old Jap Miller.* My very best to you and you and you, O Envied Lockerbies!

As ever,
Jimpsy,

To Rudyard Kipling.

Grand Rapids, Mich.,
March 4, 1893.

Dear Mr. Kipling:

See what penalty your kindness has incurred. Promptly as your note of late twenty-seventh overtakes me here on

---

Hoosier Book, No. 113.

the road I write my publishers to send you my entire product of seven books. Bear with them patiently—I can't send you any more—at least for some months.

Your words do me great good, and your work does likewise for the whole world of letters; we are all refreshed and helped and heartened by it, and we are very grateful and enduringly so.

For some years I've been striving to ferret out the one evident lack or defect of our whole art guild; and I've struck it: It's *business*. We naturally hate that, and therefore avoid it. That's why we're all victims. So I've gone to work to change that status of affairs. In consequence, I'm a revelation to myself. Am making not only "oodles" of money off my books, but twice over as much again by personally reading the same to packed houses; and how I do wish you were gypsying around with me this vagrant side of my dual existence! If ever you should incline to such a deviation (for health's sake or vulgar money's) come and see me at Indianapolis, New York or where you will, or let me come to you anywhere on the face of the earth.

As ever gratefully and faithfully yours,
JAMES WHITCOMB RILEY.

To Miss Lucy S. Furman.

Detroit, Mich.,
March 7, 1893.

Dear Miss Furman:

Just now I mail to you a book of Richard Malcolm Johnston's inimitable dialect sketches. Probably his work is known to you already, though I do hope I'm sending you some special taste or flavor of it that is new. To me,

this collection has in it his choicest characters—*two* of
them, at least, *i.e.,* "Mr. Bill Williams" and "Mr. Jonas
Lively." They are simply *delectable!* Another time I'll
hope to find and send you "Mr. Absalom Billingslea"—
possibly the very best character ever drawn in dialect.

Hastily but very heartily your friend,

J. W. RILEY.

Note what minute obeisance the author makes to dialect—and what reverence he pays to simple, homely things.
He is a classic scholar and teacher, no less, though in the
commonplace is the fuller love of his ripe and sweet and
mellow old heart, be sure.

To William Carey.

Baltimore,
March 27, 1893.

Dear Carey:

Of all the manifold favors you have shown me, this last,
of turning me over to Mr. Kipling has not its fellow in
the blessed list. What a bright man he is, and what a
sound and good one—his gentleness, and the sweet ripe
home-heart in him—why, I want to write poems to him.
You should have been with us that night! Do you remember what you said you hoped I'd never find out about
myself? Well, in that respect that lovely man is safer
far than I,—what greater faith in and love for any man
could I express than this? Do all you can for him, and
watch over him; and I'll bet you God'll whirl in and bless
you for it even as I'll want to lam loose and he'p Him.

JAMESIE.

To Honorable Charles L. Holstein.

Washington, D. C.,
March 31, 1893.

Dear Charles:

Just now a brief note from George Smith acquaints me with the sad news of your father's death. Of course, I don't know what to say, but feel impelled to write you simply, assuring you of my ever stronger growing conviction that there is a good God doing everything, and doing it most wisely, however vainly we may question. What your state of grief is I can fairly estimate, being fashioned of both mind and tendency not unlike yourself, rather inclining toward the somber side of all views, and resentful even at for ever being denied a positive knowledge of God and His intentions concerning us, both here and hereafter. But I am learning to smile right bravely—recalling over and over all the loved ones favored beyond me and gone on ahead—Mother, Brother, and friends innumerable. When they went I cried out against it—(just as though the power that controls us all could err!) Now I know that that then was as it should be, and I thank God—or that Intelligence—for His, or Its will being done—not mine. Isn't this proposition absolutely clear? I hope you can find it so, as it's the only comfort I have ever found, in like need, and I don't know but that I can as honestly testify that it is all the comfort I could possibly desire. So try to see it this way, and smile on very bravely with a fellow.

With best cheer, faith and affection,

Yours,
JAMESIE.

To William Carey.

Indianapolis,
May 17, 1893.

Dear Carey:

Am prompt as can be with return of this, but getting more settled at home again. Can be steadfastly prompter. So send along.

Some notes marginal I could not resist. I can never get in dialect correct "morning or evening" in type. Your proof-readers take away my last "g" terminal in those words always,—therefore making the word or termination New England, southern, etc., etc., but never *Hoosier.* We say 'comin' and goin' '" but never, never, never "mornin' or evenin'." Help me club the over-vigil vandals out of my premises at all hours o' the day and night as well as mornin' and evenin'.

Best regards to everybody.
As ever yours,
JAMESIE.

To Edgar Wilson Nye.

In the following Riley refers to the publisher of *Nye and Riley's Railway Guide*, who paid little or nothing for the rights.

Indianapolis,
June 14, 1893.

Dear Nye:

Your letter is a characteristic delight to one, alas! who hears from you, these piping times of peace, too all-fired seldom. That I was glad to see your hand-write once more, and note the free lush flow of your long pent thoughts, goes without saying; but when you trench upon power-of-attorney matters, and breathe a hope that we may some time jerk a few strippins of justice out of one —— —— ——, I experience a quality of rapture that is simply grand! In regard to your query as to my having any "paper" of his—or Isaac E. Adams',—contract-form or instrument, etc., I have not; but were any such ever in my hands it is very likely that I turned them over to Walker; and you might inquire of him if ever I did—for of course I don't know anything I ever ought to. So it is I again enclose to you the Maher & Gilbert law letter, retaining their address, as you suggest—that in case I should find my scrap of correspondence from said publishers, bearing on said claims of our'n, I can send same said matter to our said counsel, as aforesaid, 'ydoggies!

But ain't it good to do nothing?—or are you really at it yet as I am? . . . I just won't work, after the long undying struggle for bread on the platform. Coming in, I've stacks of accumulated duties that ought to be attended—but dam' ef I will! And every night I say that softly over and over in my prayers.

When are you going to Chicago—or wouldn't you just rather not go anywheres again on earth? Oh, I'm gettin' worse than pore Mark Twain about seeing and hearing and going; and you're in the same awful state, I'll bet.

For your *Gutenberg and Poet* article I wait chafingly—for I know you'll git 'em, as you only can!

Also I will pant for your new *History*—your real facts on the United States—suppressing, as I trust, absolutely nothing. In a month or two look also for another of my charming little volumes.* The Century Company is doing it, and I'll send you earliest copy I can lay hands on.

Poems Here at Home.

As ever, with best remembrances to your mother, wife, children, kith and kin,

Affectionately,
JAMESIE.

To William Carey.

Indianapolis,
June 29, 1893.

Dear Carey:

All right.—*Poems Here at Home* is best choice for title.—Glad you made it. 'Tain't much to write a book, but, my Gawd! to name the thing that's what takes Genius! I am anxiously waiting opening chapters up to page fifteen. Hope you will send soon, as I am about striking into the timber for a month or two's loaf.

As ever,
JAMESIE.

To Honorable Charles L. Holstein.

G. A. R. Committee.

Greenfield, Ind.,
Aug. 2, 1893.

Dear Walpurges:

Having dwelt on your letter and request of this date with full deliberation, and concluding that you mean September sixth—not August, as you have written it,—I can agree to read "Good-bye, Jim"* for the Boys, positively providing that I'm not to read in Tomlinson Hall. There I can't be heard, or I'd not object. Tell 'em three or four times I've fractured my reputation there, when all that

---

*"The Old Man and Jim," *Hoosier Book,* No. 200.

was heard during my efforts was cries from the audience of "Louder!" So for reputation's sake solely I must appear elsewhere—church, opera-house, Masonic Hall, or *The Universe* with a hem-stitch run around it—any vacuum of space but that dread "Ultima Thule" of Tomlinson's Hall!

As ever,
JAMESIE.

To Honorable Charles L. Holstein.

Minneapolis, Minn.,
Nov. 17, 1893.

Dear Charles:

Packed house to-night. A great compliment, considerin' I'm plum' wore out here.

No use waitin' for the real worthier time to write you— that time simply does not and will not arrive. So take the best I can do here and now. All has gone, and is going, well with the little man. Especially does he find himself blessed when your letters or papers reach. Then he sprawls out at full len'th on the bed and dreams o' heaven and home-made bread, like old John Henry!* And, peradventure, he also dreams that this dodgasted show-life is a thing of the awful past, and he's livin' like other folks— At Home—where all God's children ought to be in both this life and the next. Just got Mrs. H's letter. God bless her—only, in one place, she must need Matthew-Arnold me for not writing her sadly about our dear Cora's death. Tells me she can't imagine why I never referred to it in any way. Well, tell her it was just 'cause I someway

---

*"Old John Henry," *Hoosier Book,* No. 215.

felt that neither Cora nor God would like us to be worry-
ing about her in the least. And I'll bet she's smilin' now to
see this very sensible observation put down in black and
white, once and for all! . . . You know, she understood
me always purt'near better'n anybody ever did. So she
will not fail to understand me now. She is happier than
ever before, and I'm sure wants us to smile right on till
we've caught up with her again. That's all. I'm worried
just now about my program here to-night. This is my
fourth appearance here—and just this instant a card
comes up from R. H. Maple, your "babes-in-the-woods"
kinsman. Ain't it funny? . . . and he's been talking, of
course, of Cora—but he's sound enough on the ethics of
death, and has agreed with me fully—yes, and with most
wholesome spirit,—and I know, too, from what he in-
directly betrayed, that his presence with the broken family
did them good—especially "Lil."

* * * * * *

An old school-teacher of mine was up a while ago, and
it was good to see him—really. He never whipped me
very hard—and never at wrong times. He was so glad to
hear me say that, that shore-enough tears kindo' loafed up
and lounged around his kind old eyes. Ain't a real good
man good?—just about next to God. How I do wish I
could see "Lottie"—'cause' I jes' know she's mighty tired
layin' there all this time. Two or three times, thinks I,
"I'll ist turn in and write her a letter 'at ain't for none of
ye on'y ist her!" but somepin's allus in the way. *Dog-
gone!* Ef I don't git a chance purty soon, I'm go' to git
wite mad and swear like *mens;*—'ll swear like "Johnnie"*

---

*"Johnnie" is Mr. Nickum and "Lottie" is his wife who lived with their
daughter, Mrs. Charles Holstein, in the Lockerbie Street home.

swears when they don't put no 'lectric light on Lockaby Street—*"add-dam their triflin' souls!"*

As ever,
JAMESIE.

To Honorable Charles L. Holstein.

Minneapolis, Minn.,
Nov. 19, 1893.

Dear Charles:

This is merely to beg you to give shelter to a box of summer clothes I am just expressing myself in care 26 Lockerbie; and to ask you, when the same arrives, to git somebody to kindo' open and shake 'em out and hang 'em—'cause I want you all to see a sorto' mute symbol, as the feller says, in them-air pore, lone, disconsolate gyarments, and empty, holler, homesick counterpart of

Your old wandering Jew
BEN JAMESIE SCHUFFLEBERGER.

To Major Charles Holstein.

Rochester, N. Y.,
Feb. 2, 1894.

Dear Charles:

Will write you at just, length and care, Sunday—when we're to have one day out of the seven undesecrated by either travel, committees or dam' untimely and importunate callers. My Gawd! for even one day, to myself!

We've been having splendid business and success every way: Victory not only perched but positively roostin' on

our banner. Sherley* may be, in fact is,—happy, aye, and
flushed with it all,—but I've had about enough o' fame,
and heart and soul o' me seem about qualmish and on the
verge of a sorta' wholesale disemboguement of the whole
unsavory mess.—

> Fame, says I, go 'way from *me*—
> *Please* go 'way and *lem me be,*
> I'm so tired out, and so
> Dam' infernal sick of "show"
> That the very name of you
> Palls, and turns my stomach, too.
> See, O Fame!—I know and *plead*
> To you, in my poor knock-kneed
> Fashion—I fall at your feet
> Like a hat-rack—wrecked complete,—
> Therefore spurn the dam *debris,*
> And go 'way and
> > > *Lem*
> > > *Me*
> > > *BE! ! !*

JAMESIE.

To Mrs. Charles L. Holstein.

Feb. 10, 1894.

Dear St. Lockerbie:

This page I hasten to you in answer to your Wednesday
letter, in which you're sorry for sending me the Sunday
one—which is the very best letter you ever did write, and
don't need no apology of nobody's! The one just here
hain't no slouch,—but the Sunday letter! ah! that's divine!
That's why I had to write you pure poetry† in the answer

---

*Douglas Sherley, who appeared on the platform for several readings
with Riley.
†See preceding poēm.

which by now you're smirkin' over, thinkin' what a dod-
gasted fool I am when you've a mind simply to press the
button thataway!

Of course I'd like you to come on with the Doctor and
surprise us in New York—only my ever leaving there
while you remained would be the awful consideration.
Will be in frenzy the few days there, as it is—So—No. I
don't want you to come. In fancy now I undergo that
awful trial which so certainly awaits me there—as always
it must and will. On the stifling-purple depths of blues, to
which I descend in any coarse, big vulgar city, with its
sweating, reeking thousands, elbowing, snarling, fighting,
chasing and striking and trampling and kicking each other
into Hell. . . . My God! My God! I'd rather hot-foot
rush into my casket and slam the door to after me! Still all
this is not meant to discourage your intentions—for I
know you like New York almost as much as I detest, ab-
hor and hate it. Therefore if you're well enough, and the
doctor thinks so, and will accompany you, and the folks all
there at home agree, and can give you up and likewise
promise to hold me wholly blameless in the matter every
way,—why, come—and God have mercy on your pore
vain soul! ! !

Mighty glad to hear you're going out again. That I
know will help you, and gladden, too, your friends. Remember me to all of them—only don't go anywhere when
old hoary-headed Winter stands shakin' his icicley finger
at you! To hear your cough is better makes me merry as
griggs—"Whatever griggs is."*

JIMPSY.

---

*Quoted from Dickens.

To Honorable Charles L. Holstein.

Amherst, Mass.,
Feb. 13, 1894.

"Out of the bosom of the air,—
  Out of the cloud-folds of her garments shaken—
Over the woodlands brown and bare,
  Over the harvest-fields forsaken,
    Silent and soft and slow
      Descends the snow!"

Dear Charles:

For one half-day and a solid night it has been snow-ing—snowing—snowing! Snowing too on a world al-ready muffled to the ears with the awful, smothery, star-ing, glaring white wash and surge and billow and drift and foam and spume of the vast waste of the now recum-bent storm that whelms the earth till its veriest tumult is but as a pent whisper in sinister conspiracy with the sleuth-like, cushion-footed silence of the Universe.

Occasionally we hear sleigh-bells, and in fancy shudder-ingly see, and estimate the hardihood of, the fur-sub-merged pleasure-seekers as they whirl on into the hush again. Truly this is New England as we read about it! All vehicles are on runners; and driving to the storied old hall last night, I thought grimly all the way of an horrific picture that used to fascinate me when a child—of some outlandish Russian sledge over the Steppes, or boundless barren chaos of Siberian snows, being chased by wolves, and the frenzied woman occupant lifting from the furs, and in the act of throwing her little shrieking babe to the ravening pursuing beasts, already leaping, snapping, lolling their hot red tongues out in close expectancy over their dainty feast. Then I wanted to throw Sherley out to some like doom—to feed him to some howling herd of particularly hungry beasts who made a speci'lty of large, fat, dopey men who stayed eternally good-natured and even happy, no matter what dire weather or conditions were turned on 'em! Nor has he let up yet; even as I write, he's out sleighing with some dam' "Esquimos" someplace,—with the blank, bleak, wan climate all around here lit with his raw, red face! (I will kill that man ere long,— maybe to-night.)

Last evening we trod holy ground: We stood on the self-same platform where, in the Great American past, have stood Emerson, Longfellow, Lowell, Thoreau—all truly illustrious in their time, no doubt, yet wearing knit socks and kip boots, and little dreaming that in such a climate Mr. Douglas Sherley* and I would come capering later on the scene in patent-leathers—and no socks at all to speak of—especially Sherley's.

Now, do write a fellow—why don't you? I get your papers, God bless you! and an occasional word on an envelope; but never poem or letter any more. 'Spect I've made you mad at me. Always when I jes' whirl in and really *like* any one, they're sure to git mad at me in return. Guess I'm too dam' *pestiferous* er *somepin'!* Want my friends, who are but mortal, to be gods. With best love to all,

As ever,

JIMPSY.

---

*Talked on same lecture programs with Riley one season.

To Mrs. Henry Eitel, a sister.

Boston,
February 16, 1894.

Dear Elva:

Lovely letter you send a fellow, but have wasted all my time on the "Valentine" you ask for. 'Smatter with you?—wantin' such a thing from your pore woreout brother 'at's purt-nigh bedrid' fer want o' sleep! Glad you're all better. Keep at it. Awful winter here. Love to Henry.—Yes, and all the friends. Great highjinks here over our show—and us. Best and first people "usin" 'round with us jes' as common-like as your kin-folks! As ever your afftnte bro.   JIM.

A Custom-Made Valentine
for
My Sister Elva Riley Eitel.

If your imperious command,
    O gentle sister mine,
For prompt impromptu verses and
    Pictorial design,
But gave me time from '94
    Straight on till '99,
Then, only love and art *might* shape
    Your *worthy* Valentine.
                JAMES WHITCOMB RILEY.

The one addressed is unidentified.

New York,
March 5, 1894.

Dear Mrs. Reid:

Thank you heartily for correction you have made for me in sonnet "When She Comes Home."* Also glad to hear you don't favor Ambrose Bierce contagion ravaging the otherwise really Pacific Slope. Wish I knew Miss Ina Colbrith so I might write her in congratulation—for if Bierce "counts out" her poetry, she may be certain of its superior worth. Bierce edits God, you know, and His Universe; Mr. B. considers its imperfections (all tremblingly submitted to him), as falling very little short of an impertinence on the part of Deity.

To George Smith.

New York,
Mch. 9, 1894.

Dear Grandpa!—I say, *"dear Grandpa! !"*——

We are just turning in here for much-needed rest. Simply with two weeks' rest I will be well every way. All is made desirable as can be during rest.—Arrangements made to stay at Players' Club—very exclusive, as you know. Rooms I'm to live in—next to Booth's and just vacated by Mark Twain, who sailed yesterday. In this connection I desire to observe that he is the kind o' man I love clean through and through,—is simply honest—natural—direct,—this last virtue leads 'em all. God will

*Lockerbie Book, No. 374.

make it very pleasant for him when He lands him in home
again.—If I were Mark Twain's wife, and got a letter
from him, one paragraph long, I would simply turn the
pillow of my bed to the foot and read that serial all night:
Indeed, you may gather from this that it is as positive a
pleasure for me to respect Mr. Clemens as to love him.

Hastily but heartily—and with best cheer to Johnson,
Bradbury, Parker, *et al.*

JAMESIE.

To Mrs. Louise Chandler Moulton.

Indianapolis, Ind.,
April 24, 1894.

"They stood together in the blessed noon—
   They sang together through the length of days:
Each loving face bent upwards like a moon
   New-lit with love and praise."

My dear friend:

Two days ago on the street here at home I met my just-
returned Hoosier friend, Miss V——, who was visiting in
Boston when I met you. In her talk of you and your
gentle womanly loveliness I caught myself liking her even
more than for State-pride and clannish reasons. You may
remember she is hard of hearing—but she is not hard of di-
vining, I can attest: for she talked to me of you. . . .
(Never until you and I talk long together, will you wholly
comprehend how most serious I am when seemingly trivial.—Even Miss fellow-citizen V—— never guesses such
a thing!) . . . And you've been in New York, where, had
I minded the doctor, I should have remained. But I'm
ruined—soured with travel—always elsewhere than

home,—so that even, I feel, should I happily die, I've a
ready apology to the hotel for so doing it in. Mind! I've
been for about fifteen years on the road,—and am, therefore, just a trifle biased toward a somewhat acrimonious
disposition, not a confirmed believer in, but favoring, fortunate happenings. You were of the latter—but, behold
the penalty! What little I saw of you—was later to see—
and what promise on ahead? . . . Nor, never again until
I see you, can I assure you of the certainty of the Hereafter. Know, as best you can from my word, that there
is no death (yes, and bravely lighten every future verse
of yours with this real universal feeling). Your Whittier
and mine is strictly right:

> "I know not where His islands lift
>   Their fronded palms in air;—
> I only know I can not drift
>   Beyond His love and care."

"When John said that, he was a full wise man."—That is
why we instinctively look upon all our dead as our supe-
riors: my baby sister, my younger brother, no less than
my old father. Therefore be comforted. That is enough—
have nothing to do with Spiritualism—it only vexes—
never answers. It promises, but doesn't. One's native,
brave, "John-Greenleaf"-faith surpasses everything.

Wish I could come to London while you're there—but
don't know what the Fates devise for me. Am largely a
fatalist—regarding myself, at least. What I most desire
is generally denied. And yet I feel and know perfectly
that God's hand's on the helm and His breath in the sails!

As ever your affectionate

J. W. RILEY.

To Meredith Nicholson.

Indianapolis, Ind.,
Oct. 11, 1894.

Dear friend:

Your written comment was, and will remain, a special favorite among "Armazindy's"* tributes. The book, as you know, is meant for *all parts* of the audience—less, even, for the crowned heads than for Tom, Dick and Harry—that exacting coterie, in fact, with which I feel more at home than Royalty. Indeed the knowledge of your full appreciation of that standpoint of mine is equally gratifying with the praises you accord. May the gods prosper you!

As ever most gratefully
Your old Hoosier friend,
JAMES WHITCOMB RILEY.

To Eugene V. Debs.

Indianapolis,
Aug. 6, 1895.

Dear old friend:

It's mighty glad your cheery letter makes me, with its "rushing flume," "whirring spindles," "shifting shuttles," and the rest of our moving oratory's darling timber. It minds me gloriously of our old sessions of delight, which, please God, we're to have over and over again, as wholesomely as ever in the rapturous past. But just now I'm virtually bound hand and foot from any near hope of an-

---

*The poem "Armazindy" introducing the book of this name is No. 131, *Hoosier Book*.

swering your good request for your "Railway Times"—
being, aside from engaged magazine work, at labor on
two separate books—else I should at least make an attempt at some just and worthy contribution, honoring, in
most reverent Longfellow spirit,

"The nobility of labor, the long pedigree of toil."

But you will be patient with me, I know—just as you are
patient with everything—and hale of soul and stout of
heart.

With this I venture to send you a copy of the best book
I've read in last ten years—Ian Maclaren's *Beside the
Bonnie Brier Bush*. Do, please, don't have read it, long
ere my copy reaches you—as *I* want to give you this vast
and all-indulging ecstasy myself.

As always your faithful and affectionate friend,
                        JAMES WHITCOMB RILEY.

To William M. Carey.

October 5, 1895.

Dear Mr. Carey:
My old friend, Mr. Newton Booth Tarkington, is going
your way and I want you to know each other as near like
as we know each other as possible—so I charge you both to
like each other at once as "vera brothers."
                As ever yours,
                        JAMES WHITCOMB RILEY.

To William Carey.

October 15, 1895.

Dear Carey:

Mr. Booth Tarkington—an especially gifted and "versi-talented" young friend of mine—is going to New York to "brush up ag'in' things" gently in the art, dramatic and literary line; and just now I've given him a letter to you, believing that your very alert perception and adroitness of management could do the boy a world of good. In a histrionic way he has proved himself an embryo Irving. And in dramatics has written his own play; while in art and literary lines he is a youthful Du Maurier, and mark! none of these talents he has yet ripe for marketing, only he wants and desires to see and know the real producers at their desks—in their dens—studies—clubs, etc., etc., and as the Irishman said of his Savior "Spake to him the same as one man would spake to another."

In anyway you can serve the young man you will be favoring me, already so very much your debtor, but still have no end of desire and readiness to prove myself any kind of a friend worth having in return.

As ever,

JAMESIE.

To Mrs. Louise Chandler Moulton.

Dec. 10, 1895.

My dear friend:

You are so good in my behalf—so more than kind and generous in welcoming my likes and interests and friends—that my pen can but falteringly stammer and fail in any attempt I make in striving to express the vast expanse of my gratefulness to you. Were Indianapolis indeed a suburb of Boston, woe worth the name! but I should be continually knocking at your portals with ever newly invented speeches, phases and phrases of thanks and never-dying obligations; therefore, for your sake, I doubt not the long-headed wisdom of Fate in plumping me down 'way out here where I can't possibly get to you but by mail, and then only in visits no longer than a sheet of paper

But you must give me a line about my friends—how and when they came to you, and if you liked them and how much—for I know they liked, and must ever continue to like, you—O gentlest of my friends!

Already I have heard from them both, and, although they had not yet seen you, they were in such radiant states of impetuous expectation I could but envy them their nearness to you—wishing, achingly yearning, that I were there personally to present them.

Like yourself, I can not indorse the *snow*—nay, nor any kind of winter weather. Even should I be eternally lost, and consigned to that peculiarly tropical climate "where Hell's heat festers" even to Swinburne's extremest fancy's focus, I doubt not that many times I shall ask the Devil kindly to close the door after him, as there seems to be a draught entering somewhere. But to be really serious, I do shudder all winter long—no matter where it be—Boston, Indianapolis, San Francisco, or Atlanta, Ga.

You ask if I believe in so-called spiritual manifestations. I do believe in many of the manifestations, but not the Spirit part. Beware of that. The manifestations of slate, pencil, etc., I have seen tested, and myself tested, and believe in; but am persuaded wholly that it is not spirits, but a new phenomenon, ere long to be clearly explained and utilized to some good end. I can not believe that God meant us to know certainly of our spiritual existence after this life; for did we possess that certain knowledge, would we not all be hurrying and crowding there before His own good time? Let us, therefore, continue to trust Him.

As ever truly and gratefully your friend,
JAMES WHITCOMB RILEY.

To Joseph S. Riley.

December 30, 1895.

My dear Kinsman—for if you're the son of Dr. John Schlick Riley you're a cousin of mine, however you might wish to conceal the fact! Certainly I am very proud of the relationship—for, longer ago than you would ever guess, I knew—romantically—of my Texas cousins, recalling particularly, "durin' the Army," that I had "a nuncle" in the Confederate ranks, who was a surgeon, and who, according to dire rumors, was taken prisoner by our forces. That, to my boy's mind, meant of course, an awful thing; judge, therefore, of the harrowed apprehensions of a very small boy who visited his grandmother living alone in her own little-Dame-Crump cottage across the town from my father—then away from home, a captain, in his country's service. Judge, I ask, of this boy's state of mind, when he discovered this Southern brother of his own father, smoking a very sequestrated but peaceful pipe with the good old mother, who adroitly answered my juvenile curiosity regarding her peculiar guest, that it was "John Slick"—an old relative of their Pennsylvania people. Though, at once, I guessed it was my own father's brother—an escaped prisoner here in the heart of the

North—in fair safety, again meeting his old mother from whom he had been separated for years and years. Tacitly, therefore, I bore about a brave secret, for one of my very tender years and patriotic training. Vividly, too, I recall his constrained interest in this "son James of Reuben's"— as the very dear, gentle and utterly lovable old mother and grandmother put it.

Indirectly—as you list some of your characteristics and ambitions, I have to smile:—they seem so to belong to my father's side o' the house,—therefore, like at least six brothers of his that I knew. And, even now, as I recall them, I make of the group a veracious composite of what you are like—and I'll bet big money that I do you most full and accurate justice: You have an unusual zest— physically and mentally—in life; your equipment, both ways, favoring you. Your afflictions weaken you not, in the main, but strengthen you.—You can be awfully grim and pitiless as you are natively tender and compassion- ate. Knowing you so well, I feel as proud of you almost as I am sorry for you. God, I doubt not, understands and will get around to our especial needs in His Own good time. Anyway, one thing I like about God is, He is not so intolerant nor impetuous as some of us Rileys, hence I think He can really be depended on even beyond the old Bedford County (Pa.) Rileys. What you read some place of my having "nobly" helped my old father in his need, etc., is all wrong—mere sentimental, whole-cloth, "reporting." If ever I have been truly noble, it never has, nor never will, get into the papers.

Give me a line when you can, and know always that your well-doing, and your family's—the beautiful-mem- oried wife—the child—the dear old parents—your affec- tionate interests are mine abidingly.

JAMES WHITCOMB RILEY.

To Mrs. Eugene Field.

Indianapolis,
Jan. 31, 1896.

Dear Mrs. Field:

Something—and a very wise something I think it is—has kept me from any effort at prose introductory for the dear boy's book. Instead, I send a *sonnet**—which tribute, I feel assured, would better please "Gene" than anything in prose I might attempt,—for however poor my verse, my prose is far inferior—as he knew, and knew moreover, that I knew it.

So explain to your publishers, with express instructions to set sonnet entire in Italics—widely "leading" the lines—and certainly sending me proof-page of same here, which I will as promptly attend and return as it is received. As always,

Your sincere friend,
JAMES WHITCOMB RILEY.

To Mrs. Edgar Wilson Nye.

Upon the death of Nye, Riley wrote the sonnet with the line, "Such silence—after such glad merriment." (*Lockerbie Book*, No. 289.)

Indianapolis,
May 6, 1896.

Dear Mrs. Nye:

Your good letter of hope and cheer is at hand, and by it I am again reassured that the brave and gentle hero is ever present with you and sustaining you, as his blithe and

---

*"Eugene Field," *Lockerbie Book*, No. 260.

steadfast spirit only could. So too his loving arms are about the children—and always, always is his presence bright and pleasant as the veriest sunny summer weather. To his brother Frank he was thus manifest (as he told me, on his return this way after the final parting) and to me he continues absolutely his halest, realest, living happy self,—just as I knew and loved him from the first, so I know and love him now, and with the same feeling of securest, never-changing, mirthful happiness.

All this beautiful strangeness of his absence and yet presence certainly is just like him; and the cheer I gather from it, time and time again, makes me smile and laugh and thrill with the veritable old-time delight—just as though he were secretly rejoiced at provoking this novel state of mourning—smiles in lieu of tears—laughter in lieu of any lightest moan of sorrow.

With best love to the children, whose future can but be wholly worthy, with such blessed guardianship, I remain,

As always, your grateful friend,

JAMES WHITCOMB RILEY.

Tell the children my next volume*—nearly ready for printer—is entirely of my own childhood, and I mean to send them the very earliest copy, that they may see what to avoid in youth that might tend to make any of 'em poets.

*"The Child-World," *Hoosier Book,* No. 251.

CHAPTER VI

Books

A Child-World—Thomas Bailey Aldrich—Judge Oliver Wendell
Holmes—Kate Douglas Wiggin—"Doc Sifers"—Homestead Edi-
tion of Complete Works—Peculiar experience with poem to
Stevenson—Clara E. Laughlin.

To Thomas Bailey Aldrich.

Oct. 27, 1896.

Dear Mr. Aldrich:

Your kindly acceptance of my last book of home-made
poetry (*A Child-World*) lifts me into altitudes of delight
long yearned for but never heretofore attained. Frankly,
I have felt always that the limitations of my verse product
poorly warranted a welcome at the hands of the elect—so
that now your generous approval falls on me both as an
unexpected glory and deserved rebuke. Therefore, in my
exaltation and confusion still must I lean wholly on your
mercy, but with a most heartening, grateful and reposeful sense of that ripe worthiness of yours that has so refreshed and quickened my own.

What you say latterly of *The Flying Islands of the
Night* is to me a matter of rejoicing beyond even that
awakened by your opening comment. But (Alas me!)
yours is almost the only voice of praise breaking the dense
hush that seemed to close over that book at its very
birth.—Joseph Knight, the other notable exception, wrote
me from London a good stout letter favoring the perform-

ance as "a creation" and an "important" work. Smilingly
pardon a fellow as he thus childishly puts on exhibition his
most particularly "strong weakness."

Most gratefully and truly yours,

J. W. RILEY.

To Judge Oliver Wendell Holmes.

Oct. 28, 1896.

Dear Sir:

Your kindly word for the simple, old-home verses of
the *Child-World* is most gratifying to me; and with all
fervor I thank you for the help as well as pleasure that
your comment gives me. It is one thing for the writer to
approve his own rhymes, but quite another to have his
auditors approve them. As foremost, then, among these
whose estimate is of *real* value, to find you favoring my
effort, and its simple theme as well, is an enduring joy and
benefit to me. And so over and over again I thank you.

Have you not by this time another volume of the
speeches—or essays—addressed to your audience—that
higher, wiser, more exacting one,—whose answering applause must be indeed the highest, most inspiring of all
conquests intellectual?

Most gratefully and truly yours,

JAMES WHITCOMB RILEY.

To Norman Gale.

Nov. 28, 1896.

My dear friend:

For full two weeks, at all available intervals, I have been browsing through the pastoral dales and dingles of your *Songs for Little People.* And while I hope I am not very little People, I have to record the fact that had these songs been written expressly for me they could not have pleased me better. True I am not drawn toward them all with one plain level of affection, but, as Mr. Pepys would say, "they all do please me mighty well." They are possessed all with the becoming graces of Childhood—the little fellow's native endowments of simplicity, purity, utter artlessness, unfathomable faith in everything, and fresh and dewy sweetness of spirit. This, in fine, is the lovely little Bartholomew son that you have sung,—and lo and verily!—

> No mother has
> A sweeter one.

As I write I am reminded of my last hasty letter to you in which I failed to answer your query: "Do I know anything of John Claire's poems?" (or was it Clare—or was it Davis?) Your writing of the word blurred me, I remember—nor did I know either of the names here as a poet's. But we have poets here of most genuine stuff— and I mean to get *stacks* of 'em all together and send you when I can. Maybe not soon—for my physician (I speak of *"my* physician," observe, as every tongue-coated cuss on the scalp of the globe does—just as though I had an *in-*

dividual one—same as a hairbrush or a horn comb or—a cowlick.)—Well, *ahem!*—my physician informs me that I must indefinitely avoid all mental cares, tasks and responsibilities,—so, of course, flattered by the therapeutic savant's implied belief that I have even breaded brains, I am now turning my large wan eyes in quest of health, and, in consequence, overlooking far worthier things. Also I am taking—along with much medicine—more serious views of life, meanwhile eating—in a sorto' lackluster way—large gouts and poultices of oat-meal and other health-food of like demned moist unpleasant characteristics. Cheer me up with a line when you can.

As ever very gratefully and truly your friend,

JAMES WHITCOMB RILEY.

To Mrs. Kate Douglas Wiggin Riggs.

Indianapolis,
Jan. 14, 1897.

Dear Mrs. Riggs:

The supernal book—poem—picture—all—all are here, and I am radiant as a—as a—radiator! How glad I am now that I've persisted in my determination not to read the book till I'd wrested a marked copy of it from its all too-modest author. (And for a time I was fearful you were going to prove so like other women I'd be having to write it *authoress*.) At last I think I'm liking you again—only you do mature so slowly! Wonder if it's your kindergartening so much? Then you must give it up in time—forswear it—"pluck it from your bosom though your heart be at the root!" You are to do great huge deeds in story and in song. But, pardon—lest you think I'm invading the shooting-gallery of the young idea.

Of course I'll send—the promptest post—my mildest photograph. I've one in particular that looks like shaving-soap smells—and with one accord all forms of government indorse it as an almost human likeness.

Very truly and gratefully yours,

JWR.

To Mrs. E. W. Nye

This letter is to the mother of Edgar Wilson ("Bill") Nye. Frank is a brother of Edgar. Reference has been made to one sonnet to Nye. Another which appears in *The Lockerbie Book*, No. 198, may well be read in the spirit of this letter.

Indianapolis,
March 10, 1897.

Dear Mother Mine:

And you are still remembered, though your boy James doesn't get the time to write it down as often as he wants to—that's all! Why couldn't you come to Frank's when I was there? I expected you—missed you, and, with all the others, wished you would come, but, like too many of our earthly longings, it was not then to be granted. Very bravely I shall keep the faith in the Sometime just ahead when we shall meet, all the happier for the long delay. Of course we talked of you. Oh, but you'd be flattered if you knew the good things said behind your back! And we were glad and sad—rejoiced and grieved; but mainly, I think, we were happy—happy in the assurance about us all the time that our dear Edgar was there and wanting us to be happy, and wholly so himself when we were. In all sacred truth do I believe this, and am so resigned. So again and again I told Frank, and more and more I think he feels the same, and will grow only the more certain of

Naples, Aug. 25 –
– 1891 –

Dear George:

If you happen at all to remember the book=pack=
age you charged me not to lose, as we rode about
in the cab in search of the ever=evanishing Kip=
ling, why then you will at once understand the
meaning of the enclosed Lost Property notifi=
cation, which same I beg you to answer in
my stead, taking unto yourself, to have, hold,
and possess, the two unemasculated copies
of my new English book, the contents of
said package as aforesaid – providing,
strictly, that you at all consider them
worth the attendant trouble and expense,
for which latter I can think of no way
of reimbursing you, as I haven't but
one English coin to my back, and what
that is in value, I affirm, I've not the vaguest
idea in the world.

Or turn the paper over to Dr. Hays, who may
be with you by the receipt of this.

Your friends all asking after you and the
Journal jokes. — All well, joyous and "holdin' fast
to the horns of the altar." My best to Mr. and Mrs. New.
and to Harry, Mr. Moffett &c. &c. — Jamesie.

it as the years go by.   First my mother, years and years
ago,—then a brother, twenty years of age,—then my
father, four years since—all gone away, but not dead I
know.   "Surely," I think, "everybody must share with me
this blessed assurance and be glad thereof till God's hand
beckons us."

With all best love to you and yours always,

> Your affectionate boy,
> JAMES WHITCOMB RILEY.

To Miss Lucy S. Furman.

With all fervid

> Easter Greetings
> Apl. 18, 1897.

Soul of Mankind, He wakes—He lives once more!
    O soul, with heart and voice
Sing! sing!—the stone rolls chorus from the door—
    Our Lord stands forth.—Rejoice!
  Rejoice, O garden-land of song and flowers;
  Our King returns to us, forever ours!
    (Hymn Exultant)*

> J. W. R.

Lockerbie Book, No. 233.

To Miss Lucy S. Furman.

Indianapolis,
May 3, 1897.

Dear Miss Furman:

I *s'pose* you're thinking, about now, that I've forgotten all my obligations to you and given my attentions up entirely to a rapt and continuous contemplation of "Doc Sifers."* Well, I really can't but confess that "Doc" has been in my thoughts "a heap," as he himself might phrase it,—but in strict justice to all facts, I've been trying to do some real work, of late, and the same has been, and is, mighty hard sleddin'! But slowly, slowly, I feel that I'm getting back to something like the old spirit—such as that is. One thing has been vexing me for months,—and that's a story I've got—out of real fer-shore life—that is just panting to be told and printed, bound embossed and tooled and cased, and so imperiously tossed into the lap of the foolish fond old World. But I can't tell the story myself, 'cause it's prose and I've sworn I'd try never to try prose again. So, at last I've almost decided to hand it over to— whom? Two writers, of human heart, art and righteous sympathy, have I thought of as worthy of so rare and priceless a gift as my patriotic and pathetic theme presents.—Mr. Kipling is one of these; Miss Furman the other. Which shall it be?—which shall it be?—I've only time now to say that the story is already complete, in its home-history and fact of life-occurrence. It needs only the master-art of written utterance—the simple, yet all-forceful speech of the Inspired of God. Have you read

*"Rubáiyát of Doc Sifers," *Hoosier Book,* No. 250.

any of Kipling's stories with children in them?—like *"Ba, ba, Black Sheep!"* etc. Of our prospective story, I will only further say that, while tender and pathetic, it is wholly strong, ringing, mainly most pleasant, yet per-vaded with a spirit that will—or ought to—make all man-kind better, prouder, more grateful for this human life with such real heroes in it as our child-hero of the story. So now go to reading Kipling's children—the "Black-Sheep"-ones in particular. Then, too, his "Drums of the Fore and Aft"—and, for further spirit and patriotic fire, baptize your being in Hale's *Man without a Country*—and if you haven't any of these at hand, please let me know and I will send them.

Your sincere friend,
JAMES WHITCOMB RILEY.

To Robert J. Burdette.

Indianapolis,
May 15, 1897.

Dear Burdette:

Can't you arrange to get on here for a lovely week with our Western Writers' coming annual at Warsaw, Indi-ana, June twenty-eighth to July second? Bring the sister, too, and the Prince, if they can or care to come—there will be all beautiful home-people present. Out of Kansas, Gene Ware (Ironquill) and William Allen White, who wrote the crisp and peerless editorial on "What's the mat-ter with Kansas?" and "The Real Issue," short stories so simply delectable; are coming with their families; and numberless other members of the Society likewise, Myron W. Reed, of Denver—Young E. Allison, of Louisville; Editor of Forum, Boston—in fact as glorious a gathering

as can be found in the whole literary universe. You'll
want to see your publishers, here about then, and I jucks!
they'll be at Warsaw, too! Gimme line at once, saying
yes.

Always your affectionate,
JAMESIE.

To William Carey.

Indianapolis,
May 29, 1897.

Dear Carey:

Just sending you complete—"Doc Sifers"—returning
with same your revision. I have made several alterations,
but fear in most I have only hopelessly confused them.
Think you'd better turn them over to Kemble to complete
volume and let him absorb and soak them up with all his
human heart and soul—he can do wonders with old "Doc,"
I know, but he must as delicately treat him as he would his
old father—never without a cheery, wholesome humor and
a reserved dignity—never even approaching on the ridiculous, though this element may be found in "Doc's"
eyes and face—give him all the pathos of any one in his
experience he may choose to depict.—His ministration to
the poor in simplest homes, homes no less with all the cares.
Dress him very simply, carelessly but not slovenly—
"Doc" is always orderly.—Straw hat or felt but inexpen-
sive. And Doc always wears boots—not with his
"breeches" in the tops but boots ever and always!—his
horses—or team smeared with mud—top-buggy no approach at style or speed but comfortable. I can see Doc
now picking up the old tramp and making a companion of
him utterly unconscious of the charity of his act or any

sense of personal superiority. Tramp thinks he has struck
it rich; but ain't gettin' no more out of it'n old "Doc," I
bet! "Doc" wears fur cap and great big fur mittens in
winter—(these mention). Why doesn't Kemble glance
through Indiana here? He'd get enough inspiration here
in just a few days to last him for years. I see the South
in his work, and the East, but he really needs to know this
quarter. Tell him I'll meet him and personally conduct
him and come right now.

As ever,

JAMESIE.

To William Carey.

Indianapolis,
Aug. 6, 1897.

Dear Carey:

Here's proem-form for the space you marked for me in
Relyea's* "dummy." The lines immediately follow dedicatory page, and thus appear as addressed to my friend.
Hope they'll strike you as about the right thing every
way.—Also hope Relyea can *exalt* my suggested little vi-
gnette tail-piece for same. Therefore tell him that sketch
is meant to illustrate the two concluding lines of proem—
that the scene is a sort of *Hoosier Valhalla,* gorgeously
drawing on the rapt vision of the now beatified "Doc,"
as with his angelic retinue of shadowy followers, he
emerges from the beech forest, crosses the twinkling wa-
ters of the little creek and rapturously rides on into the
eternal splendor of the morning sun.

As ever,

JAMESY.

---

*Relyea was the artist who illustrated *Doc Sifers.*

To Charles M. Relyea.

Indianapolis, Ind.,
Sept. 6, 1897.

Dear Mr. Relyea:

Mr. Carey is very greatly pleased with your Doc Sifers creation. But he is not more pleased than I. In my estimation it is strong—firm—fine, and most simply individual, natural and therefore effective. But I want you— if not too late—to give your masterpiece a better pair of feet.—They only are out of character. I don't try to mend 'em with my pencil, but they should be modified in both size and shapeliness. Doc's foot is not with corn or bunion even, but fair-sized, strongly shod but symmetrical,—and widen his right boot a little at the ankle-front going up his trousers. If, too, the chair he sits in were commoner, he would be more at home, like. I can't see your background in the blue-print, so I've filled one out in pencil—all, of course, meant dimly to show. See Doc's patent shelf, hinged to his glass bottle-case. Push the hinged cleet or prop below, and the flap folds down out o' the way and flush and smooth with the sill. Also I've tried to make open window, with vines and roses suggested outside, and a perky little bird that, of course, knows Doc personally, cocking his head on the window-sill.

Please give me a line at once, but don't let me or my suggestions bother you. All I humbly beg or ask you now is to save Doc's feet if it be possible in any way.

Hastily but very heartily yours,
JAMES WHITCOMB RILEY.

Doctor Hays and all your friends here send you greetings. The Doctor and I had a great sprint one week ago through Brown County,* and the scene of your sojourn. We drove into Nashville in fine season for dinner— roamed about the really beautiful hill-country till four o'clock,—then sent our first rig back to Martinsville (our starting-point) and, with a clicky old Nashville turn-out, went ricochetting over the slopes into Columbus. Supped and slept there—then on home by rail in the morning. Glorious day and experience!

To Charles Scribner's Sons, Publishers.

Indianapolis,
Sept. 27, 1897.

Dear sirs:

It may seem a rather novel complaint, but this check of yours is much too generous—even had I meant to ask or take any money for the Stevenson† poem,—which I did not, though perhaps I should have more clearly indicated that fact to you. Still you make me oversordid; for if— instead of this immoderate check—Mr. Stevenson's most worthy publishers would send me his books in red buckram I should feel—(even as now with their gift of Kipling here on my shelves)—additionally and continually their debtor.

Very gratefully and truly yours,
JAMES WHITCOMB RILEY.

---

*Brown County, a remote Indiana county and a favorite with artists to-day.

†The lines, "On a Youthful Portrait of Stevenson" (*Lockerbie Book,* No. 246), are explained in the second letter following.

To Arthur H. Scribner.

Indianapolis,
Oct. 12, 1897.

Dear Mr. Scribner:

It is pleasant to hear of your safe home-coming, and a far-away western friend joins in your general greeting— even though from the throne of your desk you again demand tribute of him in prose! For three days therefore I have gone mooning and muttering about, and yet no fitting result. Prose, simply, likes me not, nor can I mix its elements with any skill, or knead or bake the stuff to any proper finish.—I will get in too little "XXX Family Flour" and too much baking powder.—In fact, prose is the only verse I write that is worse than my other verse. And that is why I've just been thanking heaven that the worst of it was about over with in the two volumes you have happily escaped by being at "the other side of the world." But on next page I will copy and submit the best paragraph I've got together—and it's, of course, subject for any change you may choose to suggest.

Very truly and gratefully yours,
JAMES WHITCOMB RILEY.

. . . At sight and inspection of "The Homestead Edition" I desire to acknowledge to the Publishers, Messrs. Charles Scribner's Sons, the deep sense of personal satisfaction their perfect work affords me. Presenting my simple product, as they are, in so superior a way, I can but feel the honor they do me and mine, and most fervently therefore do I assure them of my thanks now and continual gratefulness.

To Clara E. Laughlin.

Indianapolis,
Oct. 28, 1897.

Dear Miss Laughlin:

This is no letter at all—only a long-distance clapping
of hands over your lovely "Revelation of Christopher"—
yes, and the fine, strong, heartening letter I'd been silently
applauding since its inspired creation on the nine-
teenth,—for even a full day prior to its arrival the spirit
of it smote me like a sort of anonymous glory. Of course
I shall never be able to thank you for it—though certain
am I that you already know the righteous sense of my appreciation. But you must not think it is "the oft-recurring gnat"—the rabidly erudite little critic you so recently
were afflicted with—that vexes me seriously at all. *I'm*
the fellow that gets after me the most effectively and relentlessly. Now, however, I'm at peace with even myself
again, and no end of good things are coming round my
way. Wish I could see you and talk some of 'em over at
you! What do you think of this, for instance? I've a
youthful photograph of our beloved Robert Louis Stevenson, and I wrote some maunderings to it,—nay, to the
lovely man himself,—sent picture and lines to a magazine
and publishing house,—and they wrote to say portrait and
verses would appear in their Christmas magazine, and enclosed a great corpulent check which I had not dreamed
of in such connection—so returned it, coyly saying even if
I had intended the lines for money, their check was in vast
excess of their worth,—but if, in lieu of such sordid compensation, Robert Louis Stevenson's publishers were to
send me a set of his books, it would seem to me about all

the recompense I could bear.—Well, now here's where only a poet can humor and account for the doings of Divinity: As I stepped out into the golden morning-edge of my very recentest birthday, Robert Louis Stevenson was blithely seeing to it that his books were being then and there delivered into my hands by the expressman who looked and acted just for the world as though he were delivering the package to me.—Even made me sign something to that effect, I think!

Very truly yours,
JAMES WHITCOMB RILEY.

And don't you
ever give this
letter of MS. to
anybody!

To Robert J. Burdette.

Omaha, Neb.,
Nov. 20, 1897.

Dear Burdette:
    Your inspiring hail across the spaces—

> "Fills me and thrills me with life divine,
>   Till the purple flood
>   Of my bounding blood
> Breaks into riot of bloom and bud!"

There now! See what a rapturous go-devil you've let off in my midst! To-morrow I'm to miss divine service at All Saints Church, and a Thanksgiving dinner with the Rector thereof,—but have I not your sacred page with its largess of compensation for all I am denied elsewhere— by blessed reason of my not having brought along a frock-tail coat—which reminds me that The Wise Purveyor, he knows. . . .

And mayby, while you're wunderin who
You've fool-like lent your umbrell' to
And *want* it—out'll pop the sun,
And you'll be glad you hain't got none!*

By your list I see you've been "usin' " round about old
Indianap'lus—so I'm most earnestly hoping that you had
a stop-off there—long enough to see the folks at your
Lockerbie home—bless 'em for lovin' you as they do!
Fact is, old feller, I believe I'm a-lovin' you just a little
more and more, and gentler and gentler all the time.   Is
it 'cause I'm a-kindo' clockin' along to'rds the dusk of
things?   No odds!—it's very lovely, just the same; and
my Thanksgiving impromptu, all honestly and fervently
reads:-

To all, each day—or blithe and gay
With summer sun, or drear and gray
With winter weather—come what may
It yet should be Thanksgiving Day.

Send us along an ahoy every chance you get.
                              As ever your affectionate
                                             JAMESY.

To Samuel L. Clemens.

Dec., 1897.

Dear Mr. Clemens:
   For a solid week—night sessions—I have been glorying
in your last book†—and if you've ever done anything better, stronger, or of wholesomer uplift I can't recall it.   So

---

*"Wet-Weather Talk," *Hoosier Book*, No. 23.

†*Following the Equator*.   Letter was printed in *Mark Twain, a Biography*,
by Albert B. Paine.

here's my heart and here's my hand with all the augmented faith and applause of your proudest countryman! It's just a hail I'm sending you across the spaces—not to call you from your blessed work an instant, but simply to join my voice in the universal cheer that is steadfastly going up for you.

As ever gratefully and delightedly,
Your abiding friend,
JAMES WHITCOMB RILEY.

To Frank M. Nye.

New York,
Christmas Day, 1897.

Dear Frank M. Nye:

Best greetings of this day to you and yours! Your letter of twentieth is just here—forwarded from Indianapolis, from where I've been just one week—called here by both business and pleasure, but more particularly the former. In fact, the pleasure I get out of a large city is indeed out of it—as now I'm just back from Bronxville, where for two days I've been "in clover," so to speak, visiting Edgar's old friend and mine, Edmund Clarence Stedman, whose boast is that he must, as always, live in the "roaring town," and yet hies him away perforce to the silent sanctity of the suburbs. Edgar, as you know, also lived here,—and tried, God knows, to like it and believe it was good and as it should be.—But he—inwardly—knew the utter dearth of it, all the time, and wanted to get back "elsewhere,"—where we *all* naturally belong.

For a long, long while I've been at hardest work, and lost wholly in it. All else has been—not forgotten, but denied.—Just as though I complacently were thinking I had a check for it and could go and call for it any future time.—But I am realizing that this is not the state of things, by any means, as age comes on.—So, I think, Edgar realized, in far advance of any of us. Where is he now, meditating such serious things under the old disguise of levity? Truly, I want him here again, yet truly am I assured he is still in far advantage of this mortal "lay-out." (What I want to say is something to suit him.) Always I am thinking of him—as I have repeatedly told you—not mournfully, but as though some certain wholesome glory had occurred to him and he were striving to "Whack up" with his poor old needy pardner. And that's exactly as it is, I feel and know.

Glad you like the new book. Have worked, every line of it, to make it natural, native fact,—which same it is, in every detail,—and you'll be glad to know—as I here know from publishers—that its sales already predict its confirmed tangible success. Have heard—and most gladly— that Mrs. Nye's loss is not—everything, as first reported by "the joyous press"—as I think Edgar is smilingly phrasing it. With all cheery love to the mother and hale Christmas greetings to the wife and children all—And God bless us every one!

Your affectionate friend and brother,
JAMES WHITCOMB RILEY.

To Mrs. Charles L. Holstein.

Nashville, Tenn.,
Apr. 10, 1898.

Dear St. Lockerbie:

All happiest Easter greetings to you! As usual in the North, so the day here is marked by the full citizenship in dress-parade—all in near spring suits and utter satisfaction. I even grew enthusiastic enough to entirely unpack my stuff and "rag out" in my new suit.

Yesterday, however, was an opportunity even more to my liking,—for, although not a day of such splendor overhead (for many times, indeed, "it came on to rain"), I was taken out to the famous town of Murphreesboro, and the scene of the great Battle of Stone River. This excursion-melancholious from ten, morning, until two in afternoon, and then (God be thanked!) to the country home of Charles Egbert Craddock—Miss Murphree. A young lawyer here, John Bell Keeble, was my sponsor and companion—he being almost a member of the Murphree household from his boyhood. Well, it was an unpretentious home, but very evidently happy. The family entire—the bright old mother—more than eighty—and her two equally bright daughters,—Miss Fanny, the older, whose serial novel you may have seen in *The Atlantic* a year or two ago,—and Miss Mary, the more famous of the two. The pair are inseparable and therefore both virtually recluses, for Miss Mary is in some way crippled—has been so from her childhood, Mr. Keeble told me,—but I was rejoiced to see how strong otherwise she was—even robust,—and hale and wholesome, too, as her best heroine. Her lameness evidently is in the feet,—for though she received us standing, she held firmly to her chair with one hand and immediately seated herself after our introduction. Miss Mary is a tireless worker at her desk; Miss Fanny, a like worker at household affairs. She writes some—but, as her sister laughingly said, "She writes with her hat on and a parasol under her arm"—(just as she comes from market, I fancy she meant). The old mother doesn't write, but every day of her blessed life she devotes an hour or so to her piano—a practise, Mr. Keeble told me, she has strictly maintained since her far-away girlhood. But the details of the entire visit I reserve till I can better give them when I land at home.

Best love to all, and trusting one and all of you are well and happy, I am as always.

Yours,

JAMESEY.

CHAPTER VII

A visit South—Poems set to music—Bliss Carman—Nicholson's tributes—Professor Beers—Verse selected for an Anthology, *Literature of All Nations*—Maurice Thompson—Riley's violin—A visit to Harris and Stanton—Riley writes a "Bre'r Possum" story—"Leonainie" hoax still echoes—Henry van Dyke.

To Frank L. Stanton.

Asheville, N. C.,
Apl. 28, 1898.

Dear Stanton:

Just now I find you in the May *Current Literature*—a splendid portrait frontispiece and group of superb songs. All congratulations and may your melodious deservings ring for ever in all grateful homes and hearts. Soon, now, I'll be again at my own desk, and then will institute a series of afflictions for you in the shape of better thanks than this—with books, pictures and all else. Speaking of pictures, I must have yours,—so don't delay in sending me your photographic portrait—to Indianapolis, where I'll be by thirtieth at farthest.

Yesterday visited our dear Nye, at his grave and at his home—nor did I doubt his cheery presence throughout the lovely day—nay, nor throughout the evening's program whose best half was his again just as of old.

Love to Uncle Remus and all.

Your always affectionate

JAMESY.

To Bliss Carman.

Indianapolis,
Aug. 30, 1898.

My dear Mr. Carman:

Over and over I am joyously reading your sagacious
and yet generous estimate of "Mr. Riley's Poetry"—until
indeed you seem to me the featest, fairest critic in the
lettered world and *The Atlantic,* the very first of mag-
azines on earth! "When that I was a little tiny boy,"
my first worshiped contemporary was an old poetic farmer,
with his mind a trifle canted—sufficiently at least to invent
a flying-machine which he used to lecture on—not fly. I
shall never forget his startling hand-bills, opening thus:

> "The time long wished for is at hand,
> When man, grown tired of sea and land,
> On artificial wings shall fly,
> And navigate the liquid sky," etc. etc.

And one awesome night I heard him lecture, in the court-
house, on a pasteboard model of his machine; and I came
away through the thick-sweet summer night, in a rapt
state staring up and toward the north for the lecturer on
his way home on his machine,—for then I doubted not
that he could fly—and now I know I can. And, even so,
behold me in the far azure heights, eerily lifted and
havened there by the inspiration of your tribute to my
late lowly—but now lofty—rhyme. And that you grant
the same a too great honor, as I fear, at times, only makes
me flinch into newer intrepidity of flight and praise; and
as you name me the first American Eagle of them all, I
simply just spread out my wings and loll there in the
central heavens

"——faint and white
(Yea, and light)
As a schoolboy's paper kite!"

At the last New Year's Watch-night at The Authors' Club, I for the first time met your poet friend Roberts, whose worthy verses I must needs take in as mountain air. And he talked most righteously of your fine strong work, and, all incidentally told me of this very estimate you were then fashioning for *The Atlantic.* So, although not wholly unprepared, I have still most frankly to confess that its high appreciation in main spirit, together with its hale sincerity of weight and measurement, combine for me a state of satisfaction never before surprised into tingling life and action. What you say, in every way touches me as would the grave judicial counsel of the nearest wisest friend. Your conscience no less than your magnanimous heart—your subtlety of observation, analysis and vivisection of living facts—all astonish even the upbuilder—nay, the *framer,* I would better say—of the fabric that you sound and gage and classify minutely, as the master mental architect you are.—Yet here am I—as far from thanking for it all as at my opening page. But I do thank you—beyond words,—with brimming heart and soul. And, some other time than in this now and in this way, I hope to "even up" my vast indebtedness.

To me, as to your world of comrade-friends, it is a joy to see the steadfast march that you are making. God keep your blithe soul ever young and lyric as when He first unleashed it on the morning heights! You have been greatly made and greatly launched and furthered on a great career—and already, too, greatly are you arriving.

Fraternally, as ever and always your friend,

JAMES WHITCOMB RILEY,

To Meredith Nicholson.

Indianapolis,
Sept. 15, 1898.

Dear friend Nicholson:

Thank you heartily for your clear and bracing hail out of the far West. That's as good to a fellow, even, as the far eastern one you so endorsingly refer to. Hence is it that my vast gratefulness reaches from coast to coast—from the "Atlantic" to the Pacific verily.*

But what you mean by going so far away, and for so long a time, and never giving me a chance to get your borrowed book back to you, is not at all clear to me, nor fair, either, to my intent of returning with it some like worthy volume which I was first to make sure you had not already in your list of varieties—likewise some choice brand of cigars, as I've been furtively considering might prove a remembrancer of my especial obligations and appreciation of your kindness in welcoming with me our southern friend, Frank Stanton. All of which I cease not to remember, and shall yet in some material way justly respond to.

As to your appointed high place in the literary galaxy, you have but to go and occupy it.—And long may you shine! Your very earliest start was high, and higher steadfastly have you gone, and are still rising—soon centrally to locate in the pure serene of divine singing, for all time, I pray.

As ever, fraternally your old friend,
JAMES WHITCOMB RILEY.

---

*Mr. Nicholson says: "This reference to the Atlantic harks back to some verses of mine printed in Indianapolis *Journal* at the time "Old Glory" appeared in the *Atlantic Monthly*. They were called "Riley in the *Atlantic*."

To Prof. Henry A. Beers.

Cir. Autumn, 1898.

Dear friend:

Again I have been reading and loving your delightful
sketches under title *A Suburban Pastoral*—and they are—
all—the veritable delicious things that must have occurred—just as an unconscious master has set them down.
A very rare gift is yours, thus to make merest common-
places extraordinary and things everybody knows with
utter familiarity seem rarely fresh and dewy. But I am
not wholly content.—I want your verses. And your rare,
exquisitely actual "Bumble Bee" I want in your own
"hand-write." So please send it promptly to

Very truly and gratefully your friend,

JAMES WHITCOMB RILEY.

To Julian Hawthorne.

New York,
            Christmas Day [probably 1898].

Julian Hawthorne, Esq.:

It makes the day more memorable that your request
has been forwarded to me here,—asking for any line of
mine for your *Literature of All Nations.* My consent to
any wish of yours always consider wholly certain, as it is
utterly grateful; and, as you find me involved with publishers, fail not to press my wishes as your very own—and
they have all been steadfastly kind and indulgent to the
interest as well as to the desires of

Your long-time most grateful friend,

JAMES WHITCOMB RILEY.

To Prof. Henry A. Beers.

Indianapolis,
Jan. 17, 1899.

Dear Friend:

That written copy of your deliciously intemperate "Bumble Bee" is now "jugged," so to say, in the fitting duress of a golden frame, along with like culprits, such as Stevenson and Twain, and Nye, and "Artemus," Irving, and Uncle Remus, and other beworshiped literary gentles. As to your volume,—it has already become a text-book with me, and is at my desk's easiest shelf by day, and my bed's easiest reach by night.—So, you see, for no blessed instant am I left uncheered or unuplifted. And I've been reading—both to myself and friends, equally delighted, your "Suburban Pastoral" stories,— in their way showing their exquisite selves as blood-kin of your verse. Over and over I recall my pleasant visit with you and the friends all as we foregathered.* To Professor Lounsbury my especial greetings!—and do put Professor Phelps upon his guard, as I mean, the first chance I get, to pick him off with a letter.

Your always grateful, faithful friend,
JAMES WHITCOMB RILEY.

---

*"This one dated Jan. 17, 1899, was after a dinner at Professor Scripture's, I think, at which Lounsbury, Phelps and I were present. Mr. Riley had been giving a reading (which I attended) at The Hyperion Theatre in New Haven, unless my memory is at fault as to dates."—Prof. H. A. Beers.

To Maurice Thompson.

Indianapolis,
Jan. 20, 1899.

Dear Mr. Thompson:

Your good letter, just here (with its inclosed copy of your letter to Miss Gilder) grieves me with the evidence that your recent kindly comment in *The Critic* of my homely verse should have—in any phrase of it—called forth any critical charge against the fairness of your motive in the utterance. Is it not the reviewer's office to point out these very trifles of defects which to the erudite are only the graver errors for being passed over undetected by the general reader? In frankest truth, while I am far from fond of having the lint lifted out of my pseudo-literary pelt, I have long since learned to know that such castigation helps more than it hurts. So, even for your deflected intent I am grateful—and how much so you can smilingly estimate when I tell you that, since I first read that particular line of indictment now in question, I never doubted but your charge was absolutely true; nor, till your present letter, have I dared look up the wee, timid, cowering little beastie of a poem—assured that I should be confronted with the monstrous error you had unearthed. But, God bless us! no vaguest harm is done but the little chuckle in which our voices all blend for an instant's rolic-brawling, then ripple back into the deep dusk pools of infinite silence. And now, lest you might miss the not wholly irrelevant paragraph and the wholesome laugh attached, I paste this clipping from the "Bubbles-in-the-Air"-man's cluster of brilliants in the morning's *Indianapolis Journal*.

As ever gratefully and truly yours,
JAMES WHITCOMB RILEY.

"I know," pleaded the little bride, humbly, "that I make a good many grammatical errors."

"They are nothing," said the young husband, "to those mother used to make."

To Miss Constance Maud.

Oct. 12, 1899.

Dear Miss Maud:

Certainly—set the "Song of the Road"* to music of your inspiration. Nothing could flatter the author nor make better the worth of the lines originally inspired—for he, like you, doesn't know why they insisted on singing themselves. But do send me an earliest copy of your melodious interpretation—not forgetting a like one to our dear rapt genius, Madame Sterling.† Always I am remembering you—and gratefully,—though I refrain as best I can from reminding you of a memory that positively will not out! Nor do I even lispingly forget your books—your prose music—possibly even more beautiful, to my inland senses, than all the "long, low Australasian washes" of your native waves of Song. And I'm right now going to copy for you another song—which here in America at least "belongs," as our mutually beloved Mr. Kipling would say. So, better than other further written talk, take thou *the Song.*‡

Your always grateful and fraternal,

JAMES WHITCOMB RILEY.

---

*"A Song of the Road," *Lockerbie Book,* No. 236.
†Madame Antoinette Sterling.
‡Here follows a copy of "Where the Children Used to Play," *Lockerbie Book,* No. 48.

To George A. Carr.

Indianapolis,
Dec. 5, 1899.

Dear George:

Your good word of the second is like a cheery hail out of our boyhood times, and it's the first letter I've tried to answer for many weeks—for I've been ill and shut in for an age, it seems, and am just beginning to sit up. As to your query as what to tell the oft-recurring interviewer, I'm sure your own taste will direct you wisely, though I do hope you'll recall the happy and often ridiculous, incidents of our truant days,—such, for instance, of our boyish escapades as are in likeness of our open-day raid on Grandpap Huntington's "mush"-melon-patch, and his unlooked-for descent upon us, in our very lair, and the deft handling of that buggy-whip of his as it swishingly sorted us out, over the old slat fence. There was "poetic justice"! Then there's that only fight we ever had,—at night, you remember,—with not a solitary witness to keep us from the dread encounter, or to interpose when we really yearned to be separated. And Ed Howard was with us, I think, when we swiped a whole basketful of spring-clothes-pins out of the new preacher's back yard, and fringed our roundabouts with 'em, and clamped 'em to our ears and noses and played "Injun" and ransacked the town, till, alarmed at last, we went into concealment from the outraged citizens, and, long after nightfall, were found in our stable, all sound asleep in the old top-carriage with all the curtains fastened on, etc., etc., world without end!

As ever your old friend,
JIM.

Kindly remember me to your father, mother, wife and family all.

To Peter Cook.

Indianapolis,
March 5, 1900.

Dear Sir:

In the *Indianapolis News,* this date, I am particularly attracted by a Muncie special, headed, "A Violin with a History," in which your name (with address) is given in relation to your being the possessor of a rare old violin, bearing (as the types insist on having it) the inscription "Paglo Albani, In Boston, 1691." When a boy—from about seventeen to twenty—I was a large enthusiast of the violin with a very small gift of execution. But, being a true worshiper of that peerless instrument and its history and that of its master-makers and manipulators, it was evidently ordained that I should meet with some appropriate reward for that devotion. So, one afternoon, visiting an old musical friend at his home, where often I went to hear him play upon a high-priced, burnished violin he doted on, I saw his very little daughter promenading about the back porch trailing after her a curious doll-cart, which same miniature vehicle proved, upon my inspection, to be an old "fiddle," with the "belly" off, the "ears" and "apern" gone, but otherwise intact. It had been, in its day, my old friend explained, a fairish instrument, but he had long ago discarded it, with the constant caving in and over-gluing of the top. And then he volunteered, with a superior twinkle, that, having the broken top somewhere in the wood-house, if I cared at all to tinker at the old "shell," I should have it—ending derisively with an outright laugh, that, if patched up half-way decent, it would still make a better instrument than the one I owned. So I took him at his word, and—awaiting till dusk—I carried the old fiddle and its fragmentary top home with me.

Its insides seemed caked with the dust—the dirt—the very mange of ages, and yet how gently, tenderly and reverently I worked upon it—till, all gradually uncovered to my rapturous sight, on about an inch-broad and three-inch-long square strip of sallow paper pasted in the bottom, I read the printed inscription,

"Paolo Albani, Botzen
1650.". . . (Mark *this* date.)

Well, I hadn't much money, but all I had went to dress up that old instrument in something like befitting style. And when all this was accomplished—and not till then—I proudly brought my treasure before the public eye. And what did that public do and say?—I doubt not, Mr. Cook, that you surmise. In vain I battled with all skeptical insinuations. But even my nearest, dearest friends smiled at my youthful credulity and ardor. At least out loud they, as kindly as they could, assured me that my violin was but "an imitation"—a brazen pretense—a vociferous and self-acknowledged fraud. "But," I urged, "if an imitation, why had not its cunning fashioner shaped it after the manner of some well-known old Cremona master—one of the famous brothers Stradivarius for instance?" Then I said "Ha?" and waited. Then they asked "Where was this-here 'Botzen' where the thing was supposed to be made at?" And I couldn't answer just then, and not being an expert in either Geography or Ancient History, it took me about six weeks to reply,—but I did find out—from Callicotts' *Encyclopedia of Geography,* I think—that "Botzen (was) a town of Tyrol, population 9000," etc., etc. And then I began scratching and combing through all the maps, till there too at last I hounded it down and put my paw across it and lay there and panted. Even as to-night—all my then glorious victory revived by the brief outline of your kindred possession—I turn the *Century Atlas* (of the *Century Dictionary* Series,) to map Austria-Hungary, No. 90—about two inches inward from left margin and four upward from bottom, and find again the city "Bozen—or Botzen," where, in all sincerity, I doubt not, by the same old master-hand, and at their respective dates, your noble violin and mine were made.

Very truly yours,
JAMES WHITCOMB RILEY.

To Joel Chandler Harris.

Indianapolis,
April 11, 1900.

Dear friend:

Have just been writing things in the fronts of a set of Homestead Edition especially for you—which same will be boxed and expressed this afternoon, per care *The Constitution.* Have been an invalid the whole-indurin' winter, else I'd 'a' been a-writin' you whole reams! Now am just well enough to travel for my health, and I'm coming down your way to look for it, Mr. Dickey, my manager, accompanying me. We go first to Bon Air, and will leave in a few days, passing through Atlanta, where Mr. D. says we'll have two or three hours stop—the exact date of which I'll let you know, praying you'll meet and greet a feller on his bright sunny way. And, if you will, bring Stanton with ye. Very hastily—for even now I'm packing—

Your ever grateful, faithful
JAMES WHITCOMB RILEY.

To Mrs. Charles L. Holstein.

Augusta, Ga.,
Apr. 18, 1900.

Dear St. Lockerbie:

The journey here seemed but a few hours, and the gradual development of real spring, with the blossoms and green in the trees, has been simply glorifying in effect. At our three hours' stop at Atlanta we were met at station by both Harris and Stanton, who lunched with us, right across at the Kimball. Robert Geiger was not there, but had left a note explaining his unavoidable absence. But I expect to see him in week or ten days, when I'm to visit Mr. Harris briefly for few days. Am already much better in this truly invigorating air—mild, clear, pure and balmy—penetrating medicinally to the basement story of the invalid's immortal soul, as it were. We've experienced but one trouble,—that of hotel rates and location: but at last are in double-room on parlor-floor, very materially assisting the landlord to pay his yearly rent. Soon as settled and trunk unpacked we took street-car for Augusta, whose spacious streets I paced with Col. Richard Malcolm Johnston and old "Jonas Lively," in fancy, on either side of me. Did Robert (who was to reach Atlanta day after us) send you marked illustrated notice of Harris, Stanton and Me? Saw a copy here but couldn't buy one in the market, or would have sent you that. Hope all are well at home and that the real spring weather is arriving there by this time. With halest love to all.

Jamesy.

To Joel Chandler Harris.

Indianapolis,
May 8, 1900.

Dear friend:

The last two weeks have been simply a bewilderingly
gorgeous dream to me—when as the guest of your lovely
home and family I have known the highest honor and
happiness of my life,—all of which—(since all is sacred
truth—you must be wholly conscious of, without one word
of mine)—I'm not going to *plague* you with, but instead,
ignore, knowing you will be the readier to bear with other
themes.—To begin at the exact beginning.—"How Bre'r
'Possum came by his Pocket." It all came to me in scraps
and minute particles as I fitfully slept and dreamed, wak-
ened and slept again, all along my way home: First,
Sis 'Possum, having scarce a friend in the Animal world,
outside her own family, and being continually chased
about from pillar-to-post, went to the Animal Creator
and begged for peculiar protection for her "chilluns,"
which same, in her hurried flights, she was continually
spilling along the way, thereby, as well, discovering her
very path of safety to her enemies by the little 'possums
marking it with their ostensibly dead bodies. So the
Creator listened, and at Sis 'Possum's very wise suggestion, smiled and gave her brackets, growing out upon her
in most convenient localities. These for a season she
tried with poor success,—her chilluns, in her mad flights
for safety being "breshed" off by low-hanging forest-
boughs and "onderbresh." So she again appeals—this
time for a series of little individual drawers, in which each
little 'possum could hide himself—pulling the drawer shut

with a snap and locking it from the inside. Again the Creator patiently listens—and, even more smilingly than at first, grants Sis 'Possum her "Beseechment." But for the third time she returns, asking for a change of some kind which (gracious knows!) she's got no s'gessions ter make no more,—but that the drawers des won't work, less'n she stand straight up whiles the chilluns hunts round for their dratted little keys—and blows the chinkapin crum's out'n 'em and onloks and pulls the drawers out—which more'n ha'f the time they're stuck so, she haf to take and turn in and pull em out her-own-sef, etc., world without end. So this time the Creator don't crack nary smile, but say He done know from de start what Sis 'Possum need, and s'po'n dat ef she on'y look clost enough, and "Know thysef," lak de Good Book say, she'ull certny fine a pocket already-made-and-waitin', ef she on'y got sense enough to snip de bastin'-threads with her teeth and pull 'em out with her toe-nails!

All day yesterday and to-day I've been setting up my (not Gram-o-phone, but) Zon-o-phone, which the Co. says is by no means so complicated. Well, at last, I've mastered it; and with ten introductory disks—and one from your duplicates, I am now giving a great show, and all we Lockerbie people wish you-all were of our enthusiastic audience. Your disk holds favorite, though we have one phenomenal one which I'll order duplicate of forwarded your way at once. Halest greetings to you one and all.

As always your grateful and affectionate

JAMESY.

To Joel Chandler Harris.

Indianapolis,
June 8, 1900.

My dear friend:

And here's your favor of the second of June just being answered the eighth—and what'll you be thinking of my "hanging fire" like this? Simply I've been away again, and only now bursting into your long-waiting letter like a belated explorer into a new continent. But content you, nor be you vexed the least.—The pictures are all all right,— only it is I who should be clamoring to pay for the entire order, since (do please remember) it was I who "proj- icked" you into the scheme—and, with the happy result here in my avaricious clutches, I'd count myself the gainer, at a dozen times the price. So, over and over again, I charge you not to fret in the least, since all the affair is of my doing—written, signed and sealed—yea, and dismissed,—only that I'm still your debtor, and will, in some good way, acquit myself. God bless you! how I've tanned in the glow of your proposition of sending me a check when that same is, in strictest justice, due from me to you. Therefore, like the distressed Sancho, I cry: "Peace! peace! in God's name, peace! lest I cast myself from the window!" Nor are you to be vexed one further shadow in the matter save in writing me—on slips of any paper pastable—your signature—to be framed with the portraits—even as my own shall be sent to you, if so be you even dast to hint you want 'em.

Well, I've been trying to get you two or three of my favorite disks for your Gramophone, but there's a delay at headquarters, and if I'm not soon supplied, I'll send you mine—for I simply know they'll delight you. And this reminds me that you asked if my Zonophone were better than your instrument. No, I think not, so far as sound and clearness is concerned. In some minor details of the mechanism, perhaps, it has advantages: The crank is at the side—not top; and the disk slips on, without delay or need of fastening it in place with tap. That is all— simply a trifle less complex—though it takes about twenty more revolutions than yours, to wind up the dod-gasted concern.

I've ravenously consumed the first part of your Lincoln story. It is a brave intrepid theme you've struck; and, better yet, it is as veritable as history, the way you're creating it. Over and over I think as I read, "How this would please the shrewd Lincoln himself!" All glorious like success attend you! Wish I were with you "cheek-by-jowl and knee-by-knee"—and, in truth, very often it seems as though I were—and very likely I am. Anyway, it's pleasant so to humor my fancy. Truth made out o' lies like that-un's good enough fer me! So with halest ahoys to you, and to every blessed one of your ever-blessed family, I am

Your always grateful and affectionate
JAMESY.

To Joel Chandler Harris.

Indianapolis,
July 30, 1900.

Dear friend Harris:

Well! weeks and weeks ago my publishers here jumped on me and said they must have a new book—so I went at it—(you know),—and as you are also aware, no man with a Waterbury intellect can do two things at once without losin' his nomnitive—I have kept strictly to that task; and now that it's over—this day—I thank God that I can say at least one coherent word to you. All the between-whiles I've been 'sociatin' with you and "Sister Jane"; and I must say it's mighty good company I've been in! That—it seems to me—is the way to let a feller's pen talk. Utter sincerity and stark truth must and does command delighted universal attention. Lord! but I wish I were back there on the porch—to sit there and discuss a few artistic things in betwixt the ruther superior remarks of the mocking-birds! Soon, though, I'll get to you, and observe (as Dickens would say) a very great number of things. And what do you think?—Yesterday the express brought to me three of your favorite disks—so that the major part of this day has been absolutely glutted with melody—*Larboard Watch* and *Little Nell* a-both a-playin' on my feelin's like a checker-board! And I'm always layin' off to send you some o' my favorites and I will, before a great while now—as I'm beginning to breathe again. Have heard—with joy—of Julian's* advancement—so that I'd like to be you—God bless you! Up and down and through and through your house, at all hours of the day and night, goes striding a phenomenally bow-legged ghost. Accost the cuss some time, as he dallies with the dipper in a drouthy way, and see if he doesn't answer to the name o'

JAMESY.

All hail to ever'body!

---

*His son, Julian.

To Mrs. H. F. Hovey.

Mother of Richard Hovey, who with Bliss Carman wrote *Songs of Vagabondia.*

Indianapolis,
Sept. 5, 1900.

Dear "Mother of Poets":

Your letter declaring me one of your beloved clan touches me to the tenderest quick of sympathy as well as pride. Most truly do I feel the signal honor you confer, and its especial sacredness, as relates to your dear and gifted son who now makes Heaven fairer for his radiant eyes—the Anthem richer for his rapturous voice. God comfort you and hold you ever proud and glad and grateful—since so surely He has blessed you, being, and ever to be, the noble mother of that noble son.

With halest faith in the All-Father and in the dear boy's now unchanging happiness, his ever loving friend and yours,

JAMES WHITCOMB RILEY.

To Mrs. Robert Louis Stevenson.

Indianapolis, Ind.,
Christmas, 1900.

Dear Mrs. Stevenson:

Since your brief visit to our city here, last winter, I've been remembering you and your kindness every day, and, in fancy have written down—hundreds of times my thanks to you and yours, once, when first well enough to get down-town, wrapping a photograph for you of the very well man I *used* to be. Finding the portrait this Christmas morning, I someway think it good-omenish and so send you the long-belated thing, together with a copy of a recent book in which are most affectionately set some old and some new lines of tribute to the dear dear man who is just away.* How I loved him through his lovely art! and how I loved all he loved and yet loves—for with both heart and soul, and tears and smiles, he seems ever near at hand. Therefore my gentlest greetings on this blessed day go out to him as to you.

Fraternally,
JAMES WHITCOMB RILEY.

To Meredith Nicholson.

The poem referred to below, a favorite recitation of Riley and designated by him, "a perfect poem," is "Brave Love," by Mary Kyle Dallas, reprinted in Biographical Edition, III, p. 539.

Indianapolis,
Jan. 9, 1901.

Dear Friend:

Belatedly, hastily, yet with all heart I thank you for your last best of letters, and, with an equal measure of thanks, ask to be remembered to Mrs. Nicholson. Tell her, too, how proud I was of her praise over the St. Louis readings, and proud likewise that her choice of the selections has long been my own, though I am not its author— save only as imperfect memory and unconscious editing may dubiously claim. The real author, whom I have been seeking for long years, I have only now first trace of.

---

*The references are "To Robert Louis Stevenson," No. 262, and to "On a Youthful Portrait of Stevenson," No. 246, *Lockerbie Book.* See also "To Hattie—on Her Birthday," written in *A Child's Garden of Verses* and describing it,—Biographical Edition, IV, p. 11.

When full evidence is in, tell Mrs. N. I shall send her a copy of the original, which, though in pinchbeck dialect is no less a golden poem at heart.

While I've tried to speak face to face with you of your new book, I feel, still the more as I read and reread the volume, that you have accomplished a truly high and notable work. *The Hoosiers,* as the book takes its place in my estimation, is a striking and distinctive contribution to our American literature and history. While it is unusually entertaining—with no lapse of that delighting quality throughout—it has full seriousness of verity, and a conscience and a dignity like a fine strong man's. So, with one wide sense of fervent gratefulness, I congratulate the author and the public.

With all best New Year greetings,
Your grateful and fraternal
JAMES WHITCOMB RILEY.

To Paul Lemperly.

Indianapolis,
Jan. 17, 1901.

Dear Mr. Lemperly:

Yes, I well recall the Foote inquiry regarding the Ainsworth Dictionary with the faked Poe-poem in faded ink written on fly-leaf of the volume.* The book I had entirely forgotten (until his letter)—then all details of the old fraud came back, and most vividly I recalled, first having my artist-friend, Sam Richards, do that *copy* in fine Poe-*facsimile,* and then of my joyously wrapping and hugging the treasure under my arm, and so personally bear-

---

*For further references to the "Leonainie" hoax see letters of November 22, 1886, and July 23, 1877.

ing it (by rail from Anderson to Kokomo) to the hands personally of Oscar Henderson, the editor of the *Dispatch* in
his sanctum, where, after a brief but rather "chortling" session, I left my smiling friend, locking the priceless volume
in his office-safe. . . . Since that hour—as I hastened to
inform Mr. Foote—the book's fortunes or adventures I
had no thought of further—until, as stated, came Mr.
Foote's inquiry,—saying he had bought the book and was
now writing to ask me if the fly-leaf poem therein were
Poe's or mine. So, of course, I was no little embarrassed,
forced thus to confess myself the author of the spurious,
pinchbeck thing—not justly doubting he would place the
least value whatever on my word when I assured him that,
had he priorly asked, I should have told him that the poem
was not Poe's, nor was the book the lawful property of
whoever had sold it to him—but that it was my property,
as originally,—though now, I said, in *his* (Mr. Foote's)
possession, he was wholly welcome to it—though I regretted not having had any vaguest thought or chance of
averting his purchase of an utterly fictitious value—the
more shameless, since whoever had disposed of the book
in Kokomo must have known positively the poem was a
fraud and that the book was not his property to dispose of
in any way.

To Arthur H. Scribner.

Indianapolis, Ind.,
Feb. 21, 1901.

Dear Mr. Scribner:

Thank you for your good letter of late sixteenth. Its
contents throughout are so agreeable that, with accelerated zest, I go on with the building of the twelfth (prospec-

tive) vol. for The Homestead Edition. For some time this particular volume has been outlined, to my own satisfaction—and I trust it may meet with the publishers' tolerance if not entire approval. As long designed, I have wanted this to be a thorough Child-book—nothing but children in it—and happy, wholesome children. All kinds,— the natively lovable, and decorous—rare as they are; the lisping genius, poet, composer, orator; but especially I want the lawless little fellow represented. And by *lawless* I mean simply that type of child whose gravest defect is in his speech—not his morals.—A bad grammarian, but the best of all good children. Child-poetry—real poetry— make believe poetry—very dubious poetry—and oftimes invisible poetry—down to the nothingest of nursery rhymes and jingles,—but all of the halest worth of joyous spirit.*

Well, the original first edition of the book I should like to see appear with ample list of illustrations—these to be on same simple lines of fact as found here in Hoosier life—from which, of course, mainly springs the matter of the volume. Then, after this edition, the book to be expanded, in like text, into uniform size, and making it the twelfth volume of The Homestead Edition. All this accomplished, I want to lie down som'ers in the shade and pant!

The copy for eleventh volume I have very nearly shaped and will forward in few days. Wish I could send with it the book that is to be; but all I can do now is to assure you that I'm at work on that consumedly. Ooh! if only the public should be half as fond of it as its visionary author, with all the courage of his vast conceit!

As implied, the prospective volume has been nowhere offered or promised. So if, from so filmy a prospectus,

---

The Book of Joyous Children, published 1902.

you think your house would care for a look at it, I will arrange to send you the first comprehensive part of it I can get together.

Very truly yours,
JAMES WHITCOMB RILEY.

To Slason Thompson.

Slason Thompson wrote as Field's biographer. The poem is "The Artemus of Michigan," explained in letters to Nye dated April 6 and 7, 1886.

Dear Mr. Thompson:
　Yes, the

"H.

Y.

Potts"

—poem is mine, though first introduced to the public by our dear Field in his Sharps and Flats column—at which introduction—as I recall it—he clearly gave proper credit,—though I remember, shortly after he again gave just credit, by correcting Dana's New York paper, I think, which had copied the lines from Sharps and Flats, doubtless not reading Field's introduction or thinking same fictitious naturally.

Hastily but heartily yours,
J. W. RILEY.

To Dr. Henry van Dyke.

Feb. 27, 1901.

Dear friend:

Your note of cheer is as uplifting as your books—so that I seem speaking across exalted heights if not quite up to the level of your altitude,—in truth a thin rare air, for general breathing purposes, but wonderfully sweet and reviving to the grateful soul. Of late months I have been steadily saying good-by to out-going friends, till it is growing rather a lonesome life I'm lagging in—this side of it,—so many of the dear fellows over There. But, as I say, or would strive to, such voices as your own are lifted now and then, and one eagerly listens, and, hearing the blessed hail aright, thanks God for calling him again to his mortal fellowships and higher duties and more serious delights. Two things I want now directly from your hand, O friend of mine!—Your portrait (a copy of the photograph you gave our mutual friend Mrs. Moulton) and—signing that—sign also a copy of your Whippoor-will poem. These I want for my nearest deskmates— along with "Uncle Remus," Henry A. Beers and his "Bumble-Bee," etc. Oh, you shall be of joyous company!—such even as will inspire you, 'way yonder in your remotest Eastern fastnesses. So prays, with halest affection, your old Hoosier friend,

JAMES WHITCOMB RILEY.

Am, all unasked, sending to you by this mail a photograph of a western admirer of both your verse and mine— yours he frankly thinks superior, but as he's no critic of plumberless profundity I gainsay him not, but silently saw wood.

To Joel Chandler Harris.

This letter followed McKinley's assassination, September 14, 1901. Riley wrote his "America" and "Even as a Child" at this time. (*Lockerbie Book*, Nos. 305 and 320.)

Indianapolis,
Sep. 23, 1901.

Dear friend:

I've just had a flickering evasive glimpse of you, through a characteristic visit of Mr. Geiger—who, all unexpectedly, materialized on one train and evaporated on the next. Brief though his stopping, it was mighty good to have him here, and to listen to his word of home-news right out of the wholesome heart of old Atlanta. Long ere this arrives he will have, doubtless, boomerang'd back into your startled presence with my best messages from out the North. Three or four several times, in the long awful weeks just past, I've been on the verge of writing you, but mercifully stayed my hand, feeling your measure of woe was already brimming, like my own, with the anguish of the piteous tragedy through which our nation passes. God of Heaven! the almost helpless heartache of it all! How I wanted to trail off into some desolate path of exile, and bide, bowed and mute and hidden, until Christ's own voice came down and found me and said "Lo, I will stay thy soul now as it lifts and sings the supreme faith—and love-song of thy land and mine."

> "So runs my dream,—But what am I?—
> An infant, crying in the night—
> An infant, crying for the light—
> And with no language but a cry."

Evelyn* got the books, sent in his care, I learn from Geiger—but did you get Venable's *Dream of Empire,* and did it please you?

How is the boy by this—for I've heard he's been back newspaperin' again, which you tell him his old "Uncle Sidney" thinks he orn't be a-doin' till he's entirely and teetotally restored to perfect health. In meantime, how's your own health—and what you drivin' at? Hope you're not overlookin' the delicious little songs as you go along,— for it's my forecast that our last work is to be the ripest and the juiciest and sweetest of our lives. Lord! to be for ever young! I want to hear, too, of the Complete Edition. And when soon we've jointly rounded that, le's git off together somers for a little holiday of about ten or 'leven years, in which we will grow young again indeed. With all best remembrances to your household one and all,

Your always grateful and affectionate
JAMES WHITCOMB RILEY.

---

*Harris's son.

CHAPTER VIII

Poetry and Life and Death

Letter to a child—A letter in dialect to "Uncle Remus"—Yale confers honorary degree—Friendship with Professors Phelps and Beers—Death depresses Lockerbie Street—*An Old Sweetheart of Mine* and *Out to Old Aunt Mary's*—The painting of the Sargent portrait—McCutcheon cartoons *The Old Swimmin'-Hole*—University of Pennsylvania confers degree of Doctor of Letters—Easing Up.

To Miss Dorian Medairy.

Dorian was the little niece of Riley's friend, the poet Edith M. Thomas. The charming correspondence of Riley and this little child was printed in full in *Harper's Magazine*, December, 1917.

Indianapolis,
Sept. 25, 1901.

Miss Medairy Dory-Ann
Cast her line and caught a man,
But when he looked so pleased, alack!
She unhooked and plunked him back.
"I never like to catch what I can,"
Said Miss Medairy Dory-Ann.

My dear Miss Medairy Dory Ann:
No use trying, for I just can't tell you how proud I am of your letter and the portraits too—though to save me I

255

can't see, by your picture, which arm it is that has been hurting so.—Strange that the artist should take the arm so lifelike and yet leave out the ache! Surely he must have neglected something, the day you sat—wasn't it a dark and damp sort of a day, so that the chemicals smelled too thick or did the artist fail to smother himself long enough under the velvet cover of his camera? Or did he, by some fateful oversight, fail to instruct you to "look pleasant," "lift the chin," "moisten the lips," "wink" like a kinetoscope and "hold perfectly still,"—all at one and the same sneezable instant! Be this all as it may, I'm rejoiced at the beautiful result—the portraits both to adorn the walls of my already storied Temple of Fame. Yes, and I'm going to *try* to take your advice as to writing more "Runaway Boys" and "Orphant Annies."

Very gratefully your old Hoosier friend,

JAMES WHITCOMB RILEY.

Our teacher Miss King,
She's the *sweetest* thing,
    And I'll tell you the reason why,—
She dresses in light
Lawn, yellow and white,
    And looks like a custard pie.

To Joel Chandler Harris.

Indianapolis,
Jan. 28, 1902.

Dear Uncle Remus:

What's it I'm a-hearin' 'bout you-all tryin' to let on you're sick. Hit's all des a scannal-a-shame, fo' the livin' God, fer a grea'-big cum'bous heavy-sot man lak you is,

Sep. 25
1901

MISS MEDAIRY Dory = Ann
Cast her line and caught a man,
But when he looked so pleased, alack!
She unhooked and plunked him back.—
"I never like to catch what I can"
Said Miss Medairy Dory = Ann.

My dear Miss Medairy Dory = Ann:

No use trying, for I just can't tell you how proud
I am of your letter and the portraits too — though
to save me I can't see, by your picture, which arm
it is that has been hurting so.— Strange that the
artist should take the arm so lifelike and yet have
out the ache! Surely he must have neglected some=
thing the day you sat — wasn't it a dark and damp
sort of a day, so that the chemicals smelled too
thick? or did the artist fail to smother himself long
enough under the velvet cover of his camera? or didn't,

Letter to Miss Dorian Medairy with illustrated stanza by Mr. Riley

by some fateful oversight fail to instruct you to
"look pleasant", "lift the chin", "moisten the
lips", "wink" like a Kinetescope and "hold perfectly
still",— all at one and the same sneezable instant.
Be this all as it may, I'm rejoiced at the beautiful
result—the portraits both to adorn the walls of my
already storied Temple of Fame. Yes, and I'm going
to try to take your advice as to writing more
"Runaway Boys" and "Orphant Annies".

      Very gratefully your old Hoosier frien'

        — James Whitcomb †

Our teacher Miss King,
She's the sweetest thing,
   And I'll tell you the reason why;
She dresses in light
Lawn, yellow and white,
   And looks like a custard pie.

a-quilin' down an' a-actin' up lak you de mos' misfo'tunate creetur wot range de wile-woods o' dish eartly worl'!

Well, it's good to hear from you, even though the news includes a hint of your indifferent health,—for I know just what ails you,—and even now I'm suffering in like way and for exactly the same reason, though in your case you do about three or four times the weight of overwork that brings me down. Of course we have side-shoots of afflictions in endless variety, but they could be lightly tolerated if we didn't positively feed and pamper them, in-directly, by deliberately supplying them with the over-jaded brawn-and-brain they thrive on—same as chicken-feed! So I won't ever overwork no more! And oh! if there's a lovelier thing than work (when the whole exquisite machinery is just a-clickin' right) I've never overtaken the unnamable rapture yet. Nor have you, I know.

But now I'll not vex you any longer.—On'y it *do* 'pear-lak to me you might find *some* rest in writin' of a shore-nuff letter to the livin' sinner who is a-tryin' so hard to "keep his eye fixed on de Polyar Star!" With best greet-ings to all,

Your ever grateful and affectionate,

JAMESY.

To J. Ray Peck.

Indianapolis,
Feb. 14, 1902.

Dear sir:

For the package of books (herewith returned), sent for my signing, will you not kindly accept the requisite auto-graphs on inclosed slips, to paste in the volumes—thus sav-ing, at one and the same lick, not only a hurried man but one who knows no terror comparable to that of unwrapping and re-wrapping and tying and stamping and addressing and carrying and loading into the book hopper a ding-dasted book.

Very truly your friend and mine,
JAMES WHITCOMB RILEY.

To Joel Chandler Harris.

Riley refers below to *The Book of Joyous Children*, in process of publication. Riley dedicated this volume to Harris. The dedicatory poem, one "To 'Uncle Remus'," and a third, "Ef Uncle Remus Please ter 'Scusen Me," will be found in the Biographical Edition, V, pp. 198, 114, 360.

Indianapolis,
May 5, 1902.

Dear Uncle Remus:

What's all this good news I'm ahearin' about your recovery! Both Evelyn and Geiger have been keepin' me informed; and now "the Geiger" tells me that you're not sick at all, and that he actually caught you down town a-tryin' on some bran'-new gyarments at the Clothin' store! Well, you rascal! you might jes' as well quit your 'possumin' from this on and take and whirl in and pay me what you done owe now for months and months! But—most seriously I am rejoiced over your happy restoration—so much rejoiced, in fact that I've shot up into such perfect health and gratefulness myself that I've dedicated my new book to you in three Eulogistic stanzas that ought to curl the hair of any man's immortal soul! The volume is as yet a closely-guarded secret, but solemnly swearing you to divulge no word of it, the Scribners are to publish it, with profuse illustrations—a letter yesterday from Mr. Arthur Scribner thus opening: "We have taken the greatest interest in reading your manuscript and are more than pleased with it. It should certainly make a most popular and successful book, and you may rely upon our doing everything in our power to further this." So you can readily see why I'm a-feelin' sorto' gaily.

> As I write—as I write—
> With such a certain victory in sight!!

The book is solid child-verse—about half and half dialect and my best English,—but all of it right next the ground—wholly simple, natural and wholesome. Fact is, your doin' of such good work these days of your continuous youth has inspired

Your always admiring and affectionate
                                        JAMESY.

Gen. Fitzhugh Lee lectured to great and enthusiastic house here last night—the G. A. R.'s nobly welcoming him, with the general citizenship—an occasion that thrilled. Send Evelyn along to me for our monument dedication. Best greeting to all the home-folks.
Am sending you *Journal* report of Lee's reception, this same mail.

To Dr. William Lyon Phelps.

Indianapolis,
May 20, 1902.

My dear friend:
You're the feller! And oh but it did astonish even my astonishment! Just to think of me trying to be coy in the

acceptance of such an honor—from Y A L E ! Well, God knows, I tried, in my deliberated response to your honorable secretary, to be calm. . . . No worthy expressions of my thoughts or thanks are in reach of this stricken pen now. But I do realize and appreciate to the full your hand and heart in it all. And I can but pray that you favor me further with such counsel as may help me, in the coming ordeal, not to wrong your estimate of your friend's worthiness.

Fraternally, gratefully, everyway, yours,

JAMES WHITCOMB RILEY.

And was it—ever—I don't know—that a woman-poet received the just scholastic honor accorded man? And who but your truly great Yale personality might be the first to honor Edith M. Thomas—as true a poet, and as proved, as any in our solely pure English—American lists.

J. W. R.

To Dr. William Lyon Phelps.

New Haven,
June 26, 1902.

My dear friend:

This is all pure magic—Dr. Riley here in your own library writing to you whose presence is so longed for! But Heaven bless you for so promptly going in your health's behalf—besides, here in your lovely home I have found your gentle welcoming mother and brother, who gave your home over to me, though I offered them fairest opportunity to leave me quartered at the hotel—for we arrived late at night and there lodged—going to find your people and explain at ten next morning.

Well I just can not realize all that has followed. It is enchantment, simply! Professor Beers has been a very brother through it all—and your brother likewise. Doctor Hadley was an inspired man throughout all the ceremonies of yesterday. Yea, and last night at reception at Art Building, where your brother took me, "and the world went well with me then, then, oh, then!" But you'll hear of the success of everything through the press and your friends—never a hitch in any particular that I'm aware of. Even read a poem (bran' span fresh and new) though in no wise pertinent to the occasion—which I priorly explained to committee, and they said give it—and I done give it and it seemed to "go" in really very great shape!* We may be going on to New York to-day, where (utter confidence) I've a new book in press—the first copy of which shall be sent to you—possibly in September—though I'll not know certainly till conference with publishers. All your home-folks send love to you and Mrs. Phelps, with this most grateful greeting of your affectionate old friend,

JAMES WHITCOMB RILEY.

To Prof. Henry A. Beers.

Indianapolis,
July 1, 1902.

Dear friend:

It's all a dream indeed, but I'm mighty glad and grateful that I've had it—in your comradeship—the pastoral slopes of the Mitchell home, the lovely daughters and the master—all of which I've tried to talk of to the reporter

---

*"No Boy Knows," *Lockerbie Book,* No. 366.

of the press who even beat me home to my ain fireside. Well, God bless you! I whizzed away ere a chance to thank you for it all—the shore-dinner—everything an utter, gracious novelty to me. Nor will I vex you with a word—knowing you know, by divine right, all I would say but can not.

Gratefully and affectionately yours,

JAMES WHITCOMB RILEY.

To Dr. Henry van Dyke.

Indianapolis,
(Probably Dec. 12, 1902.)

Dear Friend:

Your book and your poem are alike glorious to me, though my home here has long been overshadowed with the dark, dread wings of Death*, nor has it affected "God's in His heaven and All's right with the world."

Even were my head and heart and pen at their blithest, could I make you just rejoinder—even with an age of deliberation in which to round and finish, pet and pat and then pass on to you the best possible job my shop could turn out. But "Never mind!" I keep saying over and over—to myself "Jist never mind!—Some day I'll get the swing o' things in the ringin' singin' way, and then let Mr. Dr. van Dyke look out, or I'll lift him clean off his blessed feet!"† As to the exquisite stories, I have only read them incipiently, so to say—in the stress and appre-

---

*The reference is to the deaths at the Lockerbie Street home and are referred to more definitely in the letter to Miss Thomas following.

†Dr. van Dyke wrote a tribute "To James Whitcomb Riley, Gardener." Later Riley replied, "On Reading Dr. Henry van Dyke's Volume of Poems—Music." (*Lockerbie Book*, No. 316.)

hension continually about our stricken home. But they
will only be appreciated the better for this divine foretaste.
God bless the true man's—and artist's—heart that beats in
them and all your work.

Your ever grateful, faithful friend,
J. W. R.

To Miss Edith M. Thomas.

Indianapolis,
Feb. 10, 1903.

Dear Miss Thomas:
Your account of your recent meeting with the venerable
and piteously bereaved poet's poet, Richard Henry Stoddard,* was pathetic in the extreme. Over and over, as I
read, long self-memorized lines of the old master went
over themselves, all sorrowfully murmuring—

> "But when Youth, the dream, departs,
> It takes something from our hearts,
>   And it never comes again."

and—

> "My wandering feet go up and down
> And to and fro from town to town—
> Through the lone wood, and by the sea,
> To find the bird that fled from me.   . .
> I followed, and I follow yet.—
> I have forgotten to forget."

Heaven bless the stricken man and comfort him in his
loneliness with loyal, loving friends. But how tired of

---

*Riley paid tribute to the poet Stoddard in "Your Height Is Ours,"
Lockerbie Book, No. 230.

death—death—death I am, these lonesome later years! In the immediate family here in which I have a home there have been three deaths in almost as many weeks;—the dear old father of the house met with a fall which brought on his death, within two weeks; then his old comrade and kinsman, one month later, fell, lingered, in terrible agony two weeks, and died; then the third of these old relatives fell—on the day of the second's funeral—and survived but three days. Not very cheerful matter to set down here, I admit, but that the strangely coincidental fatalities haunt me at times till, like that Ancient Mariner of the glittering eye, I can only relieve my mind of these tragic, dread and *ogerish* speculations by rehearsing the dark story to some helpless friend. Yet now and here shall close peremptorily this mortuary theme.

Wish I might have seen that Sandwich Island press notice. Surely that might have checked and cheered up even the heart of a true comedian!

You will recall, perhaps, that I promised to return to you more of the first letters, should I ever find more of them, as I thought probable. Well, I have unearthed some old trunks, packed with books, papers and letters— all in dreadful confusion, but intact, and restorable to order. So I am mindful of my promise, and will institute most careful search for your letters, every one. And this makes me wonder if my own first letters to you are—any of them—preserved—and, if so, might I have a sight of them, or copies of them? Tell "Dory Ann" some unknown artist has designed and sent to me an odd book-plate. I enclose it, before establishing it as my books' hall-mark, for her advice. To confess my real feelings, I'm afraid it's a *hoodoo:* The very old-time boy carrying the books, in the first place, is a very wabbly boy, and (mark ye!) the number of the books—as I make out—is— thirteen.

As ever gratefully and truly yours,
JAMES WHITCOMB RILEY.

To John J. Curtis.

In 1902 The Bowen-Merrill Company issued *An Old Sweetheart of Mine* in an edition illustrated by Howard Chandler Christy. The popularity of the book was such as to set a record for royalties paid by any poem up to that date. Mr. Curtis was now projecting *Out to Old Aunt Mary's* and suggested that the book would have a wider appeal if the poem were addressed to a sister instead of a brother. The poet set aside this temptation to increase his royalties for the reasons explained. These poems are Nos. 54, 6, *Lockerbie Book*.

Indianapolis,
Feb. 25, 1903.

Dear friend:

Your suggestions regarding possible changes in the old poem are excellent, for some reasons, but hurtful, for tother reasons—one vital one especially, i. e.,—that the real heart or core of the poem would be weakened and its present life-force assuredly wasted if not lost entirely. Even its supreme effect (the final stanza) would be cruci- fied and the dear old woman's dying words of "Tell the *boys* to come" either wrested wholly from her lips or recast in a distortion of phrase perforce, to admit the proposed feminine character. No, my dear friend, it can not survive any further change. And—mind you—like its "Old Sweet- heart" model, its original first form must be preserved in- tact, as made necessary by their fixed form in the volumes. Hope to have a line of any comment from you at once, though I do hope you can accept my argyment as con- vincin'!   Very truly yours,

JAMES WHITCOMB RILEY.

To —— E.

Indianapolis,
Feb. 27, 1903.

My dear E.:

Your characteristic letter of the twenty-third is here. Nothing in my course of action needs explanation, if you'll just think some when you write. Of course, you expect your desires to be respected, but do you respect mine? Seemingly, not in the least. In the very first place, you ask me to do a thing I have nothing to do with on earth or in the heaven, namely, to go romping into the political bull-pen, and write a friend of mine in office a letter, begging him for a favor for another, when I wouldn't dare ask of him a favor for myself. All of which writing process—in this particular instance—is entirely unnecessary, since Senator F.* already knows, and has long known, that I am your friend. So I don't write, for two good reasons,—the first, as above intimated; the second, for the helpless illness in which your letter found me—and which illness you were promptly apprised of by my secretary. Then what do you do but bang away at me with another letter, questioning my veracity this time but with the further demand for that letter of tribute—(extolling your veracity, I suppose) which same letter for the second time, I don't write. And then you work the galvanic battery on me (still a helpless invalid) and you wire me till my eyeballs jingle, and I roll over and moan "My God! won't he ever think!" No, sir! you bet he won't, for here—Biff!— boom!—ph—th—y-zzt! explodes another letter, with its re, re, *re* iterated demand for that letter of mine, to be di-

---

*Senator Fairbanks, later Vice-President of the United States.

rected to an overburdened senator who doesn't want one other letter of that variety—especially from me. Indeed, it is possible that his friendly symptoms may be accounted for by my never having written him such a letter as his million other friends are daily sending him. Therefore help me to continue to seem worthy in his sight.—Let me spare him—and you spare me—then we'll all *stay* friends.

As ever yours,

JAMES WHITCOMB RILEY.

To Miss Edith M. Thomas.

Indianapolis,
April 10, 1903.

Dear Miss Thomas:

To-day I send you program and marked paper of late memorial services at Shilo battle-field*—an experience of very novel interest to me, being only a sort o' piping patriot—too young for our great civil war and too old for our recent bout with Spain. Truly heroic, sacred ground—yet the pathos of it all! . . .

"They pass and smile—the children of the sword—
　No more the sword they wield:
And O how deep the corn
　Along the battle-field!"

But however pathetic the ground, the graves, monuments and tablets, a fine spirit was manifest in both southern and northern elements—for, alas! we still are North and South, though very bravely striving to be one. Hence it was a beautifully thrilling thing to witness the native fine

---

*"Mr. Riley at Shiloh battle-field with Gen. Wallace and Henry Adams, of Indianapolis."

pride of the ex-Confederate orators and the magnanimous first share of the applause accorded them. Under breath a dozen times I said: "This is the way to be brothers indeed."

A very touching incident, too, occurred at the little town of Savannah, eight miles or so up the river, where we visited the Cherry mansion—Grant's headquarters. Here we were most hospitably received by Colonel and Mrs. Cherry—shown over the fine old house, with its Grant relics, and tragic associations,—the down-stairs room in which General W. H. L. Wallace died, and the room above in which died General Smith—close friend of General Lew Wallace of our party, standing reverently and with tears where died his comrade more than forty years ago. At the house and in the dooryard were assembled the entire town—school-children and all. Speeches were made from the piazza by everybody—and everybody truly inspired. And as our boat lingeringly left the thronging shore, the voluntary song *America* came to us, and I saw tears in many eyes—spangles of tears. Pardon me that I can so forget all other things to write of and ask about. In your last letter there was a reference to a threatened illness of your sister. By this I hope you can tell me of her recovered health with the like good health and high-heartedness of the little daughter Edith—(Never, never shall I call her "Dory-Ann" again till her mother is well and strong and home with her once more.) The poems of Lorrimer Stoddard I have to thank you for, finding them of especial interest for his sake and the mother's and father's—God bless them and make them as one again.

As ever your grateful and fraternal,
JAMES WHITCOMB RILEY.

To Dr. William Lyon Phelps.

Indianapolis,
April 20, 1903.

My dear friend:

What word can I speak to you at such a time?—when the Mother's voice speaks not nor will be heard again, however you may yearn for it with tears and prayers. Ah, but the glory of the Promise! Surely you must be upheld by that. How beautiful here has been her life and her life-work,—how for her family has she lived and lovingly wrought; and, with her great generous heart and gifts, how she has wrought for the world's good and won its gratefulness and love. Why, even here her life was an inspiration and her vision divine. Then what must be the measureless, changeless happiness of the World she walks in now.

> "And the heart kept tune to the carol of birds,
>   And the birds kept tune to the songs which ran
> Through shimmer of flowers on grassy swards,
>   And trees with voices Aeolian. . . .
> And under the trees the angels walked,
>   And up in the air a sense of wings
> Awed us tenderly as we talked
>   Softly in sacred communings."

God comfort and bless you here continually, and, in His own good time, bless you even as now He blesses the beloved Mother.

My gentlest sympathy to your family—all.

Always with fraternal affection, your friend
JAMES WHITCOMB RILEY.

To Dr. James Newton Matthews.

Indianapolis,
Apr. 27, 1903.

Dear old friend:

Well—well—well! It was funny—your experience as to the "Sandie McPherson" sketch,—for—as you surmised—I did hand a clipping-copy of it in to the *Journal,* that other admirers of Buchanan might happily come upon it, aside from the many copies I marked and sent, even as the one to you. Telepathy, as you say. To add to my great enjoyment of the story, I'm just "lickin' my chops" over Jane Carlyle's letters, with most agreeable, genial, direct and indirect testimony that Carlyle was not the sour, dour, sorehead, selfish old Scotch bear he has been pictured, but, indeed, the very character of *jocoserie,* (at times) as this Buchanan reminiscence indicates. So you have your "Sandie McPherson"—and he's in the penitentiary? Mine ain't, but, damn him, he ought to be! Have you any of Buchanan's poems? They're our kind, and I'll try hard to get them for you—though, fine as they are, they seem hardly known, and can only be found among "out of print" lists. But I'll institute search at once—or send my volume. So write.

Your description of the Effingham entertainment made me blush like an embarrassed rainbow. How I wish I had been there invisibly,—to have, at least, heard your part of the program,—the other "numbers" I have heard for,

"A thousand years, my own Columbia!"

And your boy, and my namesake, is a poet sure enough. Reading his first poem, I turned 'way back to mine,—and

he beats me.   That's what!   God bless him—and every one
of us.   Your affectionate old friend and songmate
JAMES WHITCOMB RILEY.

To Bliss Carman.

Riley was on his way to sit to Sargent for the portrait which
is the frontispiece to this volume.

Indianapolis,
May 7, 1903.

Dear Carman:

Your letters "come" slower than butter by the old churn-
ing process, but they're equally rich and oleaginous when
they do "come."   Just as this last one arrives I am packing
my trunk for a brief and lonesome *pasear* over toward
your way, for I can't possibly attain New York—but I'm
inspired to hope that you can come the differing distance,
as my guest, mind you,—joining me at Philadelphia
(Hotel Walton), where I'm to arrive the coming 10th—
and to remain three, four, five, or six days.   And now—
do come, and we'll have a glorious session of real serious
hopeful, helpful interchange.   You will find me weller
than you've ever seen me, and you'll see me growing better
and better wisibly, before your wery eyes!
JAMES WHITCOMB RILEY.

To Mrs. Charles L. Holstein.

Philadelphia, Pa.,
May 11, 1903.

Dear St. Lockerbie:

This page of promptness is by way of tangible evidence
that I have really reached destination, though the perverse

Fates have kept steady pace with me from the start. But I'm here, and in a fire-proof house—trunk, hand-bag, overcoat, and even umbrella—all safely under one ceiling—so I find myself a truly grateful little man, though a very weary one. Slept little in the car last night, as I had the porter leave the window well up, for air, and the result was, splendid ventilation but chill sleeping. Mr. Fletcher was not at train, but sent his friend Mr. William Frederic Stilz, an old-time Indianapolis man who well knew your father and Charles, and spoke tenderly of them. Mr. Stilz proved himself a Mascot, for he took my trunk-check and dived under the station—I curiously following—where the baggage was being wheeled in from my very train before my very eyes! And as one load after another came trundling in, still with no trunk of mine among 'em, I begun to nurse "a fearful joy" in the prospect of its having jumped off the train again at Indianapolis, but, lo-and-behold-ye, the presence of Mr. Stilz was too much for it, so here it coyly came, at last, on the ultimate last truck-load of the whole shootin'-match! So, as you can imagine, I am installed in veritable content in this regard. Indeed everything seems auspicious—from weather to like bright and golden expectancies. Even ventured half a dozen squares from the hotel all by myself—and, mystery of mysteries! here I am, safe back again, all calmly setting forth the almost incredible fact.

As ever your affectionate

JAMESY.

To Mrs. Charles L. Holstein.

Philadelphia, Pa.,
May 12, 1903.

Dear St. Lockerbie:

Now everything is all well and settled into positive course of real accomplishment. Am just back from Mr. Sargent, after a casual little sitting of above five hours— two before luncheon and three following—at studio of Mr. S's friend, Mr. John Lambert. We all got on together finely—talking and laughing throughout the magic growth of the portrait; and when at such times the magician rested his brushes and bespelled subject he would beguile us with interludes of wizardry at the piano. My impression of him was (in whispered thought)—"What a truly, simply, naturally great man you are!" But to see the wonderful speed yet most accurate skill of his work! Why, with but this first sitting, the picture looks as though it had had the elaborate and exacting labor of a week. We lunched at the storied old home of Mr. Lambert—his mother presiding,—proud of her artist-guest and proud of her artist-son. Proud, too, of much very old and quaint china, and the historic, venerable home. Not a palace of its ancient day or now, she intimated—for the rooms were neither vastly spacious nor high of ceiling; but they had well known the presence of such distinguished friends and disciples of that old-time elect that owned the sway of that most striking, brilliant leader, Mrs. Gillispie—whose worth I know far better than how to spell her name. Nor must I forget to tell you that doors of the old house were of solid mahogany—over which we were preparing to marvel, till our laughing hostess informed us that solid

mahogany woodwork was so common in the old-time resi-
dences that they could be found to-day in poorest tene-
ment-houses, painted over with the cheapest paint—and
absolute truth. Just think of it!

    With best wishes and abiding love as ever,

JAMESY.

To Mrs. Charles L. Holstein.

Philadelphia, Pa.,
May 16, 1903.

Dear St. Lockerbie:

    The good work goes on apace, and but a few days
more'll see me home again. Of course Philadelphia is not
to be compared to New York for crowds and tumult and
bewilderment, yet it serves! Already I am verging upon
hysteria with the swirl and worry, and most heartily yearning for utter immolation from it all. The friends here are
finding out where I'm at and swooping down on a fellow
in ever-increasing numbers, together, too, with all kinds
and conditions of men who want me to call on them, in
return, at No. 11296 E. 'Steenth Street, Old Mesopotamia
Bldg., Court Entrance N. W. 9th floor, Rooms 920 to
984—just a step from the Spencer & Pphencer Street University Park Square below Penn Place New Gubernator-
ial Agricultural Institute—just a step from my hotel—
but *might* take the street-car or a cab though just a step—
just a step!—Can't possibly miss it! Well, just the same,
when I agree to go anywhere, some one's got to come and
git and lead me there like a blind man who has seen better
days!

    But I have met some great folk here, as well as Mr.
Sargent and Mr. Lambert—great artists, musicians,

travelers and cosmopolites, both of them. And it was in
their studio I was destined to meet Dr. Weir Mitchell, and
most happily indeed. Mr. Sargent has just put the very
last touches upon a most striking and picturesque portrait
of Doctor Mitchell, for some notable institution of the city
here, where the gifted doctor is universally loved as well
as honored. Last night I dined with him and his family—
most inspiredly, be sure—for the table at which we sat was
once George Washington's.—And I'm certain, too, that
as the distinguished, courtly host thereat, the former could
never have surpassed the present one. Then to the library, with a wake of aromatic coffee—and cigars. But
I can't begin, even, any report of the treasures there, ransacked from all climes and ages. A book of poetry with
the owner's name therein writ thuswise W. Raleigh. But
I read no line of the verse; it was in Italian. Robert
Burns' copy of Pope, also, was even a lovelier volume to
reverently lift and hold and have, for some minutes wholly
mine.—But all—all the list of like opulent treasures I
must reserve till home again. Have vainly hoped for a
letter from you. One letter from Mr. Dickey, however,
assures me of your steadfast improvement in health—the
news I most of all desire to hear. Hope, too, the Mother
and all are well. Am coming some time next week—will
write exact time soon as known. With all best love and
cheer.

JAMESY.

Have found a fascinating dealer in curios and everything,
who is trying to find our chandelier. All best greetings to
the friends.

To Booker T. Washington.

Indianapolis,
June 20, 1903.

Dear Sir:

With all heart and spirit I thank you for your fine life-story, *Up from Slavery*. You have, I believe, started out and are going on with an inspired life-work; and with increasing faith and joy I see, by the press, that your righteous first purpose in that chosen field of earthly duty is not to be deflected by any honors whatsoever.

With hale congratulations and godspeeds.

JAMES WHITCOMB RILEY.

To John T. McCutcheon.

Indianapolis,
July 29, 1903.

Dear Child-heart:

What a literal lovely bit of boyhood you have drawn!* The picture is just here, and I'm taking down an old master to give the gang and the dawgs a fitting place in my fine art's inmost shrine. Oh, but you do lift back into realest life the utterly, unobjectionably, ornry boy of my happy childhood—till I see him again—hear him again—*follow* him again—and am him again—even to his starkest gymnastics at the swimmin' hole after his abhorrent anointings of himself with fishin'-worm oil—melted on the barn-roof, in a big-mouthed bottle by the sun in dog-days,

---

*The reference is to McCutcheon's inspired cartoon showing the barefoot gang painfully picking its way down the railroad track in the blazing sun to "The Old Swimmin'-Hole."

where the heat beat hotter than the core of a "bile" and
the clabboards warped and turned up like a burnt boot!
Wherefore and therefore, I am your always grateful, faithful and loving little playmate,

BUD RILEY.

To Joel Chandler Harris.

Indianapolis,
Aug. 12, 1903.

Dear friend Harris:

Our old friend Geiger has just been here on—for him—
a long, leisurely visit of three whole days. Can you realize
the truth of such a statement? Well, we enjoyed his
presence, though at no one time did he sit down long
enough to get up again without pitchin' sideways. Bob's
a lovely, gentle, infinitely tender cuss, but, in all seriousness, I sometimes half suspect he lacks repose. Upon his
return to Atlanta I meant to sag him with an extra load
o' news for you,—but Bob don't leavetake after customary
fashion.—Oh, no!—He doesn't want to disturb anybody,
possibly, and so he always gets out o' the house like a
burglar gets in, and we never dream of his being gone till
we go to call him to breakfast—mind you, a special breakfast, outlined, designed, fore-ratified and approved—then
patiently and deliberately executed—for a dod-gasted
renegade, at that minute, doubtless, flooding his dam'
gutless insides with union-station-coffee, and waitin' for
a "wild freight" in which he can really be as dad-dam'
humble as a just-scrubbed-out caboose'll let him! Well,
as I started to say:—I meant to send some particular
word to you by Bob, but lo! he was not! Wanted, too, to

stick a few books in his "grip"—which reminds me.—
Please tell me how many copies of Author's Edition of
Joyous Children you can possibly use. Hastily, on receipt
of edition, I sent you all I could crowd into the box at
hand, but I want you to have not only all you want, but
more than all you want,—so give me early word, and with
any instructions as to my autograph in 'em, or left un-
stained, and white and fair as any fainted snowflake. And
do tell me—isn't the little compressed volume exquisite—
in each minute detail—press, paper, binding, form,
size—everything?

This hain't no letter—but the best I kin do now. All
best greetings to your home-folks, every one—even the
prospective daughter,—for from many sources I gather
that your brave good boy Evelyn is to marry soon, God
bless him!

As ever your grateful and affectionate old friend and
porchmate,

JAMESY.

To Meredith Nicholson.

Indianapolis,
Aug. 14, 1903.

Dear friend Nicholson:

It's a feat pen that you wield, and the grace and the
play and the point of it, all combine to warn a mere
buckler of swashes cunningly to call your attention to
some opposite view of the landscape and then brain you
with a swift, coarse, pig-iron paragraph entirely foreign to
the matter in controversy. At all events I'm not going to
try now to make legitimate rejoinder to any page of yours,

save that which most strictly bears upon the weather—and even upon that topic I shall not commit myself as endorsing your high praise of it, but will, rather, reservedly admit—as Joe Long once did to the twelfth man in succession who told him it was a fine morning,—"I have heard it very highly spoken of."

But it's good to hear anything of you—especially of your improved health and that of your wife and children. But I can see when you talk of your return and the prospective house-warming of the new home, that your family's united heart is right here in old Indianapolis—high Heaven's sole and only "understudy."

Your old fraternal
JAMES WHITCOMB RILEY.

To Eugene V. Debs.

Indianapolis,
Sep. 1, 1903.

Dear old friend:

If it be possible during hurry and stress of prospective appearance in your beloved city, I eagerly engage to be your guest, but should that longed-for privilege be denied me, through any reason, I'm at least going to call upon you and Mrs. Debs in your blessed home that has been made to seem my own since my first welcome there. However, my manager, Mr. Dickey, who alone arranges all things defying time and tide, will do his level-best for me in this instance, and I shall most yearningly pray that I am to have far more than a casual session with you at your ain fireside—for indeed it has been an age since the Fates have permitted just opportunity, to say nothing of proper length of time, in which we might once more set in commensurate motion "The whirring spindle and the rushing flame!" or again, with patriotic ire and tossing palms and pulsing hearts and pounded breasts, recount how "in the early gray of the morning of the 12th of April, 1861, the roar of a mortar and the shriek of a shell, followed by the report of fifty heavy cannon, warned the little Garrison at Fort Sumter that its stay was short. Charleston was drunk with excitement. Thousands flocked to her quays and crowded her streets in proud exaltation; the bells pealed a merry chime and cheers rent the air!"

Thus it is I am projecting myself into a vision of the future which I most earnestly trust may become, in near time, a wholly tangible reality all happily to be permitted and brought about by Providence and Mr. Dickey.

With ever the halest greetings to you and yours, and especial thanks for your invitation of this morning, I am

With affectionate esteem

Your old friend,

JAMES WHITCOMB RILEY.

To Robert Underwood Johnson.

Indianapolis,

Sep. 12, 1903.

Dear friend:

You are eminently right as to the inaccuracy of rhyming "were" with "fair," even though Hood's authority admits it as perfect and the entire quorum of Elizabethans have not winced in so employing it. Likewise you justly mark the error of intruding the moral question into the lyric.* My only defense of the song is that it was born

---

*"The Old Days," *Lockerbie Book,* No. 339.

artlessly—with these birthmarks rather than piquing what native grace and beauty it possessed—for me. Indeed, as the feller says,—"I'm prejudiced in its favor" *yet,* to that extent I can't bring myself to overhaul it, as you suggest. Later on I may be able to do this. Then you may look for what I hope may be a happier if less artless result.

As ever your grateful, faithful
JAMES WHITCOMB RILEY.

To Miss Dorian Medairy.

Indianapolis,
Sep. 19, 1903.

Dear Dory-Ann:

Your last letter was so short I couldn't laugh over it only just a little. And then you choose such small words and write them in so big a hand on such a weenty-teenty page, that just about the time your letter gets to tasting good-and-creamy, I've got it all licked up! So I think, when you hint about some folks being "pretty mean," that you must have in mind a certain girl I know—and that's you your-own-sef! (and I spelt self thataway a-purpose.) But the other day I was a little mean, I guess,—when my little third-cousin Helen broke away from her Pa (my second-cousin) and his Pa (my first-cousin) and ran right in front of a street-car and almost under the wheels, when her Pa grabbed her, and she was 'most about to cry, and I laughed at her and clapped my hands and said "Goody! goody! goody! you come purt'-near-a-gittin' run over! Goody!—Goody! that's what you git when you're only ist somebody's third-cousin!"

All right about the turkey that died of old age, waiting for me to come help eat him!—If that's a picture of him you made, why, I think he wasn't the kind of turkeys folks eat, anyhow—'cause you made him with four legs, like a work-stand, so you ought to have made casters on him— 'stid o' toes! Eatin'-turkeys has only got *two* legs. Here's a picture of a eatin'-turkey—

And here's a eatin'-turkey poem:—

> When Dory Ann she gave a tea,
> She specially invited me,
> With other children, two or three,
>   And asked us all to *come* quick—
>
> "Because," she wrote, "dear friends I've got
> A turkey for you, steaming hot,
> And each of you—forget it not—
>   Shall have a savory drumstick!"
>
> But when her four guests came, and she
> Cut off one turkey-leg for me
> And one for her—why, there were three
>   More guests might suck their thumbs slick!—
>
> A Eatin' turkey's hapless lot
> Is two lone legs, more guests or not,
> Two lonesome legs is all he's got,
>   And nary other drumstick!

Ever yore obedient servant and well-wisher ever thine
                Yours respectfully write soon
                                BUD RILEY.

> With joy too great for pen to state
> Or tongue to dare articulate.
> And I like you—and better too—
> Than angel-cake or rabbit-stew!

To Edmund Eitel.

Nephew, and subject of "The Rider of the Knee," dedicatory poem to *Rhymes of Childhood;* editor of Biographical Edition of Riley's Complete Works.

Indianapolis,
Sep. 25, 1903.

Dear Ed:

Your old uncle's mighty tickled with your letter, though I'd no idea how short it was till I looked it all over carefully and found, by both page and envelope it wasn't a telegram. If I could write letters as short as that, I'd answer every one fired at me, and so just measle the universe daily with a bird-shot splatter o' letters! Guess I'll bang away at you with one of that kind now! Glad your first impression of Cornell seems favorable to the University. That's right. You speak kindly words of and to it always, when you meet it on its lonely rounds. Bring ever a smile to its wistful features by chucking it under the cornice and patting it on the cupola! Not only your *parents* are missing you, but your poor old relative here at his desk, trying to write you cheerily while his brains are simply clabbered with the agonies and distresses of taking on poetical ballast for a three months' cruise on the public high seas of ever choppy platform work. This prospective work begins the coming Monday, and I enclose to you press notice marking exact itinerary. So inform with my best greetings, any friends of mine you may meet—especially the Nyes—and do write when you meet them and tell me all about them, every one.

As to your best intent, effort and attainment I am

thoroughly assured. No sound right-minded man can fail in this world or the next.

With all faith and affection of your

UNCLE JIM.

To George Ade and John T. McCutcheon.

Des Moines, Iowa,
Nov. 30, 1903.

Dear friends:

Ever since our parting I've been having a steady flow of bright surprising ideas—not the least of which is naturally in the interest of our sadly declining Drama and to the effect of obviating the present coyness of the general public in being discovered in questionable propinquity to the Box Office. In brief, the idea is that A's next play be written expressly for and around us three fellows.* Say! Won't that fetch 'em! Only thing troubles me is that I didn't think of it and spring it for discussion at our joyous "Bird Center" Social Function and Banquet in the Jury Room last night.

Hastily but ever heartily yours,

J. W. R.

All this, of course, strictly mum, but think it over!

To Miss Dorian Medairy.

1903. (undated)

Dear Miss Dory Ann:

Here's a new-old Hoosier game of "Authors." Of course it's a popular game here in Indiana, where the

*See letter from George Ade, Appendix, p. 334.

citizenship of the state is composed almost entirely of authors, as you may already know. As yet, however, I have not learned the game, as nearly all the other authors are playing, night and day; and, being somewhat clannish, I have registered a fatal vow that I will only play with mine own people. But, should you, there, in the freedom of your eastern unconventionalism, feel an inclination to test the indubitable recreation afforded by a practical knowledge of the subtle intricacies of the game, you will find full directions for the same clearly printed on the under-interior of the top of the case enclosing the deck— or, more elegantly, perhaps, the pack—of cards herewith so simply presented by

One of the Authors.

JWR.

To Wilbur D. Nesbit.

Mr. Nesbit showed this letter to a print-shop superintendent and he sent the following riposte: Mr. Riley's verse is fully appreciated but

> God made the printers, one and all,
> And rather than *damnation,*
> To those who master authors' scrawl,
> He gives His commendation!

Jan. 8, 1904.

Dear friend:

All belatedly my last book went to you yesterday— care *Tribune,* same as this. The book I've been purposely holding from you, through reason of its many *typic* errors, which same I've long since marked for correction;

but that edition, for some unaccountable reason, refusing to "jell," I send you the first in sheer despair.

> The first book far too bad to go
>   Till later plates were cast,
> And this last volume lost, you know,
>   I send the first at last.

Indeed I would mark the book's multitudinous errors but that I know your own glittering eye'll spot 'em—and grow dim with sympathetic tears too as you read a fellow-author's awful doom so pitilessly brought about by the all-justly bedamned printers! Surely—*surely*—for *their* sakes—there must be some fit Eternity of *indamnity!* Hah! then, in sooth,

> The Devil's feelings e'en were spared
>   His last humiliation,—
> If God would just damn *printers* there'd
>   Be plenty of damnation!

(Also there's a rather fairish number of other errors in the dainty brochure I'd like to saddle on the printers.)

But Hail to you, this New Year opening and throughout it! And to your household, all. How comes on your own Book Beautiful—and how the *prose* one, O Sweet historian of the heart?

As ever your grateful and fraternal
                        JAMES WHITCOMB RILEY.

To Jesse Y. Burk, A. M.

Indianapolis,
Jan. 11, 1904.

Dear Sir:

Your message, regarding the action of the trustees of the University of Pennsylvania, tendering to me the Honourary degree of Doctor of Letters—to be conferred at your University Celebration of Washington's Birthday, the coming February twenty-second,—is a welcome message indeed; and, with the tender, in all its implied requirements, most acceptable to me.

Profoundly sensible of the high honor extended, I am
Most gratefully and truly yours,
JAMES WHITCOMB RILEY.

To John Townsend Trowbridge.

Indianapolis,
Jan. 14, 1904.

Dear Mr. Trowbridge:

Surely magic is at work, just as I am reading the last pages of your all-enthralling history, *My Own Story,* and yearning for yet more and more of such a helpful, worthy life and such a human wholesome heart, here comes along the identically just comrade of the first volume—your *Poetical Works.* So I repeat all softly to myself and with the indrawn breath of awe of a delighted child,— Surely—surely magic is at work! As perhaps I told you in our recent meeting, much as the greater portion of your writings has appealed to me, your poetry has ever held first place in my regard, though not until now have I been blessed with but the meagerest bits and fragments of it, gathered and treasured, from my first serious boyhood's likings and selections; and now, that I have your own choice of all that melodious product, and gathered in one sumptuous volume, and from the gentle master's hand given over into mine—truly, truly, the voice of my joy and gratefulness can only quaveringly sigh where it should shout aloud, and lisp in broken whispers where it should break into song. But still am I assured of your clear and kindly comprehension of my appreciation of your noble gift and all it means to me now and, please God, shall mean to mine hereafter. Know, therefore, how deeply always I feel myself your debtor.

The friends you met here, all, are friends indeed, and your praises on their lips die not away. The especially favored group that sat with you about the board at the University Club recalls your presence there as the occasion of the happiest, most inspiring session ever brought about by any gracious guest. So you are remembered, honored, aye, and loved by my people; how then may my own esteem for you be measured but by my ever selfish claim to them that I knew and loved you first.

My friend, Mr. Dickey, was no less delighted than I at the extreme kindness shown in my behalf, both in the inscriptions of your books and your comment on your treasured letter of my truly callow days.* And again and yet again do I thank you for the great and lasting good which that recognition—by your honest heart and hand—inspired in the hope of my own heart and future possibilities. God bless you so continually.

Your ever grateful, faithful,
JAMES WHITCOMB RILEY.

---

*Riley tells how Trowbridge encouraged and influenced his early efforts in the letter to Rosalind Jones, August 4, 1880.

To Joel Chandler Harris.

Indianapolis,
Jan. 16, 1904.

Dear friend:

Wasn't it a rather curious happening that just the evening previous to the arrival of the personal copy of your beloved latest book of *Wally Wanderoon and His Story-Telling Machine*—a new enthusiastic neighbor brought me the volume—which same delectable dreamery I'd had some night-hours revel in when Your copy came in the morning. Truly, you've a way of making me positively young again, at times—and not only young, but grinningly, gigglingly, rapturously childish—just as I first was, when the whole world about me seemed a tingling delight—the morning summer-sun a dazzling, dewy, blossomy sleight-of-hand performance that made a youngster catch his breath in just such hysteric ecstasies as overtake him in the first long sweep and swoop of a woodland swing. . . . M-m!—how swirlingly, swooningly sweet!—sweet enough to cry over—yet you haf to laugh! Well, it's all somepin' like that. Anyway, I know you'll know everything I would say and can't. And it's good, too, to read between the lines your youthful buoyancy still manifest—still young in—

The childish faith in fairies, and Aladdin's magic ring—
The simple, soul-reposing, glad belief in everything.*

That's your glory, and I try to make and hold it mine—and *yit* I know I'm *a-age-in!* But the good Lord has us

---

*From "The Days Gone By," *Lockerbie Book,* No. 77.

in His care and keep—even as He has His Noble twain* of soldiers just passed on to their divine promotion. At their passing, mourning and love are universal, and the morning sun will smile on South and North as in serenest token of the changeless peace of God.

When you can—without neglecting your work—do please give me a few random lines,—'cause I'm a-beginnin' to think you're a-overlookin' my real importance in your estimation!—Oh, yes! that reminds me of a genu*ine* old Hoosierism I heard only a day or two ago—of an old-timer who declared against eating soup first at any meal.—"I've allus et my soup *last*," he said, "after all the substantials—so's to sorto' fill up the crevices."

With all best greetings to Mrs. Harris and your family all—and praying they too may urge your writing me,

I am, as ever,

Yours fraternally and affectionately,

JAMES WHITCOMB RILEY.

To Bliss Carman.

Indianapolis,
Jan. 21, 1904.

Dear Carman:

How I would like to join you in that truly fine library of poetry, but just now I'm showing some really serious symptoms of long overwork, and my best friend, who is first a physician, says I must at once rid myself of all responsibilities now so weighing me lop-sided—and instead of any work, for a long indefinite time I'm just to shed my literary overalls and go gamb'lin' round the

---

*Generals James Longstreet and John B. Gordon.

pastur'lands a-doin' nothin' but browsin' and grazin' on the coarsest grass and fodder findable—and no more tryin' to kick the stars loose for a long, elaborate, listless, loitering, lazy year, anyhow!   Have seen your friend Mr. Bryan—and glad to see him—but had to talk this way to him,—but "more dulcet, delicious and dreamy!"—so mildly, indeed, I'm half fearful now that he quit me, thinking I was favoring his proposition—as God knows I would favor it, were there a living, breathing chance for me to do it—I mean—to join with you in the certainty of the success awaiting the now almost completed and most worthy work.   But—as I tried to say to Mr. B.—if there is some indirect way in which I might be of service, you are to command me.   Can't you take a recess yourself for a few days and come help me loaf, and we'll talk, anyhow?   Other friends here, too, want a sight of you, well as

Your always fraternal and abiding friend,

JAMES WHITCOMB RILEY.

Postscript.

Indeed not until I *do* find you in *talking*-range can I at all hope to be able to express to you a tithe of my still increasing gratefulness for your recent gracious words of tribute to my latest chirps, cheeps and twitterings—which voice of praise, in veriest truth,

". . . can shake me like a cry
    Of bugles going by."*

---

*From Carman's "Joys of the Road."

CHAPTER IX

THE END

Last books—More letters to Dory Ann—"Riley Days" and the children—Honored by the Institute of Arts and Letters.

To Bliss Carman.

Indianapolis,
Apr. 21, 1904.

Dear Carman:

Here's a real ringing poem and its history in my memory and experience:—At its original first appearance (evidently) in *Scribner's Magazine,* June, 1875, I read it—thrilled by it, have been remembering bits of it ever since, and vainly trying to recapture it in its entirety. Well—a few months since I asked a friend here on a paper, and next day he picked up a just-published volume and Behold! "The Song of the Savoyards."

The volume—under title, *Selected Poems of Henry Ames Blood,* Washington, D. C. The Neale Publishing Company 431 Eleventh Street, N. W., MCMI.—The copyright line thus: Copyright, 1901, by Mary M. Blood. All of which means that I hope you can be the first to give it to the general world in your Anthology. So I've had copy of it carefully typed and send it herewith. Do write me it's not too late. And I've another bang-up MS. poem—a great dialect poem, by a preacher; and it's called

292

1903

Dr. William Lyon Phelps —

My dear friend:

What word can I speak to you
at such a time? — when the Mother's voice
speaks not nor will be heard again,
however you may yearn for it with tears
and prayers. Ah, but the glory of
the Promise! Surely you must be
upheld by that. How beautiful here
has been her life and her life = work. —
how for her family has she lived and
lovingly wrought; and, with her great –
generous heart and gifts, how she has
wrought for the world's good and won its

gratefulness and love. Why, even here her life was an inspiration and her vision divine. Then what must be the measureless, changeless happiness of the World she walks in now.

"And the heart kept tune to the carol of birds,
    And the birds kept tune to the songs which ran
Through shimmer of flowers on grassy swards,
    And trees with voices Æolian.....

And under the trees the angels walked,
    And up in the air a sense of wings
Awed us tenderly as we talked
    Softly in sacred communings."

God comfort and bless you here continuously, and, in His own good time, bless you even as now He blesses the beloved Mother. My greatest sympathy to your family — all.
      Always with fraternal affection, your friend
          — James Whitcomb Riley

"The Widder Plunkit's Kittle." It simply beats the band, and ought to be preserved throughout the ages. Write and I'll promptly find and send it.

As ever your affectionate

JAMESY.

To Bliss Carman.

Indianapolis,
May 7, 1904.

Dear friend:

When your Pipes of Pan volume III came yesterday I gave a great ecstatic jump, upon finding it dedicated to—myself!—truly the last man in the world I'd expected—therefore the now happiest and most grateful. All my night-session of reading and reveling I gave to these Songs of the Sea-Children—and over and over I said to you aloud, "God bless you, this is fine!" and "What uplift is in this—what force, and yet what grace and loveliness!" and "what dewy freshness of the very morning is here—newness—your own ringing statements of your own thoughts!" And 'way in the night I wrote and pasted a scroll in the eerie *Pan-scape* in the front of the book— across the center foliage of the trees and a copy of which scroll I make this morning and fold herein—hoping you'll likewise paste it in your personal volume. Have creased scroll just as it should set in hinge of the pages. And if you're not the most skilled of pasters, better look out or the dam' thing'll curl up on you to hell-and-gone!

As ever and always your grateful and fraternal

JAMESY.

To Miss Edith M. Thomas.

Indianapolis,
May 25, 1904.

Dear Miss Thomas:

Yesterday I sent you some news-clippings and menu-card, and came near enclosing a letter with same—but it's real summer, at last—at last! and I'm just too mortal-lazy for anything but outdoors. Your last letter shall soon be answered—when I can escape the dumb dull spell of indolence.

Our city has, for about a week, been entertaining Oriental Royalty—Prince Pu Lun. We count ourselves especially favored therefore by reason of Ambassador Wong selecting our town for the American home and schools to which he brings his wife. Mr. Wong—as he is called here generally, is universally liked, and deservedly. Though in dress throughout he is Chinese, he is subtly English in speech—or, rather, subtly American—a graduate of Harvard, no, of Yale. Is a notably good after-dinner speaker, with all the suavity, grace, and glance and play of wit and spicery the featest of these orators possesses. Last Sunday night the extreme honor was mine to take Mrs. Wong out to dinner (in about an equally blended party of Hoosiers and Celestials) though not permitted to sit at her side, but immediately next to the Chinaman who did. Anyway I humored the situation as amiably as possible, seeing the chair allotted me was next to that of His Highness', on the right. Certainly as wholly enjoyable a dinner, as Pepys might exclaim, "as ever I eat in all my life!" And oh, yes! Do tell Dory Ann that the Prince is just like us: He can't get enough

ice-cream!—As the colored waiter said, at a recent banquet: "W'y, that Chinaman Prince is the beatinest man
for ice-cream ev' I see!—I done give him three holpin's!"

As ever yours,
J. W. R.

To Meredith Nicholson.

It was a habit of Mr. Riley, among his friends, to burlesque a
certain type of unctuous itinerant preacher, just as he burlesqued
the pedagogue in his famous "The Peanut" recitation. This
letter to Mr. Nicholson is an example of this sort of badinage.

Indianapolis,
Sep. 3, 1904.

Dear Brother Brookwarble:
Truly there is both uplift and helpful furtherance in
your gladsome hail of recent date, and back I send you, in
promptest rejoinder, like greetings and godspeeds. Your
reference to your vernal surroundings and cloistered se-
clusion from the world, stress and tumult of the fevered
town comes to me, in veriest truth,

> "With a Sabbath-sound as of doves
>   In quiet neighborhoods,"

as that grand poet, Oliver W. Longfellow, so tersely puts
it in his own inimitable way. Every day I go up to The
Reader office, but guarded as are my approaches, Mr.
Howland contrives some way to evade my friendly call-
ings. Indeed I am half fearful he is giving himself over
to the allurements of the World, and that he is losing sight
of "the harvest of the quiet eye," and more and more be-

coming attaint with a moral strabismus, if I may thus
waggishly phrase it. Wish I could be with you and your
other noteworthy guests, and trusting that *The Master* is
not least of these, I remain

Your ever faithful fellow-pilgrim,

BROTHER BALMOOZLE.

To Honorable Harry S. New.

From Harry S. New to Librarian of Congress: "In 1904 I was
in charge of the Western Headquarters of the Republican Committee at Chicago for the campaign of that year, by designation
of Hon. George B. Cortelyou, who had been elected Chairman to
succeed Hon. M. A. Hanna. The attached letter, written in a
facetious vein, was written to me by James Whitcomb Riley,
the Hoosier poet, whose only purpose was to make sure of a
visit from his friend, Frank M. Nye, then a prominent lawyer of
St. Paul and a brother of Bill Nye (Edgar Wilson Nye) the
famous humorist, who was an associate and companion of Riley's.
The signature—'The Little Iron Harvester'—was one Riley occasionally employed in his personal talks, as well as his letters,
and, of course, it was employed with reference to his pretense of
the rôle of a farmer."

Sep. 9, 1904.

Honored Sir:

Word comes that you are again in the saddle once more
with the grand old party in the van till all hell freezes
over! Therefore God's most patriotic blessings rest upon
you till the cows come home! Old Marion is with you,
Harry, either on the firing line or at the polls. Every
time and all the time you can count on your old Hoosier
friends that has knowed you in the vanished past and still
is a-standing at your loyal back midst the clash of arms,
the shirring spindle and the rushing flume. See to it that

the best speakers is sent here to rouse up every sleepy hero nodding in the wild tumultuous ranks. Send Roosevelt, in all his peerless panoply of dispassionate diction: send Cortelyou, the cushion-footed cougar of the inner council: send each and all of your perfect pick of ornatest orators, and first and last and always, send us the Hon. Frank M. Nye, of The Great Northwest. Ever your old Standard-bearer and warm personal friend,

THE LITTLE IRON HARVESTER.

To Miss Dorian Medairy.

Indianapolis, Ind.,
Sep. 9, 1905.

Dear Dory Ann:

Thank you for the lovely post-card and message. Oh, no! I ain't dead at all, but just loafin' round, like the doctor said, or I would be took down, first thing I know, and wouldn't maybe be my old se'f till I was 'bout seventy years old—which is the vurry age which the Bible calls it "three skoren ten." So, you see, I got to be "connomizin' " in regards to also my health and my sole's welfare.

> "Sister, sister, come and see!
> 'Tis not a bird—'tis not a bee.
> Now it rises—up it gose—
> Now it settles on a rose."

I just write this poetry 'cause the other was beginning to sound like it was poetry too. Dozent it, allmost?

If your Aunt who is so grand a poettess was to see this poetry I spect she would be envious and spiteful with emotion! Long ago I wrote her a letter, and she has never

so much as wrote me a word in responce. All right for
her, say I!—Yes, and I *exclaime* it too with an ex-
claimenation-point!

Here come some strangers to see me, but I know what
they want, by their looks:—One of them is going to tell
me that the other one is a poet, and then the poet-one will
want me to "kindly" read a few reams of a poem he has
just begun and give him my "real" opinion of its merits—
"or demerits"—at which word, the janitor enters hurredly
to say I'm wanted at once in the directors' room above.—
And I don't never get no chance to discover the first
hemisphere of that beautiful poem!

Very truly yours and all the folks;

Bud Riley.

Write soon—and my! your composition is getting finer
and finer right along.

To Bram Stoker.

Bram Stoker the author of *Dracula,* was Henry Irving's
manager and lifelong friend. See "Henry Irving," Lockerbie
Book, No. 318. The poem appeared in *Collier's Weekly,* October
28, 1905.

Oct. 21, 1905.

Dear Mr. Stoker:

Every hour since the passing of your friend—and
mine—and the world's, I've been steadfastly seeing him
as at first, in the gentle Vicar's part, when, at the old
clock's signal, the brave head sinks over that awful duty
that is his to do. So even seems the stress and trial of his
lifework.—And even as invincibly his most honorable en-

actment of it. Now his rest is won, and with it his immortal glory. Show this, and proof-slip tribute, to the dear son I met when you were last here. God comfort him and his—and you and yours—and all who mourn. Amen.

As ever truly and in all sympathy,
JAMES WHITCOMB RILEY.

To Bliss Carman.

Indianapolis,
Nov. 2, 1905.

Dear Carman:

To hear again the voice o' your pen is a glory unto me! Just as for the thousandth time I was wonderin' why under the heavens you didn't write, here comes your blessed message, with the same old serenity and solidity of repose that simply anchors a feller 'way out in center of the roarin' deep o' Cark, Care & Company, where he can ca'mly address such remarks to 'em as, To hell with ye!

Well—it's mighty glad I am you're back home, where, once more entrenched from the weather's frosty shears and the bradawl jabs of the dam'd over-jocund winter, you may find true peace and comfort by your own most radiant and uproarious ingle—even as your likes is settling to it right here and now!

The publishers here have been getting another series of my old rhymes together which they named *Songs o' Cheer* (that is,—all I had to do with it was the little o'). Well, *"Cheer,"* of course, kept me thinkin' of you,—so I've dared to dedicate the volume to my dear old friend, Bliss Carman, who will now, I trust, cheerfully proceed to take his medicine. Your own personal copy of the book (the very first in my hands), with signed dedication, together with another—which you might care to send overseas—or cast within,—are en route, with this, by express. In God's name don't electrocute me for electrotyping you! Come instead, and sit by my fire and spin.

Mr. Howland*—Nicholson—Bobbs-Merrill retinue and ever'body that ever met you, send you halest greetings with these of mine. And God bless us every one.

JAMES WHITCOMB RILEY.

Hope you'll write me for any extra copies of "Songs o'" and gladly I'll sign and send any number you'd care to have seen by your friends any—and everywhere.

To Miss Dorian Medairy.

Dec. 14, 1905.

Dear Dory Ann:

When I got your nice, long really-truly letter I sprang right out of the doctor's care, exclaiming,—"Oh, it's a letter from Eidith Eudory—Ory—Ann,—thank you, maam!—Oh, thank you, *Mam!*" And it was so lejibbly wrote—I mean written, of course—and its words of languidge was so well—so well chozen, and speld so currect and jeudishous that—

---

*Mr. Hewitt H. Howland, later editor of *The Century Magazine*, was very close to Riley both as friend and in his capacity of editor of The Bobbs-Merrill Company.

Being a Jimpsy-jumpsy boy,
I Jimpsy-wimpsy jumped for joy.
And, now I've got *this* poem done,
N. Y. C. I's *another* one.

So now you can take a few home-lessons in equation and quotation from your Aunt Edithia Academicia; and then, with shining morning face, trip away to Miss Schoon-maker and quote at her the above striking lines, let the chips fall where they may!

I am very sorry to hear your arm isn't well and hurts so to be treated, but I bet your arm doesn't hurt as bad as both my eyes when the doctor puts more Tobasco Sauce in 'em and says "they're just a-lookin' fine!" Well—well—well! we mustn't complain about any old hurt. The very noblest men and women in this world, they hurt and hurt, all their lives and then left the brave words after them that it was really good to be hurt, while hope and faith and cheer always helped 'em to stand it. So always, mind you, we're to take new heart, with every new, accommodating hurt, and really thank it for being so obligingly overcome at last. Now, there's a very amiable hurt going to call to-morrow—as every day it has been calling on me for many long months—and it's the pure truth I tell you— I'll welcome its coming with an ever-growing pleasure, as compared with my first dread of its pitiless visits. Soon, though, I'll be able to read and write again, but now this is the longest letter I can write, so you must show it only to your folks—for it is for all of them as well as for you-your-own-se'f.

Yours respectfully, ever thine, your humble
Servant and well-wisher. Write soon.
BUD RILEY.

Merry Christmas to all!

To Lee D. Mathias.

(Indiana Society of Chicago.)

Indianapolis,
Dec. 14, 1905.

Dear Mr. Mathias:

Along with the invitation to the first annual banquet of the Indiana Society of Chicago comes your personal request for my presence, thus doubling the high honor conferred, and, alas! for me, doubling the weight of regret that bears me down even as a helpless, hopeless burden, realizing that you all want me and I all want you, while a perverse fate has implacably arranged to hold us separate—at least, upon this particular occasion—for it *is* particular, and to share its certain glory would be a lasting joy to me—for, while life lasts, my love for Indiana—even as yours—shall endure.   How the Good God has blest us, giving us such a home that even when the ever questing truant heart has ransacked the world and you have hacked a name of renown on the hip of the oldest pyramid ever "stacked up" on the oldest Ptolemy who died ages before he could spell his name,—many of you will recall how, even then, the thought of the little old crick-bridge or culvert 'way back home som'er's in Indiana, antedates the pyramidal age and claim,—since there your boy initials first went down in the gritty sandstone, along with—ooh, my boy! along with those of the little silent twilight girl at your side—ay, *still* at your side—and still silent.   And you hear the way the old brook used to sound—such a bewildering blend of liquid, plaintive, dulcet sweetnesses of music as the hearing yet, in memory, weeps over as it listens 'way back Home!   So, honoring our childhood's home, we honor too the sacred memories of father—mother—still wistfully awaiting our return—either by the lamplit window or the starlit skies.

Gratefully, loyally and fraternally yours,
J. W. R.

To Mrs. Madison Cawein.

Indianapolis,
April 12, 1906.

Dear Mrs. Cawein:

Your recent good letter has been answerless because of an illness from which only now I'm recovering—with friends, doctor and attendant all warning me that every attempt at, or thought of, anything like work must be avoided, at the peril of my life! Well, this page may kill me, but as I'll die if I don't write it, please know how sincere is my desire to be of service to you and my regret over my utter helplessness in the matter. To-morrow—for first time—am to try the fine Outdoors; and will soon know again, I trust,—*"God's in His Heaven—All's right with the world."* Wanted to be in Louisville the Old Kentucky Home coming and the Stephen Foster Monument unveiling, but alas! am not to be so favored. My best greetings and love to Madison (he to share same with Young E. Allison). Likewise to you all the best remembrances of Mrs. Holstein with these of

Your old Hoosier friend,
JAMES WHITCOMB RILEY.

To Mrs. Juliet Strauss.

Mrs. Strauss was the author of a popular column, "The Country Contributor," in the *Indianapolis News*, and *The Ladies' Home Journal*.

Indianapolis,
July 9, 1906.

Dear Mrs. Strauss:

When you started out by saying you didn't like Maeterlinck, I knew better,—'cause he looks at things from such new angles and with such fresh and refreshing insight, you (of all the capsicum elect) would just naturally *haf* to like him! So it was no surprise when your letter ended in his praise. Of course Lanier's another kind of battery and shocks us dulcetly—so to say: We like each poet's purely original thought and mode of speech;—though wholly unlike we like 'em alike. There! isn't that lucid? And you're agreed with when you don't wholly approve the Lanier portrait—the profile one, so lavishly vignetted with whiskers—the outline of forehead, brow and nose, simply superb;—but 'las me for the *whiskers!*—One's erst-raised senses drop from the Classic heights and go to housekeepin' again and dustin' off things.

Next thing you know your gift of verse won't "work" when you fain would try its paces: It will be wrested from your charge entirely, if neglected so. As gently as possible this o'erripe most wise warning plunks in the orchard grasses at your feet. Never you mind age or lapse of youthful eye-sight, or faltering step, or flagging hope and heart and zest—just let your pen prance on at its present pleasant gait, and all the world will skurry for the happy, wholesome messages you bring. (Ain't this purty near "fine writin'"? I'm 'feared you'll think so, but it's simplest fact.)

As ever gratefully and truly,
JAMES WHITCOMB RILEY.

To Meredith Nicholson.

Indianapolis,
Aug. 11, 1906.

Dear Nicholson:

How your wild huntsman's holla makes me long to join you in the chase! What a zestful revel you must be having there among the moose and bison—"and the wild gazelle with its silvery (or redundant?) feet," of which the old School-Reader poet has so highly spoken! Can't you send us some more convincing trophy of the trail than a postal-card?—Say, the antlers of the hatrack of a primeval boarding-house or the coy, retiring "brush" of a bobcat? Every day I intend to write you, and every day I can't. The town is dead,—the candles at its feet and head,—and all my friends are "lapped in lead!" However, all best greetings to you and your happy household, even to the knightly Lionel.

As ever your faithful,
J.W.R.

To Miss Dorian Medairy.

Indianapolis,
Oct. 16, 1906.

Dear Dory Ann:

Yesterday Bud got a fine, gorgeously ineffable scarf-pin, which, (*not* being received in any near distance of his birthday) he most proudly accepts; and to-day he is strutting the streets, in a new tie and the opulent Orient splendor of his dazzling gift, till the admiring passers-by are startled at the gem's refulgent glory, and the mettled horses of the midstreets snort and rear and run away at the first resplendent sight of him! And—very best of all—*I* consider it the very most delicate compliment that you didn't send it as a birthday present. Therefore with all heartfelt thanks to you—and best greetings to your father, mother and the postman and the morning sun—and your Aunt as she comes,

Your old friend,
JWR.

To Dr. William Lyon Phelps.

Indianapolis,
Nov. 28, 1906.

Dear friend:

How much I am in debt to you—and continually!—and never but pinchiest pennies of time in which to make up my vast arrears of thanks . . . thanks for your just and fine Austen tribute—though her genius is subtly ingenuous as that of Irving in his real characters on the stage—(as hers are on the page). The Stevenson book is just here—so I've barely struck hands with it yet and clapped it on the shoulder. What a man of kidney was R. L. S. No intellectual Bright's disease about that lovely cuss! Lor' don't you love him! Sir Walter, even—for all the start he's got—won't outlast him! And now the pawkie twa o' them are aye toegither! Oh, it's hame!—hame!—hame! It's there I'm goin' to be, Wi' Weelum Lyon Phelps himsel to gang along wi' me!

All best hails to you and your household, and to your friends that are mine down around "The Academic Works." As always your fraternalest,

JAMESY.

To the Secretary, The National Arts Club,
(Gramercy Park, New York.)

Dear Sir:

With sincerest heart I thank you for your invitation to the dinner in commemoration of our Country's poet, Longfellow. Only ill health could and does keep me from answering with my presence. Even as he was a divinely inspiring poet, he was a true simple human brother of us all.

Very truly and gratefully,
JAMES WHITCOMB RILEY.

To Miss Dorian Medairy.

Indianapolis,
Mch. 27, 1907.

Dear Miss Dorian:

Thank you for your last good letter with all its good news of the home-folks—and Bud certainly wishes he could be there for the long-promised visit with you all; but doctor he 'lows his "bronical" complaint won't permit him to go nowheres—till it's real shore-enough spring-weather—which it purt'-nigh is this very day,—and so I'm down-town—almost clean forgetting and forgiving the long, long, awful coughful winter which I just love to hate! So no more at present. Ever thine. Your 'beedi-ant Servent. All best greetings to all. Wunst when it 'uz Easter Aunt Rinn sewed caliko on eggs an' biled 'em, so they had colerd flowrs on the shells till us children cracked an' chipped 'em all off an'—Et 'em!

Respectfully your loving little friend,

BUD.

To Meredith Nicholson.

Indianapolis,
Aug. 23, 1907.

Dear Doctor:

Nothing but pulling your good self out of the envelope instead of your letter could have pleased me better,—for the way your zestful comment ambles along seems de-livered in almost veritable person in your own old best form. Indeed in your crisp and breezy talk one tastes the very sea—aye, you bluff old buccaneer! and marks it, too,

> "As it lifts and 'scends on the old trail—our
> own trail—the out trail—
> 'As she ships it green on the Long Trail—
> the trail that is always new."

And I'll bet that's as nearly accurate as any man-jack of us all can possibly quote old Doc Rudyard—dam' his eyes!—"as his tackle grips the crate and his tape-worm whines through the sheave!" . . . Well!—"Get 'er *home*—get 'er *home!* where the drunken rollers comb!"—for it's home here you're wanted! and, beside the howling need of you, there's a grade of climate here now that'll meet your saddest old sea-doggest exactions.—Am tarapaulin' round, this livin' minute, in a winter suit—and so is Hewitt.—Yea, so is the erst dulcet and salubrious Mr. Bobbs. Surely there in your cold seacaves, and by your all inadequate sea-coal fire, you must be training for eyether a dash for the pole or acclimatizing your genius to the requirements of The Cold Storyage. (Only thing I never liked about Shakespeare was his brazen, shameless peccancy of punning.) Lor'! the oodles of writers international and like artists and sculptors you have there right at hand. Do go nest 'em out and bring 'em into friendly, neighborly subjection—and feed my raw regards from your naked hand.

All best remembrances to the children, and tell 'em of a certain scientist's very silent, serious little five-year-old boy, who fractured the lull at luncheon, one day, by the volunteered remark that the reason he liked radishes so much was because they were *anti-scorbutic*.

'Magine how the mature guests sat up!

All best greetings yet again to all.

Fraternally,
J. W. R.

To Miss Dorian Medairy.

Indianapolis, Ind.,
Nov. 26, 1907.

Dear Dory Ann:

Here is a 'tend-like letter from Bud, who is a-waiting here till his Publisher gets back from luntch, where he must be a-eating like a Orphant-Child, he stays so long! As usual, Bud is behind time with everything till it just seems he can't never catch up again no more! And he's a confirmed hoodoo, everything he wants and tries to a-complish he just can't. So he thinks of hisse'f about like your Aunt thinks of him,—that he's a-getting to be not a youngster no longer, but a real shore-'nuff "Oldster." And that's just what I 'spect he is! His friends, though, all tries to incurrage him, and says *"he's* all right, and the Clouds is all got silver linings, and It's a long lane, and Onward, Christian Soldier, and why don't he try Christian Science anyhow—'cause that'll fetch him out when everything else fails!"

So you write and cheer him up—even when you are visiting. And next time he writes he'll be a-feeling more like his old se'f. All best greetings to every one.

As ever your old friend

BUD.

To Booth Tarkington.

Nov. 24, 1909.

Dear friend:

It's a positive glory—your *Beasley's Christmas Party*— and its dedication to *me,* most truly "fills me and thrills me with life divine." And how is it possible for me fittingly to thank you for all the all-hallowed either or both?

When two weeks ago I gloomily oozed into the Bobbs-Merrill book store and was radiantly informed that your Christmas book was there—and inscribed—as it is—O my dear old friend and fellow—that was enough to lift the clouds and flash me, heart and soul, into a dazzling state of elation and delight that lights me like a headlight to this very hour. Three times, in still hungering succession, have I devoured the story—so when I tell you it's simply everything a Christmas story should be (Godlike, Manlike and Childlike), you may know how sacredly wholesome is my appreciation of and affection for it. Nor is this estimate an overloving one of an old friend simply, but that of the great public whose universal heart you have most tenderly touched and won to love you. So do, I pray you, accept my love with the vast world's—only considering mine as first—uttered in the long ago when you were but a boy. And so God keep you to your latest day.

As ever your grateful, faithful friend,

JAMES HUNCHBERG RILEY,

To Miss Lesley Payne.

Miss Lesley Payne, daughter of the sister, Mrs. Mary Riley Payne. See "To Lesley," Biographical Edition, V, p. 90.

Indianapolis, Ind.,*
Mar. 1, 1910.

My dear Niece:

Your good letter pleased your old Uncle very much—considering his advanced years and clouding mental infirmities. In fact, from time to time, as he first read your clear legible lines, your directness, as well as grace, together with just about the right tang and relish of cheer and humor, made him sit up like a gratefully approving fox-terrier subtly recognizing an intelligence worthy of his really very best attention and consideration. Surely, I thought—and still think—here's a young kinswoman of many gifts and possibilities—divinely endowed to make the world at large a happier place to live in by reason of her bright inspiring presence. Know, too, by this, what

---

perfect faith I have in your unspoilable common sense. Be assured always, my sister's only child, that I love you equally and pray ever for your mutual fullest happiness. Haven't seen brer John since your going, but hear of his good health. All here are well—even the writer, though somewhat overworked. We have company at home and good times, and Mrs. Holstein in unusual health and spirits. She asks to be remembered kindly to you both.

Ever thine, Niece of mine,
Write 'bout ten times out o' nine!—

to Your old UNCLE JIM.

To Dr. William Lyon Phelps.

Indianapolis,
Mch. 9, 1910.

Dear Billy:

Good for your brief hail and good for your new book! I am reveling among your literary gods—and s'prised at your leaving out Meredith. You've a way o' making me like some of 'em mor'n I would naturally, so I want you to kindo' let me in on the ground-floor of Meredith.

How very good it was to see and hear you—and so well and strong and health-ridden! We're all talking of you yet. God friend you so continually.

Remember me to Mrs. Phelps, to Professor Beers and all friends.

Your ever grateful,
JAMES WHITCOMB RILEY.

To Madison Cawein.

Indianapolis,
June 15, 1910.

Dear Cawein:

You may well wonder at my long silence, and upbraid
me an it please you to,—no less I'm not entirely to
blame—being, through gathering years, tried and vexed
with one infirmity after another, till it seems at last I've
acquired the whole measly assortment, from vanishing
teeth, wried eyesight and thick hearing, to bone-erysipelas
of my very soul!—Not one of the long calamitous list but
drills away at me, night and day, till, like the desperate
Dutchman, I feel liable at any minute to *"jump der dock
off!"* But I try not to complain—however poorly I succeed.   Ah, but now our dear Allison's long affliction is
realized and sympathized with as never before by your
like stricken friend who so often now has to request it to
"thunder again!"

And, all this time, you—God bless you—"as merry as
griggs—whatever griggs is!" Wonderful! Wonderful!
A thousand times I've said it, going over your new poems,
book after book.   And truly it *is* wonderful—your lavish
output and its unfaltering excellence.   All—all of it, be
sure, a source of rejoicing to your ever-loyal though long-
voiceless friend and fellow.

How I do pray for real summer weather!   Join in my
wild petition and roll up the sleeves of prayer.

All best greetings, dear poet, to you and yours—and to
Allison and his.

As ever faithfully your old friend,

JAMES WHITCOMB RILEY.

To Evelyn Harris.

At the close of this letter Riley refers to what was the fore-warning of a stroke.

Indianapolis,
July 8, 1910.

Dear friend:

Your favor of July fifth took me greatly by surprise and occasioned a great delight in me, be assured.

I have not forgotten my friends down your way in all these years. But for a long, long time have been in such miserable average health, or rather lack of average health,—that I have not possessed the heart to attempt writing to you when I must misrepresent so sadly. However, now, at least, there begins to show some promise of general betterment in which I hope to, in part, make amends for prior delinquencies.

Since your father's death I have schooled myself to know that we shall not meet again as heretofore, but that he is dead I can not bring myself to believe in the least. Always in fancy I see him just as he always was, as I knew him best, only the communication is down, I can't speak to him as I once did, but I feel that we are in a sense together still and so to be for ever.

My best greetings go to you one and all. Tell your good mother how often I think of our pleasant times at home there, when all were there, when even you had not yet thought of marrying. Now you are married and your sisters are married, truly it would seem like coming into a strange land indeed for me to be once more at your home.

You will kindly pardon my present typed letter, as

just now I am suffering from vertigo which leaves me
barely able to sign my mail, which here goes down.

Believe me, my dear young friend,

Yours gratefully and faithfully,

JAMES WHITCOMB RILEY.

To the School Children of Indianapolis.

After Riley's illness became known, never was a man paid more
affectionate tribute by public and intimate friends alike. Each
birthday was celebrated by the children, not only in Indiana but
throughout the nation. The Hoosier children marched to Lockerbie Street with their tributes in rhyme. The following letter in
answer to the children's greetings was read in the schoolrooms
of Indianapolis on Riley Day, 1911.

Oct. 7, 1911.

You are conspirators—every one of you, that's what
you are; you have conspired to inform the general public
of my birthday, and I am already so old that I want to
forget all about it. But I will be magnanimous and forgive you, for I know that your intent is really friendly,
and to have such friends as you are makes me—don't care
how old I am! In fact it makes me glad and happy that
I feel as absolutely young and spry as a very schoolboy—
even as one of you—and so to all intents I am.

Therefore let me be with you throughout the long,
lovely day, and share your mingled joys and blessings
with your parents and your teachers, and in the words of
little Tim Cratchit: "God bless us, every one."

Ever gratefully and faithfully

Your old friend,

JAMES WHITCOMB RILEY.

To Andrew Carnegie.

Carnegie probably called the poet "Pard" in reference to Riley's gift of a considerable portion of the present site of the Indianapolis Public Library.

Indianapolis,
December 5, 1911.

Hail Prince of Good Givers:

Your humble "pard," as you are so gracious to designate him, was delighted beyond measure to receive the kind word from you. It was like having the endorsement of the countrymen of Burns. And in my quiet modest way I have tasted somewhat of that overwhelming gratification which must be yours in your glorious work for humanity.

Let me tell you, also, how I appreciate and value the hearty commendation you give my commonplace poem of "Jim."* May I see you some day and affectionately shake your hand in living evidence of the esteem and friendship I hold for you.

Very gratefully,
JAMES WHITCOMB RILEY.

To Gentlemen of the Institute of Arts and Letters.

(Cir. January 30, 1912.)

Twenty-four years ago I visited New York to appear on the platform with a number of American writers in the interest of Copyright Reform. That was one of the pleasantest of the experiences of my life, and I have never

---

*Hoosier Book, No. 51.

forgotten the cordiality with which I was met by so many of you gentlemen of the East, strangers to me then, who have since been among the loyalest and most stimulating of my friends. I am glad to have had my small part in the work of the Copyright League, for through its efforts American Literature assumed a new dignity. Not only was protection assured the American writer, but the public became aware that authors were human beings, entitled to respectful consideration as such. And I should like to say in this connection that not only did Mr. Robert Underwood Johnson do valiant service for us all in those days, but that he and dear Richard Watson Gilder were among the first to take a stand here in the East for the westerner and the southerner and to assist in nationalizing our literature.

If I am not misinformed it is the aim of the National Institute to stimulate devotion to high ideals in all the arts, and to extend practical encouragement to beginners of promise. And with these purposes I deeply and sincerely sympathize. The West, as a contributor to the various branches of American art, has risen almost under my own eye. No one more keenly appreciates the high value of the service that may be rendered by the Institute and Academy than I do.

May I take this opportunity to express my heartfelt appreciation of the kindnesses I have received at your hands personally and as a society. Nothing has ever filled my cup so brimmingly as your generosity of a year ago in conferring upon me the medal of the Institute in the department of poetry. I have been a humbler and, I hope, a better man since that bestowal. You not only honored me beyond any imaginable deserving, but my state and "mine own people" as well. The year that has passed has been gladdened by this; but I am still bewildered that any such thing should ever have come to me.

I am sorry that, owing to my prolonged illness, I was unable to acknowledge last year your courtesy and kindness, and I regret that I am unable now to meet you face to face, to express my heartfelt appreciation and gratitude. But believe me, that we Hoosiers, while eagerly invading the world of art and not without certain strutting airs of proprietorship therein, pretend to no monopoly of human kindness. On this field state lines break down, and we are all good Americans, the friendliest, kindliest, wholesomest people on earth!

To you all, my thanks, renewed and continuing, and my fraternal greetings, and best wishes for your increasing success in all your undertakings.

JAMES WHITCOMB RILEY.

To Miss Edith M. Thomas.

Indianapolis,
September 3, 1914.

Dear Canterbury:

The older of the boys has received your letter. The younger one* is on a prolonged vacation. For many days I have been waiting for his return in order to have my good right hand to deal you a commensurate letter, but in vain. So I am writing in the old handicapped manner. It was very good to get your letter and I have used it over and over by way of reading matter. To hear that you are all well is a delight and I am gratified beyond

*The younger one was the nephew, Edmund Eitel, who acted as secretary to Mr. Riley.

RILEY MEDAL
EXECUTED BY LORADO TAFT

Copyright 1916 by
HUGH McK. LANDON

Used by permission

Above medal, the work of Lorado Taft, was commissioned struck by a group of Indianapolis men in commemoration of the public ceremonies held in Riley's honor on his last
and sixty-sixth birthday

measure, though with you I can but complain of the terrible war times, and spend my leisure in agonizing over the unimaginable horrors of it all. It must have been an impressive sight,—you women marching in countless numbers, draped in black, to the accompaniment of the muffled drums. Truly, truly, a moving sight it must have been! One can but hope that it may prove feebly effective, but I gravely fear that the elements of war have grown wild and wanton, and in no wise to be checked. All that can be done by prayers and tears will be.

As to health: I am glad to report some betterment all the time, but I fear,—after heroic treatment on heroic treatment,—my good right hand is helplessly incurable. But I am resigned and grateful for my otherwise well-being.

My best regards to the good sister and niece. Tell "Dory Ann," for me, to enjoy to the full her vacation and come back to her work again with renewed zest.

As ever, gratefully and faithfully,
the old pilgrim,
JAMES WHITCOMB RILEY.

To Booth Tarkington.

Indianapolis,
September 30, 1914.

Dear Booth:

With this I am sending you the last two books of the Scribner Edition in which please mark the dedication of *Early Poems.** I think you will recognize the portrait, as it is about the time of our first acquaintance. It is

*Dedicated to Mr. Tarkington.

eminently characteristic of that epoch as it was taken by Nottman during my first appearance in Boston. My friend, Dr. Frank A. Harris, commented on its eminent characteristics, saying, "It looks like you had just flung a cat over the barn."

With all best greetings to Mrs. Tarkington and yourself, I am

Hastily
JAMES WHITCOMB RILEY.

To the School Children of Indianapolis.

Indianapolis,
October 7, 1914.

Greetings and salutations:

Despite my well-known coyness, it has occurred to you to celebrate another birthday of mine. They seem to follow one another with great rapidity as I grow old, but I can assure you that your love and loyalty make them more bearable. Let me thank you with all fervor for your letters, poems and many kindly messages.

Most gratefully and faithfully yours,
JAMES WHITCOMB RILEY.

To Elizabeth Whitcomb Eitel.

Elizabeth Whitcomb Eitel was the daughter of the sister, Elva, and now Mrs. Harry Miesse. The entourage for the second trip south is here described. "Prough" was his nurse; Frank, the chauffeur; Katie, the housekeeper from Lockerbie Street, etc.

Indianapolis,
November 4, 1914.

My dear Niece:

I am just unloaded from the car personally to reply to your last good letter which was duly received and greatly enjoyed. It is my pleasure to coincide with your pleasure, however much I may regret your decision. But I am certainly glad to hear of your fine success and the encouragement you are meeting with to continue it. I assuredly wish you the utter fulfillment of your dearest dreams, and am happy to think that with your high ambitions you will not fail. Always think of your mother and pray her help, and all will be well with you.

We are in the very midst of our preparation for the South with all our arrangements perfected, as to reservations, etc., for our now near going. Mrs. Holstein, Prough and I go by rail, while Frank and his wife and little daughter, together with Katie and Lockerbie,* will drive down by car,—a beautiful experience, no doubt. Lockerbie will have a little fat joy ride of six or eight days of veriest delight. That you will be missed upon this, our second advent in Miami, goes without saying, and all your friends there will be disappointed; but I shall personally acquaint them of your generous greetings and remem-

---

*Mr. Riley's pet dog.

brances.   Mrs. Holstein sends her love to you, and mine, too, goes with it for ever and a day.

Your affectionate old uncle,
JAMES WHITCOMB RILEY.

To Governor John N. Slaton and The Board of Pardons of the State of Georgia.

The poet's sympathies were aroused by hideous charges against a Jew of refinement made by an ignorant witness.

May 26, 1915.

Dear Governor and Gentlemen:

May I add my solicitations to those of others on behalf of Leo Frank, that he may have further opportunity to clear his good name and vouchsafe the life and honor dear to him and to his family.   I have followed the case throughout, having faith that the tenderness of human sympathy would not see an extreme penalty inflicted, unless utterly certain that such is deserving.

Very fraternally yours,
JAMES WHITCOMB RILEY.

AFTERWORD

It is possible that some readers of these letters, observing the full-hearted encouragement that Riley gave to literary aspirants, and the unstinted praise, "weighing out gold for silver," that he bestowed on books and authors of only moderate ability, may think he was easily deceived by mediocrity and that he was without critical judgment. The facts are otherwise.

His own early struggles were so severe, his appreciation of what encouragement he himself had received was so intense, that his naturally warm-hearted and affectionate disposition prompted him always to help rather than to hinder. He well remembered how enormously he had been stimulated and inspired by approving comment from famous authors. He felt that praise from him might spur ambitious literary aspirants to higher achievement; whereas harshness or irony would not only hurt their feelings, but possibly extinguish their spark of talent. It will be seen that he always had in mind Perfection—in his most extravagant praises he held that goal before those to whom he wrote.

He held up an ideal and gave cheer because he wanted every one to do his best. He was patient and he was generous. I have taken the risk of submitting him to the censure of cold-hearted readers, because I wished these letters to reveal his unfailing and unlimited kindness, and his faith in the elevating power of encouragement.

There is another and perhaps a better reason for including so many letters to men and women whose ambition exceeded their talents. Many of his letters give valuable instruction in the art of composition, especially in the proper use of specific words; they are also valuable as contributions to the study of dialect, in which he was an absolute master. Just as his letters must have delighted and helped his correspondents, so I believe all young people with literary ambition—which means nine out of every ten—will find it profitable to study these epistles.

Riley's belief in the survival of personality after physical death was never affected or constrained. He was not whistling to keep up his courage; nor was his faith in immortalism inspired by a fear to face realities. He did not believe in the so-called "proofs" of immortality that come from spiritualism, however much comfort others may have derived from such manifestations. He did not need any proof. I have never known any one with so natural, so unquestioning, so sincere a belief in survival. He took it for granted.

Riley has become a legendary figure, and many lusty myths are in circulation. It will perhaps do no good to substitute fact for fiction; but there are two current myths about which a word might not be impertinent. Because he wrote with such sentiment and accuracy about farm life, many believe he was born and "raised" on a farm. As a matter of fact, the family were never professional farmers.

His father, Captain Riley, was an able and successful lawyer in Greenfield; but he returned from the war, like so many other soldiers, only to face poverty. The family went from affluence to the opposite. There was a splendid library in the house, but James was antagonistic to the "learning" which his rather stern father attempted to force on him. Yet the boy grew up in a cultural environment.

A member of the family tells me that the histrionic ability of the poet may have been inherited from the father, who was distinguished for his emotional pleas in the courtroom and for his persuasive powers on the political platform.

Another famous legend is that Riley was a professional sign-painter, who in his wanderings finally acquired enough homespun literary facility to express himself in rhyme. A member of the family, to whom I am indebted for these and other facts, says: "He was no more sign-painter turned poet than Eugene O'Neill was wharf roustabout turned playwright."

Riley had no means of making a livelihood, knowing no trade. The state of affairs at home was discouraging, and his earliest attempts at writing failed to receive any encouragement. A physician told him he was threatened with tuberculosis. A roving life outdoors appealed to him as it does to every normal boy, and in his case there were specific reasons for it. He ran away from home, and for a time joined an itinerant medicine wagon of a type now extinct. The "doctor" in charge had one sign-painter and finally hired Riley as an extra hand at painting, advertising and entertaining. Here he turned his natural talent for drawing to some account, had a jolly time with an amusing set of men, and wandered joyfully outdoors.

Those who believe that because he wrote so many poems on farm life he must have lived on a farm, might also argue that his poems of the home prove that he was a "family man." He was never married.

Riley's immense appreciation of the letters he received later in life from Kipling, Mark Twain, Howells, Henry Irving, John Hay, Joel Chandler Harris, Woodrow Wilson and others ought to be easy to understand. His earliest ambition was to be a man of letters; and to be "recognized" by the leaders, and received into their company as an equal, gave him the purest happiness.

His own life was like a poem. The almost insurmountable struggles of his early years; his indomitable will and consuming ambition gradually meeting with recognition and reward; the dawn of fame; the nation-wide appreciation; the delight of finding "his soul in men's hearts," for some of his poems were universally known; and toward the serene end honors of all kinds, and what is better, the love of a people.

W. L. P.

APPENDIX

From Samuel L. Clemens.

In response to an invitation from Western Association of Writers to a dinner in Riley's honor, October 18, 1888.*

Hartford,

Oct. 3, 1888.

Mr. W. D. Foulke and Others:

Dear Sirs and Misses—For the sake of the strong love and admiration which I feel for Riley, I would go if I could, were there even no way but by slow freight, but I am finishing a book begun three years ago; I see land ahead; if I stick to the one without intermission I shall be at another in thirty days: if I stop to moisten my hands I am gone. So give Riley half of my heart, and Nye the other half, if he is there, and the rest of me will stay respectfully behind and continue business at the old stand.

Truly yours,

S. L. CLEMENS.

From Samuel L. Clemens.

Hartford,

Feb. 2, 1891.

Dear Riley:

It's a darling poem,† and I thank you ever so much for it. But—when it comes to reciting it, I can't even remotely approach you. You are the only man alive that

---

*See letter of Oct. 15, 1888, to Mrs. Andrews, p. 87.
†The poem in question is "Honest Old Sam Hungerford," published for the first time in this volume in the letter to Mark Twain, dated January 30, 1891.

can read your poems exactly right.—There are poets who can't read their works worth shucks; and if they should offer to read their poems to me I should easily have the grit to say, "Oh, gimme the book and lemme show you *how!*—You just make me tired." But I should never say that to you; no, I take my hat off to you, my boy; you *do* know how.

In the fine 'Ras Wilson* poem you've flung in some more of those things which make my mouth water for an Elder Time, and a big toe with a rag around it. One time or another you've got them *all* in, I believe—except, perhaps, p'simmons & p'cons; and maybe red haws. We hadn't p'cons in Missouri—had to cross over to the Illinois bottoms.

This is my tenth day in bed with rheumatism. There is less recreation about it than you would think.

Yours ever,
MARK.

From John Patterson.

The following letter inspired Riley's of October 24, 1891, to John Patterson.

Philadelphia,
October 21, 1891.

Mr. James Whitcomb Riley,
    Dear Sir:
In the October number of *The American Catholic Review,* (Harly & Mahony, Publishers, Phila.) the writer of an article on Edgar Allan Poe quotes a poem entitled "Leonainie" which begins thus—

Hoosier Book, No. 15.

Leonainie—angels named her
  And they took the light
Of the laughing stars and framed her
  In a smile of white;
And they made her hair of gloomy
  Midnight, and her eyes of bloomy
Moonshine, and they brought her to me
  In a solemn night.

He comments on it to this effect: "This beautiful poem is not to be found in any of the edition of Poe's works; and our opinion is that no edition should claim completeness without it. His poems are too few to allow the loss even of the most inconsiderable or least valuable; and certainly the above poem does not enter into that category; it has all the characteristics of Poe at his very best and we do not believe any other American poet could have written it!"

I have been informed and believe that another American poet, to-wit yourself, not only *could* but *did* write it. It will please me very much, however, to have your word for it, and that not through idle curiosity. I hope you will give it.

Yours respectfully,
JOHN PATTERSON.

From Joseph Knight.

This letter refers to "The Flying Islands of the Night." See Riley's letter dated Feb. 11, 1892, p. 159. Also Riley's letter to Eugene F. Ware, Feb. 9, 1892, p. 158.

London,
Dec. 26, 1891.

My Dear Mr. Riley:

Pray accept my very best thanks for your very beautiful book and for other proofs of your kind, flattering and valued interest. I hope to send you a book of mine before long. In such exchange I know I must be regarded as a robber, so much do I benefit. I am, however, very proud and grateful to be in any way associated with your original and important labors.

Your new volume is of course as much of a puzzle as of a delight. Its lyrical and imaginative gifts are of a high order, and I have read it again and again with augmenting pleasure. It is a *tour de force*. I need, however, more illumination than I possess from within, and am thinking of starting a Whitcomb Riley society. Are all the new terms simply your own invention, or is there a reference to some earlier work? What marvelous words some of them are.

I am enamoured of Jucklet, and Spraivoll is delicious. I am still anxious to know more of the plustre, and "The Tweck on the bamner stem."

Some of the later speeches of Dwainie are the loveliest poetry:

> "When girlish happiness locked hands with me
> And we went spinning round, with naked feet
> In swaths of bruised roses ankle-deep."

Exquisite!
So it all is.
But I want a little more light.

I wish you very sincerely a happy new year, and, with renewed thanks for your kindness and the high poetic rhapsody you have shown me, I am

Your ever,

JOS. KNIGHT.

From Rudyard Kipling.

Naulakha,
Brattleboro, Vermont,
Oct. 13, 1893.

Dear Mr. Riley:

It came in this morning—all gallant and gay in the beautiful green livery. The *Century* folk certainly know how to turn out a book just so. I let the morning's work slide and went through it at once—which was weak of me. Squire Hawkins's tale* of course I remember from that great night, and some of the others of course I have met in their first print dresses, but "Fessler's Bees"† was tee-totally new and I shook helplessly over it.

I can hear that tale being slowly drawled by the teller. Over some of the others, I won't say which, I choked and 'tis your blamed verses that are the only ones I know that can make me gulp. In revenge, I wish to state clearly that I don't like "Tradin' Joe."‡—It may be true to nature but it goes ag'in' my stomach. And that's all and a heap of thanks.

We've got a roof above our heads now, so if ever business brings you within ear-shot of this place you'll know where to "light an' hitch."

With kindest regards from my wife and myself.

Ever yours sincerely,
RUDYARD KIPLING.

Hoosier Book, No. 208.
†*Hoosier Book*, No. 205.
‡*Hoosier Book*, No. 206.

From William Dean Howells.

The letter below refers to the unusual tribute which was given Riley, in Indianapolis, on his last birthday. Hundreds of felicitations and affectionate messages were sent from friends everywhere, the list ranging from President Wilson and other officers of state, on through a host of those who were distinguished in the world of arts and letters here and abroad. At the banquet (to which Mr. Howells alludes as the Riley-Fest) Ex-Vice-President Fairbanks presided. Among the speakers were Colonel George Harvey, Dr. John H. Finley, William Allen White, George Ade and Senator Albert J. Beveridge. Lorado Taft, also a guest, later was commissioned to design a medal commemorating the event, which he executed with rare artistic skill.

York Harbor,
September 5, 1915.

Dear Meredith Nicholson:

I would gladly come to the Riley-Fest if I were not so nearly 79 years old, with all the accumulated abhorrence of joyful occasions which that lapse of time implies. But I can not really be away whenever Riley is spoken of or at. Give him my dearest love and all such honor as one of the least may offer one of the greatest of our poets.

Yours sincerely,
W. D. HOWELLS.

From George Ade.

Hazelden Farm,
Brook, Ind.,
May 2, 1930.

D. L. Chambers,
The Bobbs Merrill Co.,
Indianapolis, Ind.

Dear Mr. Chambers:

I will explain about that letter written by Mr. Riley from Des Moines in 1903 and if you haven't a good copy of the letter I think I can find you the original.* Mr. Riley was in Chicago on his way to make some appearances on the platform out west and John McCutcheon and I took him to the Studebaker Theater to witness a performance of *The County Chairman*. The scenes of the play were laid in Indiana along in the eighties and I was very happy to learn from Mr. Riley that the play pleased him because the characters were human beings and the atmosphere was real. During the evening he told Mac and me that he had been very much disgusted with certain "rural plays" which were supposed to deal with life in the Hoosier state. He said that *Lost River* and *The Vinegar Buyer* and other plays which he had seen on the stage were simply burlesques but he thought that our play was a realistic presentation of Hoosier life along about the time that Thomas A. Hendricks and Daniel P. Voorhees were in evidence. The day after we were with him he wrote the letter from Des Moines and proposed that I should write another play and that he and Mac and I should appear in it. I have never decided whether or not he was fooling. The postscript would indicate that really he had a serious idea in the back of his head. At any rate, the letter is most interesting and I think that Mr. Riley was expressing himself when he said that he would like to appear on the stage in character. Do not forget that Sir Henry Irving once said that if Mr. Riley had decided to be an actor he would have been one of the greatest character actors of all times.

I am, with best wishes

Sincerely,
GEORGE ADE.

---

*See letter of Nov. 30, 1903, from Mr. Riley, p. 284.

INDEX

INDEX

Academy, 90
Adams, Henry, 267n.
Adams, Isaac E., 187
Adams, Oscar Fay, 113
Ade, George, 2, 7
  explains Riley letter, 334-35
  letter to, 284
Ainsworth Dictionary, 63, 65, 77, 248
Albani, Paolo, 237, 238
Alcott, Bronson, 77
Aldrich, Thomas Bailey, 2, 37n.
  letter to, 208-9
Allison, Young E., 215, 303, 313
America, 49, 132, 136, 235
America, 268
American Academy of Arts and Letters, 7, 317
American Catholic Quarterly Review, The, 145, 330
Anderson, 64, 249
Anderson, John M.
  letter to, 16-18, 29-30
Andrews, Mrs., 87, 329
Aristotle, 61
Arnold, Matthew, 189
  letter describing, 39-40
"Artemus"
  see Potts, Hiram Y.
Art Interchange, 69
Asheville, 155
Atlanta, 203, 239, 240, 253, 277
Atlantic, 231
Atlantic, The, 226, 229, 230
Augusta, 240
Austria-Hungary, 239
Authors' Club, The, 230
Authors' Readings, The, 76

Baker, Polk, 73
Barrackman, Colonel D. A.
  letter to, 67-68
Battle of Stone River, 226

Bedford County, 205
Beecher, Henry Ward, 58
Beers, Prof. Henry A., 312
  "Bumble Bee," 232, 233, 252
  Initial Studies in American Letters, 1
  letters to, 232, 233, 261-62
  Suburban Pastoral, A, 232, 233
Bensel, James Berry, 113
Bierce, Ambrose, 5, 197
Binghampton, 39
Black, William
  Judith Shakespeare, 130
Bleak House, 16
Blood, Mary M.
  Selected Poems of Henry Ames Blood, 292
Bobbs, W. C., 49n., 309
Bobbs-Merrill Company, The, 49n., 300n., 310
Bok, Edward W.
  letter to, 107
Bon Air, 239
Boston, 36, 37, 47, 53, 113, 164, 198, 203, 215, 237, 320
Boston Transcript, The, 11, 35
Bowen-Merrill Company, The, 49n., 100, 265
Bradbury, 198
Bronxville, 224
Brown County, 219
Browning, Mrs., 27, 38, 41, 143
Bryan, Mr., 291
Bryant, William Cullen, 17, 82
Buchanan, 270
Buck, Daniel Deronda, 31, 32
Bulwer, 166
Bundy, Eugene
  letter to, 20-21
Burbank, Mr., 155
Burdette, Robert J., 127
  letters to, 215-16, 222-23

339

Marion, 296
Marquis, Don, 1
Martinsville, 91, 219
Marvel, Ik, 154
Massachusetts, 53, 113
Mathias, Lee D.
letter to, 302-3
Matthews, Dr. James Newton, 70, 73
"Current Poetesses," 41
letters to, 41-43, 98-99, 270-71
Maud, Miss Constance
letter to, 235
McConnell, Mr., 55
McCutcheon, John T., 335
letters to, 276-77, 284
McIntyre, 55, 98, 99
McKinley, 253
Medairy, Miss Dorian, 3, 264, 268, 294, 319
letters to, 255-56, 281-82, 284-85, 297-98, 300-1, 305-6, 307-8, 309-10
Merrill, Charles W., 49n.
Mexican War, 130
Miami, 321
Middlemarch, 96
Miesse, Mrs. Harry
see Eitel, Elizabeth Whitcomb
Miller, Jasper, 91
Miller, Joaquin, 181
Milton, 89
Missouri, 330
Mitchell, Dr. S. Weir, 2, 275
letter to, 108
Mitchell, Miss, 91
Moffitt, Mr., 137
Moore, Tom, 92
Morgan, John, 52
Moulton, Mrs. Louise Chandler
letters to, 198-99, 202-4, 252
Mount Vesuvius, 55
Muncie, 237
Murphree, Miss Fanny, 226, 227
Murphree, Miss Mary, 226, 227
Murphreesboro, 226

"Nada the Lily," 166
Nashville, 219

Nast, Thomas
"Landing of a Father, The," 164
letter to, 164-65
National Arts Club, The
letter to Secretary of, 307
National Institute of Arts and Letters, 7
letters to, 316-18
Neal, Mrs.
letter to, 93-95
Nesbit, Wilbur D.
letter to, 285-86
New, Honorable Harry S., 60, 137, 177
letter to, 296-97
New, Mrs. Harry S.
letter to, 177
New, Colonel John C., 110, 111, 131
New, Mrs. John C., 60
New Castle Courier, 44
New England, 52, 186, 194
New Haven, 233n.
New World, 139, 148, 160
New York, 9, 39, 76n., 79, 113, 116, 134, 136, 145, 152, 166, 182, 183, 193, 198, 202, 251, 261, 271, 274, 307, 316
New York Post, 17
New York Sun, 1, 103
New York Tribune, 11
New York World, 84n., 90, 162
Nicholas, Miss, 98
Nicholson, Meredith, 2, 6, 112, 149, 300, 312
Hoosiers, The, 248
letters to, 200, 231, 247-48, 278-79, 295-96, 305, 308-9
"Riley in the Atlantic," 231n.
Nicholson, Mrs. 248
Nickum, John R. and Lottie, 165, 170, 190
Nottman, 320
Nye, Edgar Wilson, "Bill," 3, 57, 75, 123, 126, 152, 156n., 212, 224, 225, 228, 233, 251, 296, 329
and Riley combination, 79n., 90, 93
Gutenberg and Poet, 187
letters to, 58-59, 59-61, 61-62, 70-72,